MARK TWAIN

Peter Messent

© Peter Messent 1997

First published 1997 by
MACMILLAN PRESS LTD
Houndmills, Basingstoke, Hampshire RG21 6XS
and London
Companies and representatives
throughout the world

ISBN 0–333–58566–6 hardcover
ISBN 0–333–58567–4 paperback

A catalogue record for this book is available
from the British Library.

10 9 8 7 6 5 4 3 2 1
06 05 04 03 02 01 00 99 98 97

Typeset by Forewords, Oxford/Longworth Editorial Services
Longworth, Oxfordshire.

Printed in Hong Kong

Contents

Acknowledgements   vi

General Editor's Preface   viii

1 Keeping Both Eyes Open: 'The Stolen White Elephant'   1
2 Old World Travel: *The Innocents Abroad*   22
3 *Roughing It* and the American West   44
4 *Tom Sawyer* and American Cultural Life: Anxieties and
   Accommodations   65
5 Racial Politics in *Huckleberry Finn*   86
6 Fantasy and *A Connecticut Yankee in King Arthur's Court*   110
7 Severed Connections: *Puddn'head Wilson and Those
   Extraordinary Twins*   134
8 The Late Works: Incompletion, Instability, Contradiction   157

Notes   177

Select Bibliography   228

Index   232

Acknowledgements

Mark Twain wrote in *Following the Equator* that 'Man is the only animal that blushes. Or needs to.' I have been spared many blushes by the friends and colleagues who were good enough to read parts of this manuscript, and who corrected my mistakes, suggested new avenues to pursue, and helped put me right when I had gone (often badly) wrong. So, my grateful thanks to Lou Budd, Chris Gair, Colin Harrison, Richard King, Peter Ling, Christine MacLeod, Scott Michaelsen, Peter Stoneley and Tim Youngs. And especially to Dave Murray for reading the completed manuscript. His comments provided, at this late stage, just the help I needed to make some important final revisions and readjustments. All those mentioned above helped to make this a much better book than it would otherwise have been. Any faults it still has are down to me alone. My thanks to Douglas Tallack, my Head of Department, for his encouragement and support in this project. My thanks, too, to my very patient and helpful editor, Margaret Bartley. I acknowledge my debt to the British Academy: without its grant, which doubled the sabbatical time available to me, this book would not be finished now, or, I suspect, for some considerable time. The Mark Twain Circle of America contains the most unusual collection of academics I have come across. Its members genuinely enjoy each other's company, are unselfish in their support of those working on Twain, and have a great deal of fun too. I have benefited greatly from my membership. My family and friends gave me all the support I could hope for as I wrote this. My dear father, John Messent (1912–1996), died soon after I had completed the manuscript. The example of his life and love will stay with me. As I worked on the book, my son and daughter, William and Alice, bore all with patience and even with interest. Ella and Leah, my two step-daughters, got used to my continual time at the computer, even though it meant, for Leah, that 'Jill of the Jungle' had to go unplayed. Carin, my wife, read parts of the manuscript for me, phoned every day from work to make sure I was still sane and stable, and (whichever the condition) kept me going with her encouragement and love. I dedicate this book to her with all my love.

Nottingham   PETER MESSENT
February 1996

General Editor's Preface

The death of the novel has often been announced, and part of the secret of its obstinate vitality must be its capacity for growth, adaptation, self-renewal and self-transformation: like some vigorous organism in a speeded up Darwinian ecosystem, it adapts itself quickly to a changing world. War and revolution, economic crisis and social change, radically new ideologies such as Marxism and Freudianism, have made this century unprecedented in human history in the speed and extent of change, but the novel has shown an extraordinary capacity to find new forms and techniques and to accommodate new ideas and conceptions of human nature and human experience, and even to take up new positions on the nature of fiction itself.

In the generations immediately preceding and following 1914, the novel underwent a radical redefinition of its nature and possibilities. The present series of monographs is devoted to the novelists who created the modern novel and to those who, in their turn, either continued and extended, or reacted against and rejected, the traditions established during that period of intense exploration and experiment. It includes a number of those who lived and wrote in the nineteenth century but whose innovative contribution to the art of fiction makes it impossible to ignore them in any account of the modern novel; it also includes the so-called 'modernists' and those who in the mid- and late twentieth century have emerged as outstanding practitioners of this genre. The scope is, inevitably, international; not only, in the migratory and exile-haunted world of our century, do writers refuse to heed national boundaries – 'English' literature lays claim to Conrad the Pole, Henry James the American, and Joyce the Irishman – but geniuses such as Flaubert,

Dostoevsky and Kafka have had an influence on the fiction of many nations.

Each volume in the series is intended to provide an introduction to the fiction of the writer concerned, both for those approaching him or her for the first time and for those who are already familiar with some parts of the achievement in question and now wish to place it in the context of the total *oeuvre*. Although essential information relating to the writer's life and times is given, usually in an opening chapter, the approach is primarily critical and the emphasis is not upon 'background' or generalisations but upon close examination of important texts. Where an author is notably prolific, major texts have been made to convey, more summarily, a sense of the nature and quality of the author's work as a whole. Those who want to read further will find suggestions in the select bibliography included in each volume. Many novelists are, of course, not only novelists but also poets, essayists, biographers, dramatists, travel writers and so forth; many have practised shorter forms of fiction; and many have written letters or kept diaries that constitute a significant part of their literary output. A brief study cannot hope to deal with all of these in detail, but where the shorter fiction and non-fictional writings, private and public, have an important relationship to the novels, some space has been devoted to them.

NORMAN PAGE

1

Keeping Both Eyes Open: 'The Stolen White Elephant'

When detectives called for a drink, the would-be facetious bar-keeper resurrected an obsolete form of expression, and said, 'Will you have an eye-opener?' All the air was thick with sarcasms.

('The Stolen White Elephant')[1]

I

In this opening chapter, I look closely at one of Twain's most puzzling short stories, 'The Stolen White Elephant', to identify how, in this specific case, the narrative works, and where its comic effects lie. Although my general approach in this book will be chronological, I begin with a text written in 1878, two years after the publication of *The Adventures of Tom Sawyer* (1876).[2] It might seem perverse to disrupt my main organising principle so early. I do so because 'The Stolen White Elephant' provides a particularly appropriate introduction to my analysis of Twain's work as a whole, and the problems involved in such a task.

The sheer size of an elephant, and its incongruity in an American setting, would make it unmissable. Yet, in Twain's story, it has been stolen; has disappeared from view. The detective looks for clues to find the elephant, but it is barging chaotically around the landscape as he does so. The relationship here between the obvious and the hidden is peculiarly unstable. I would argue that the stress in this text on such instability, incongruity, and shifting perspective, provides a paradigm for Twain's work as a whole. 'The Stolen White Elephant', despite its undoubted celebrity, has had comparatively little written about it; a result, perhaps, of its enigmatic quality. I start my book by giving it, to adapt a phrase from 'Jim Smiley and His Jumping Frog', my own little critical punch behind.[3] Then, in the final section of the chapter, I widen my scope to suggest the relevance of this analysis to my larger argument.

'The Stolen White Elephant' is a narrative that appears to be 'pointedly pointless'.[4] Though the specific comic techniques Twain uses can be identified, the story as a whole, like so much of Twain's work, seems not quite to add up. The reader is left with a peculiar sense of not having got the joke. This sense of puzzlement, the struggle to interpret satisfactorily a problematic text, is (self-reflexively) signalled as a subject of narrative concern when Inspector Blunt, the chief of the detectives employed to recover the stolen goods, places an advertisement in the morning papers to open negotiations with the thief. His message remains a form of gibberish for both the narrator and the reader (though their response to it implicitly differs). Shared codes break down as both are left on the outside, as it were; the point of the communication completely blunted. The detective's cryptogram is impenetrable: 'A.—xwblv. 242 N. Tjnd—fz328wmlg. Ozpo,—; 2 m ! ogw. Mum.' (p. 25).

The reader has a similar feeling of being left stranded at the conclusion of Twain's story. The enigmatic nature of the text as a whole, however, takes a different form than that of Blunt's brief message. The language of 'The Stolen White Elephant' is straightforward enough. Its cryptic element does not lie in any inability to understand the individual phrase or sentence. Rather, it is the overall humorous intent which remains obscure and causes the sense of frustrated expectation[5] already noted.

I would suggest, however, that it is in this very sense of readerly frustration and disorientation that the comic ends of the narrative (uncomfortably) lie. The story's apparent pointlessness *is* its point. A type of double effect operates here, for it is only as our initial sense of puzzlement is explored, or so I would contend,[6] that another level of humour becomes apparent. We then discover a comedy of estrangement that speaks to the very condition of the modern – a form of humour that operates at an epistemological level. The story, as I see it, finally operates as a form of anti-narrative 'programmed to go nowhere'[7] and it is here that its deeper 'joke' is to be found.

It is at this point that I need to add a note of hesitation and qualification concerning the nature of my own critical activity. An indication of Twain's mastery of the comic form is that to try to interpret or explain his humour is to risk falling, figuratively, flat on one's face. When I do so, I always have the sinking feeling I may be missing the point entirely, may be ending up as the victim of Twain's joke. The gap, in 'The Stolen White Elephant', between the myopic logic of the detectives and the elephant's random force is the main incongruity round which the story pivots. The former are burlesqued for their 'pompous assumption of infallibility and ridiculous inappropriate procedures'.[8] As I do my own critical detective work, here and in the rest of the book, trying to pin down and explain the incongruities and shifting effects in Twain's work, I hope at least to avoid a similar fate.

II

On first reading 'The Stolen White Elephant', clear parallels emerge with Twain's other humorous sketches, particularly in the use of narrative frames and of a central deadpan narrator. The title of the story is followed by a footnote attributed to the author (M.T.). This note both gives the provenance of the sketch and immediately foregrounds the potentially problematic relationship of the real to the fictitious: 'Left out of *A Tramp Abroad*, because it was feared that some of the particulars had been exaggerated, and that others were not true. Before these suspicions had been proven groundless, the book had gone to press'. A first narrator (presumably the same M.T.) then briefly introduces the teller of the main tale as 'a chance railway acquaintance . . . a gentleman more than seventy years of age . . . [whose] good and gentle face and earnest and sincere manner imprinted the unmistakable stamp of truth upon every statement which fell from his lips' (p. 1). The latter's tale is then told, in the first-person voice, with no return made to the initial narrator. The immediate sense of possible contradiction, as the reference to suspected exaggeration gives way, first to its dismissal, and then to the deep earnestness of the central narrative voice, strongly indicates to any Twain reader that the story will work as a hoax: the literary form with which he was identified from the early Virginia City *Territorial Enterprise* days onward.

Susan Gillman sees Twain's use of such a form as 'responding to an insatiable appetite, both on popular and literary levels of culture, for the hoax and the stunt, often in the form of the sensational . . . "true crime" report'. She links Twain, in this use, to the figure of P. T. Barnum[9] whose career 'exploited the national appetite for fraud'.[10] Barnum himself figures in Twain's tale, cutting a deal with Blunt, as a telegram reports, for 'exclusive privilege of using elephant as travelling advertising medium from now till detectives find him. Wants to paste circus-posters on him' (p. 18). Barnum's presence, and the comic rupture in narrative expectation and logic which has the elephant then 'plastered over with circus-bills' (p. 20) just three hours after Barnum's original despatch, while large numbers of detectives continue unsuccessfully in its pursuit, all confirm – if it needs to be confirmed – the nature of the literary form Twain is using.

Any of Twain's contemporaries reading with even one meta-phorical eye open would probably have made the connection between the subject of Twain's story and the frontier expression 'seeing the Elephant'. Forrest G. Robinson speaks of Twain's own predisposition during his years in the Far West (described in *Roughing It*) to 'fall lock, stock and barrel for the practical joke that the mining frontier amounted to'. To see the Elephant, in this mining context, was to be aware of this joke, to see through the hoax. For behind western illusions of wealth and success lay mainly 'the Elephant of gross self-deception and inevitable failure'. Robinson comments further on the way Twain's art relates to the hoax that the frontier turned out to be, when he writes that 'having seen the Elephant, [Twain] would plant a whole herd'.[11] In the title and subject matter of this sketch is the clear acknowledgement of one such (individual) literary planting.

When Marcel Gutwirth describes comic surprise in terms of 'the good laugh at [one's] own expense' that follows 'the joyous sense of having been had – in no very material sense, however – and having got over it',[12] he might have had the hoax in mind. Twain was a master of the deadpan and his earlier famous sketch, 'Jim Smiley and his Jumping Frog', foregrounds the difficulty of penetrating narrative imposture: 'because Simon Wheeler never breaks his own deadpan presentation, we never know exactly who is the duper and who is the duped'.[13] The question of the identity of the hoaxer is also a central one in 'The Stolen White Elephant'. Its main narrator, the aged gentleman, is unflinchingly deadpan throughout the story, but there is little evidence of any hoax being played on his part. His deadpan appears not to conceal anything. It would seem, rather, to be a way of representing both his naivety and gullibility. For the narrative ends with an affirmation of his 'undimmed . . . admiration' for Inspector Blunt as 'the greatest detective the world has ever produced' (p. 28), despite all the evidence both of the detective's ineptitude and of the narrator's own duping.

It is the first narrator (M.T.?) whose deadpan in this story seems to conceal the hoax.[14] He is the one who vouches for the truth of a story which contains so many patent absurdities, and who speaks of the possibility of exaggeration only to deny it. If the hoax is being perpetrated on the reader as he or she follows the plot of a detective story to its (generically) unsatisfactory ending, it is none the less of an odd kind. For two different aspects of the narrative work against each other here, and any attempt to foreground either one at the expense of the (overlooked) other cannot succeed. As I proceed, this will become a recurrent motif in my analysis of Twain's work.

Here, the comic incongruities in 'The Stolen White Elephant' make it clear that the detective story genre is being undermined. They also alert us to the fact that a 'swindle' is occurring: that the whole story is a comic fabrication. Indeed, such incongruities put us in the position of detector rather than victim of this swindle. At the same time though, as readers, we are caught up in the detective plot, and *cannot help* but follow it to its strange and elliptic conclusion. Blunt places his coded advertisement, the meaning of which remains obscure. He then leaves his client (who is also the main narrator) supposedly to meet with the criminals at midnight. Both client and reader are left ignorant of what then occurs and are left to puzzle over a series of unanswered questions. *Are* there any criminals actually involved? Does a meeting take place? Is the detective duping his client? Finally Blunt literally stumbles over the rotting corpse of the stolen elephant – if it ever *was* stolen – with no further detail given of the clues or information which led him there. The detective is then celebrated as a hero for recovering the elephant, the death of which renders that act of recovery pointless. These joint strands of the narrative ending operate in antithetical relationship to that logical clarity with which detective stories, and their closures, are conventionally associated.

Twain's comedy might be explained as operating precisely in the gap between his story's two narrative strands. The reader is aware of all the incongruities of the tale which render its status as a detective story absurd. Yet, he or she is none the less involuntarily caught within the fictional system which has been engaged; is made to follow that detective story through to its frustrating – as far as the conventions of the genre are concerned – conclusion. This may be where at least one element of the hoax lies: on a reader who has been caught between variant ways of reading and responding to a text; who is led to read a story in two ways, and ends up stalled between them. 'That is what a joke is', according to Max Eastman, 'getting somebody going and then leaving him up in the air.'[15] Twain makes us aware of having been trapped between two narrative positions. The hoax occurs in catching us mentally off guard. We realise that our minds have been 'briefly taken in'[16] as, having placed ourselves in a superior position to the main narrator, and aware (unlike him) that everything in this story tells us not to take it seriously, we nonetheless fall into the trap of puzzlement or frustration at the detective story's unsatisfactory end. We end up looking for readerly satisfaction in a form of narrative that has already been subjected to parody and which we have been thus warned not to take seriously.[17] These two readerly responses cannot be squared, and recognising that we have been left up in the air, all we can do is acknowledge our awareness that we have been taken in by this narrative joke.

III

I retrace my steps here to explore the ways in which we come to know that this narrative is a comic fabrication as we read it, and not a detective story to be taken seriously. If humour can be associated with 'the playful character of contradictory signals that come at [consciousness] simultaneously',[18] then 'The Stolen White Elephant' complies with comic expectation from the first. A gift from the King of Siam to the Queen of England, the white elephant of the title is stolen from the main narrator, a member of the Indian civil service who is responsible for conveying the present from the one country to the other. This theft occurs in Jersey City. Although there is an explanation given for the presence of the elephant in that last location – the journey has been broken in New York and the animal is in need of recuperation – some sense of (potentially playful) disconnection and of the anomalous has already entered the narrative. This occurs in different ways: in the range of geographical locations introduced; and in the presence of an exotic beast, a 'transcendentally royal . . . token of gratitude', of specifically 'Oriental' nature (p. 2), in a modernised and urban, western and republican, setting. It comes, most of all, in the mental and visual play that is released with the idea of an elephant, the epitome of loud enormity,[19] now become the proverbial needle in the haystack, the hidden object which must be found. The problematic quality of the relationship between what is obvious and what is not is placed right at the centre of the text.

The process of detection itself is parodied as Blunt proceeds to ascertain the facts of the case. The humorous nature of the narrative becomes overt as he first asks a set of routine questions which apply to missing persons, and then responds to the elephant's disappearance in the manner routine to burglary cases. From the fact that the two reactions are mutually inconsistent, and that neither is appropriate to this stolen animal, comes something of the sense of comic contradiction which now plays through the text:

> 'Now – name of the elephant?'
> 'Hassan Ben Ali Ben Selim Abdullah Mohammed Moise Alhammal Jamsetjejeebhoy Dhuleep Sultan Ebu Bhudpoor.'
> 'Very Well. Given Name?'
> 'Jumbo.'[20] . . .
> 'Parents Living?'
> 'No – dead.' . . .
> 'Very well. . . . Now please describe the elephant, and leave out no particular, however insignificant' . . .
> [Blunt takes down this description and reads it back to the narrator]

'Height, 19 feet . . . ; length of trunk, 16 feet . . . ; footprint resembles the mark when one up-ends a barrel in the snow . . . ; limps slightly with his right hand leg, and has a small scar in his left armpit caused by a former boil. . . . ' (pp. 4–5)

The comic effect stems from the obtuseness of the detective as he applies his 'strict and minute method' (p. 3) to the case in hand, as he keeps making the category mistakes on which humour thrives. Thus he has, for example, fifty thousand copies of the elephant's description 'mailed to every . . . pawnbroker's shop on the continent' (p. 5). This is the humour of incongruity – what Marcel Gutwirth calls 'a derogation . . . from that which holds together in the mind as fitting'[21] – though to put it that way is to diminish Twain's individual comic instance in the pursuit of the general rule.

Gutwirth's further description of humour in terms of the 'clash of levels' that occurs as the playful and logical sides of the self collide is, however, much more apt in helping to explain the specific effect Twain produces in this story, taken as a whole. He analyses the comic move from the one side of the self to the other, and the rupture that occurs with an awareness of the resulting incongruity, in terms of a type of 'joke played by our irresponsible, our ebullient selves upon our sober-sides logical selves trudging glumly in the inescapable tracks of purposive existence'.[22] These words can be reapplied to the nature of the comic charge in 'The Stolen White Elephant', which operates in the gap, and relationship, between the figure of the detective as Twain constructs him, with his logical and myopic approach to existence (both eyes open but seeing in a very limited manner), and the ebullient and random force of the white elephant on the loose. This is to suggest a widening of Gutwirth's frame of reference from internal to external reality, from the grounds of self to that of the represented world. A similar comic effect is then produced in the move between the high seriousness of the attempt to order and control reality and an (alternative) acceptance of its unwieldy and dislocating nature, mocking any human urge to exercise control over it. The detective here, to use an amended version of the earlier quotation, purposefully trudges in the tracks of an eruptive and uncontainable presence. He sticks to his grounds, and to his conventional operating procedures, while the elephant, a paradigm of irresponsible ebullience, leaves complete havoc in its wake.

IV

In first discussing the theft of the elephant, I compared the search for its hidden presence to that for a needle in a haystack. Such a comparison is, of course, metaphorically inept. It does, however, fit a version of the world which accords with the sober-sides Blunt methodically searching for the 'good clues' (p. 8) that will eventually enable him and his fellow 'experts' (p. 9) to find the vanished object.[23] As Blunt persists with his fixed routines, comedy continues to emerge both in the wholly inappropriate nature of his measures to the case at hand, and in the disparity between cause and effect, between the assumed difficulty of detection and the obviousness of the 'evidence', which follows. Among the measures he takes is the 'search of all suspicious persons' in the railway and ferry depots and other exit points from Jersey City. Once put into effect, Blunt turns to the narrator confidently (and comically) to state: 'I am not given to boasting, it is not my habit; but – we shall find the elephant' (pp. 9–10).

If the elephant does turn out initially to be as elusive as that needle, it is nothing like as invisible. It crashes through the local environment causing mayhem. It is reported 'dispersing a funeral . . . and diminishing the mourners by two' (p. 19) in Bolivia, New York, and '[breaking] up a revival' at Baxter Centre, 'striking down and damaging many who were on the point of entering a better life'. The elephant, now momentarily captured, also brains Detective Brown ('that is, head crushed and destroyed, though nothing issued from the debris' – p. 20) when the latter tries to identify it by looking for the boil scar under its armpit, before it once more escapes on the loose.

Gutwirth associates laughter with 'the threat of uncontained disorder', referring to 'the anarchic potential of an outburst that is apt to occur in any context'. He speaks of comedy as 'a field of force-on-the-loose'.[24] Language like this prompts me, given the way Twain represents his elephant, to a (tentative) figurative reading of it. Certainly this elephant comes to signify disruption and disorder in the text as the 'glaring headlines' of the newspapers clearly indicate. The narrator gives an example of their general tone:

THE WHITE ELEPHANT AT LARGE! HE MOVES UPON HIS FATAL MARCH! WHOLE VILLAGES DESERTED BY THEIR

FRIGHT-STRICKEN OCCUPANTS! PALE TERROR GOES BEFORE, DEATH AND DEVASTATION FOLLOW AFTER! AFTER THESE, THE DETECTIVES. BARNS DESTROYED, FACTORIES GUTTED, HARVESTS DEVOURED, PUBLIC ASSEMBLAGES DISPERSED, ACCOMPANIED BY SCENES OF CARNAGE IMPOSSIBLE TO DESCRIBE! (p. 21)

The rituals of religion and its accessories (the elephant eats Bibles), the forms of community, the means of sustenance, the patterns of work: all these things are disrupted by the elephant. The closeness of the fit between Gutwirth's theorising language and the description of the elephant suggests an allegorical relation[25] between the elephant and the comic principle itself, with Twain representing comedy as a potentially anarchic force; a threat to the established social order and all the codes and conventions on which it depends.

I am aware of treading on thin ground here, but it does seem that such an allegorical reading can, once made, then bear further development. For a common analysis of the way humour works is to show how it can be associated with misrule and lawlessness, 'chaos celebrated in relief from the oppressiveness of order . . . a release of (demonic?) energies pent up under rule'. The other side to the same definitional coin, however, is that it is also subject to containment, a force which can function only briefly as the normal authorities are temporarily disrupted, challenged, and even overthrown. If, in Gutwirth's words, 'laughter preserves the equilibrium of a culture as it does that of a group by the timely release of an outburst that dissipates animosities', then this disorder must shortly be brought under control. Laughter, in such a view, is an 'aid in maintaining whole our allegiance to an orderly existence'. Or, to put it another way, comedy is subject to a peculiar form of social policing. Seen like this, the 'disorder' of laughter is accepted in the 'well-regulated state' as a healthy part of the social process. It contributes to 'the creation and maintenance of a living order'.[26] If humour threatens and disrupts authority, the challenge it presents to the established system is always temporary (that, however, is not to say it cannot effect changes in that system) for it is to the accepted forms and norms that a return is soon to be made.

My heavy use of Gutwirth at this point suggests how closely I am following his analysis of what he calls the 'socio-integrative approach' to humour.[27] However, we might wonder, as we return to Twain, if his view of comedy accepts its hegemonic incorporation in the way that such an analysis suggests. For, to continue with an allegorical reading, the disruptive force of the elephant, once it gets out of control and commits its 'red crimes' (p. 21), is not allowed free (or even limited) run, but is subject to immediate challenge by the dominant society. It is shot at with small cannon-balls by the citizens of Bolivia, New York, and pursued by the detectives – the next best thing to the police – until it is dead, its rotting corpse found in the recesses of the very room in which the detectives sleep. The detectives regain their authority at the cost of the elephant's life. When the central narrator uses a rather odd and unexpected phrase and speaks of the elephant as his 'irresponsible agent' (p. 21) at exactly the point at which its anarchic power is most evident, might we shift the referent and read this (and thus the story as a whole) in terms of Twain's ambivalent response to his own comic art? To do so is, from one point of view, to see the white elephant as 'transcendently royal', and signifying great value: a positive agency which acts as a powerful subversive and anarchic force, and which can only be held in check by the representatives of a repressive society which constitutes it as a type of feared other ('the dread creature' – p. 22). From a different perspective, the value of the elephant is cancelled out once it runs unchecked. For its force is now identified only with negative forms of destruction, and has necessarily to be contained by the social body if that body is to continue to function properly.

If there is a veiled allegory at work in this narrative, then it is this last reading – that humour unchecked (and the humorist unchecked?) should be seen as a dangerously irresponsible counter to conventional social existence – which might seem initially the more convincing. The violence done by the elephant in the course of the narrative, the people killed and maimed, appear to endorse such a view. However, it is at this point we step back to remind ourselves that this is just a comic sketch and *not* a direct representation of reality. Humour may have the power to fundamentally disrupt social convention. So Twain will write, in *The Mysterious Stranger* manuscripts, that 'against the assault of Laughter nothing can stand'.[28] It is, though, essentially a form of 'nonviolent dissent'. The humorous treatment of both death and violence in 'The Stolen White Elephant' can only endorse our knowledge of their essentially *unreal* quality. Detective Hawes reports that 'Elephant . . . killed a horse; have secured a piece of it for a clue. Killed it with his trunk; from style of blow, think he struck it left-handed' (p. 15). This is an absurdist and cartoon violence, any aggressive quality modified by 'the consciousness of inconsequentiality',[29] our knowledge that real pain is not at issue here.

In short, there is no simple reading available here concerning the relationship of the elephant (the comic?) to social convention. Those who represent the social in the tale are themselves associated with violence, as the maiming of the elephant with cannon-balls shows. The justice and the health of the order being maintained is also open to question, for the chief detective uses the elephant on the loose to buttress his own prestige and financial position. Moreover, the violence of the elephant, contained within the comic frame of the story, can be contrasted with the *actual* violence associated with the figure of the detective in the period when Twain is writing. To move from Twain's text to its framing historical context is to be made aware of the detective's role as a violently repressive social agent. Pinkerton agent, James McParland, for instance, was accused of playing the part of *agent provocateur* in the Molly Maguires case of the late 1870s, acting on behalf of powerful business interests; part of an hegemonic order which was to sustain its position by legalised violence (the hanging of the twenty Irish coal miners).[30] Later, the Pinkertons' role in the 1892 Homestead Steel Strike would confirm the nature of such a reactionary social role in trumps.

If, then, 'The Stolen White Elephant' is an allegory about the comic, the relationship between the power of humour and its hegemonic containment is presented in ambivalent and unresolved terms. The anarchic potential of comedy can be read in two contrasting ways: as a beneficial, and potentially revolutionary, counter to a dull, authoritarian and repressive social order, or (unless properly harnessed within strict boundaries of acceptability) as a negative and destructive force which disrupts our necessary social routines and systems. The story can also be interpreted in terms of its juxtaposition of two contrasting types of violence – that associated with comedy, in its aggressive mode, and that wielded by the socio-political establishment: the physically violent means by which it exercises its power. If, in the relationship between the elephant and the comic, a one-to-one allegorical frame can be identified, the allegory only develops so far. Its point and purpose, the clarity which underlies the allegorical form, finally gets lost, to borrow metaphorically from the text, in a type of foggy indeterminacy. This may suggest Twain's own ambivalence about his comic art.

V

Whether it was his conscious intention or not, Twain's use of the white elephant at the centre of this story does encourage a figurative reading. Indeed the elephant starts off, in the text's own terms, as the ground for one such reading: its physical presence a sign or token of gratitude and propitiation. A straightforward account of the value of the white elephant is given at the start of the sketch: 'You know in what reverence the royal white elephant of Siam is held by people of that country. You know it is sacred to kings . . . even superior to kings' (p. 1). Such an account, though, does raise problems concerning figurative or representational value, for though such a creature might signify the 'transcendently royal' and the holy in Siam, that is not to say it signifies equally in the American context of the narrative. More, the question of whether we can trust our narrator's interpretive account is also at stake here. He is, after all, to be depicted in the story to come as both naive and uncritical in his reading of the events which affect him.

A white elephant is both a 'rarity in nature . . . considered sacred and precious', but also (and this is the more common meaning today) something you cannot get rid of, 'an unwanted possession' now 'up for sale'. The latter meaning, indeed, evidently derives from 'the story of a Siamese king who used to make a present of a white elephant to courtiers he wished to ruin'.[31] This might lead us to think again as to the exact nature of those 'Oriental ideas' (p. 2) motivating the King of Siam as he sends his gift to the Queen of England. And we should remember that Twain's comic fictions repeatedly play around the relativistic shift in value centres, especially regarding assumptions of cultural superiority. The question of what the white elephant might figuratively connote runs right through Twain's text as the reader puzzles over precisely what it is doing there: whether it is just a literal presence (a very unusual animal); whether the first-given figurative meaning (the sign of the transcendentally royal) is relevant; or whether the elephant signifies some other concept(s) or term(s). I would suggest that we cannot help but speculate on this last possibility. We know anyway that this is a phrase that carries a heavy figurative charge; indeed that normally we would *only* use it in a figurative sense.[32]

Marcel Gutwirth discusses the changing relationship between figure and ground as constitutive of humour itself. He quotes Gregory Bateson: 'The joke may be thought of as involving a shift between the figure and the ground, where the figure is altered or the ground is reconstituted or a reversal of the figure-ground is taking place.' This sounds complicated, but the example which follows helps to clarify. Referring (via E. H. Gombrich) to those trick figures which can be read, depending on the angle or way of looking, as either (for instance) a duck or a rabbit, Gutwirth continues:

> The mystery of illusion resides in the impossibility of capturing both views simultaneously. . . . Is laughter then the apprehension of that inability? Do we not in the art of raising a laugh voluntarily expose the single-track character of a mental apparatus incapable of focusing at once on the figure and the ground?[33]

This becomes doubly interesting when applied to Twain's story. If the elephant in its animal literalness is the ground, what then is the figure we can read onto it? Is that elephant a metaphor for the sacred and the valuable? For the principle of the unexpected and the alien (a type of mysterious stranger figure but taking animal form) which disrupts everyday logic and routine and which may suggest unknown determining influences (the intentionally malevolent gift)? For the comic spirit itself? And does the humour of the narrative arise from our confusion as readers – and from our awareness that that confusion is being cleverly manipulated by Twain – as we try and fit a 'straightforward' narrative of an elephant on the loose with a variety of clashing figurative possibilities?

What makes for the doubling of the interest is that there appears to be a self-conscious play on the relationship between figure and ground as Twain's narrative develops. His elephant, now taking the part of the figure, much as in Gutwirth's rabbit/duck example, literally disappears into the (back)ground toward the story's end. The descent of a dense fog which closes the second part of the narrative means that 'all trace of the elephant [is] lost'. The sighting of a 'dim vast mass [at] the most absurdly distant points' (p. 22) becomes just a confirmation of the confusion now reigning as the white elephant disappears into the fog; a confirmation of the fact that figure and ground have become more or less indistinguishable.

This takes me circuitously back to the relationship between figure and ground in comic theory. Gutwirth states that the 'laughter [of what he calls "frank amusement"], to come into being, has to be sure of its ground', and has to be based on a sense of the self which is 'utterly secure'. If (to use again the duck/rabbit example given previously as an analogy of the way the comic perception might be seen to function) it is the awareness of our 'single-track' mental apparatus that produces laughter, then this laughter comes from a position of mental strength. We are sure of ourselves, of our sanity and normality, and know that the mental confusion that has occurred is merely momentary. The 'pleasurable helplessness'[34] we briefly feel as our minds are taken in by that 'shift between figure and ground' depends on a more fundamental sense of being absolutely sure of our (larger) ground: the sense of our own firm mental grounding and stable relationship to the reality which surrounds us.

It is exactly such security, such a sense of ourselves, that Twain brings into question in 'The Stolen White Elephant', where the relationship between figure and ground collapses in on itself. At the narrative point I have described (to be followed only by the final turn of the illogical and elliptic ending), the sense of the relation of figure to ground – which is the white elephant and which the fog – has become completely blurred. This suggests, to me, the reason why the clash of figurative possibilities in this narrative does not function in any direct sense, as Gutwirth suggests that it theoretically might, as a source of humour. As readers, we end up half-aware of such possibilities (that the elephant is to be read figuratively) but unclear about the relationship between figure and ground. We are uncertain which of these metaphoric readings apply, or of how we decide which one applies, or indeed whether we should be trying to read this narrative in such a figurative manner at all: quite *what* level we should be taking it at. Twain dislocates his readers here: leaves us unsure of the base from which we are meant to be operating – unsure of *our* ground. Just as the elephant merges with the fog toward the end of the tale, so too are its readers unable (metaphorically) to see the elephant: to see the point of the story; the point of the joke. We can find immediate humour in the parody of the detective story, in the individual comic incident and incongruity within that story, in the burlesque of the detective business itself. We find further humour at a second and deeper level in the way we are caught between two sets of readerly responses to the narrative. But we are still left puzzled by the sense that we still have not penetrated to the core of the narrative or its comic intention: that there is some kind of further level yet, or larger meaning, which continues to remain enigmatic. We are left with the odd sense of being (like the narrator?) victims of a further hoax which we do not really understand.

VI

This brings me finally back to the 'pointedly pointless' aspect of this narrative with which I began. If Gutwirth discusses *'uneasy laughter* [as being] utterly incompatible with mirth',[35] and sees such laughter as a form of humour where we are *not* sure of our readerly ground, then 'The Stolen White Elephant' seems paradigmatic of such a form. Indeed, I would suggest that much of Twain's humour, and indeed, many of his narratives, work in this way. The theme of disorientation is a major one in this story. It is a product of the (unanswerable) questions we are led to ask about the enigmatic qualities of the narrative – *has* this elephant, for example, actually been stolen at all and, if so, by whom and for what possible purpose? It is produced, too, by the use of a narrative form where an illogicality and a lack of connectiveness are apparent, and where spatial dislocations predominate. For a geographical tracing of the movement of the elephant (exactly what Blunt does) suggests a principle of both randomness and uncertainty at work in terms of where it is going to go next, and how one can tell. In the course of a single night and early morning, it is reported as being in Long Island, New Jersey, and New York (pp. 13–14); though, alternatively, it might be in none of these places, and the reports of its presence false. The elephant certainly 'does move around' (p. 14). References to the directions it takes tend to leave the reader unmoored: 'some say he went east, some say west, some north, some south – but all say they did not wait to notice particularly' (p. 15). Further unmooring occurs as elephant and fog merge. The more the text continues, the more we lose any firm sense of our general ground. At the text's conclusion we are not quite sure what has happened nor why. The more our eyes should be opened to what exactly is the case, and to what is the narrative intent, the less we actually see. The comedy in the story is built on a base of radical uncertainty.

Twain's humour, then, from an early stage of his career, is that of epistemological uncertainty.[36] To be human in a world which lacks logic, sense, even meaning, is to be unsure of one's bearings. To get the joke, to see the elephant, is to acknowledge such a fact. The references to the illogical and the absurd within the text ('"That is perfectly absurd!" I exclaimed' – p. 18) might be extended beyond its margin to speak of the condition of the modern – note all the references to the factory, to photography, to telegrams, steamships, omnibuses and railroads in the story – where all that we can know is just how little we know; all we know of the ground on which we stand is just how uncertain it is. Indeed, in later chapters of the book, I extend my analysis of how closely Twain's work relates to an America in the process of rapid modernisation, and the anxieties associated with such a process.

But it is the sense of shifting perspective and uncertain ground in 'The Stolen White Elephant' which prompts me to use it to introduce my discussion of Twain's writing. That sense is exemplified in the unstable relationship between the hidden and the obvious which both structures the story, and suggests a quality of constant undecidability to Twain's work as a whole. In 'The Stolen White Elephant', the elephant crashes its way to the textual foreground. An uncontrollable and alien force, it stands out, in an anomalous and unsettling way, from the described background. But it also disappears into this background, leaving only traces of its presence, as the focus switches to the detective seeking his clues. Foreground becomes background, and vice versa, depending on the textual moment and on the perspective taken.

The detective is associated, at least in theory, with rational analysis, and the impulse to gain logical control over a confused narrative. But in 'The Stolen White Elephant', the elephant (and the principle of narrative chaos it symbolises) gets equal attention:

turning up unexpectedly and randomly, and disrupting all ordered sequence. A similar sense of incongruity pervades all Twain's texts, destabilised as they are by conflicting elements, changes of focus, shifts of perspective, generic disconnections, and disruptive comic effects. What at one textual moment is hidden or at the margins of the narrative, will, at the next, become a bulky and central presence that frustrates its smooth development. And if Twain thematises epistemological uncertainty in this story (and recurrently), his reader too ends up, as often as not, unmoored; unsure of her or his ground, uncertain in which direction the various textual figures are going.

In all of Twain's narratives the hidden and the obvious exist in unstable relation to one another. This is not just a matter of the way various elements are represented within his texts but affects the very way we read them. Thus, at an internal textual level, *Puddn'head Wilson and Those Extraordinary Twins* (1894) features another of Twain's fictional detectives. What his detective work reveals, however, is what should have been obvious all along: that in a society where race is determined on fractions of blood, 'black' and 'white' have become indistinguishable from one another. Indeed it is Puddn'head who makes explicit, at the beginning of the book, that without their clothes Tom could be taken for Valet, and vice versa. He already has, too, from the time of the boys' infancy, the fingerprints that clearly show a switch has occurred. But when Wilson finally exposes this switch, he also reveals the blindness of a whole society. For its members still fail to see the joke: that the absurd nature of their own racial assumptions has allowed them to be fooled. The detective himself appears also to overlook this (glaring) fact at the novel's end.

The instability of this relationship between the hidden and the obvious also carries over to the reading of Twain's texts. It is difficult to decide if the meanings of his books exist below the surface, and need to be uncovered by the detective reader, or are rather in plain view – like the elephant – and staring that reader in the face. For what critics detect in Twain's work is always, in one sense, already apparent. Recent interpretations of the ending of *Adventures of Huckleberry Finn* (1885) uncover an allegory of post-Reconstruction racial politics. This is partly because of the particular (new historicist) interests of today's community of readers. It is also, though, because of something already present in the book, and something that Twain may have intended his reader to notice. The textual elements which produce that reading have been openly available, and on view, from the time he first wrote the novel.

I am saying, in other words, that Twain's texts (like the reports of the elephant's comings and goings) move in different directions, and, as they do so, contradictions and conflicting meanings appear. We can never be quite sure what he is deliberately thematising, which elements are meant to be foregrounded and which not, or to what degree the meanings of the text emerge despite its author. Twain's role as a comic writer, and one, moreover, who ended up writing just fragments of texts, is relevant here. His humour depends on incongruity and tends to resist the type of analysis which works in terms of direct authorial intent and unambiguous meaning. Indeed 'The Stolen White Elephant' can be taken as a comic story of ambiguity about the comic, which ends with the reader not sure of the joke on any level. Humour took Twain into uncomfortable places. One of its defining qualities is the ability to express what we would normally suppress and censor, often in an unintentional and double-edged way. Twain himself, even thirty years after the event, could not quite decide whether the speech he made at the Whittier birthday dinner in 1877, where he burlesqued aging members of the New England literary establishment (Henry Wadsworth Longfellow, Ralph Waldo Emerson and Oliver Wendell Holmes) as drunken roughs, was a disrespectful snipe at his cultural superiors, or just innocent fun.[37] At the time, he thought it the latter, and was mortified to find it taken as the former. The cultural analysis and criticism in Twain's work can easily be missed by the reader. It is quite possible, as I argue in my chapter on *A Connecticut Yankee in King Arthur's Court* (1889), that he missed it too.

Among the subjects I discuss in this study are the generic instabilities in Twain's texts, the anxieties about the status of the self in his writing, and (a related subject) the way in which this writing engages the cultural dialogues of its times. I follow Steven Mailloux in looking to show how the literary text can be sited in the larger context of cultural history.[38] I pay particular attention to Twain's representation of race, of capitalist processes and assumptions, and of the larger impact of modernisation. In the last analysis, I sideline the matter of authorial intention. As I proceed, however, I suggest that Twain's awareness of what he was doing was both shifting and multi-levelled. Twain is a particularly difficult writer to pin down.

'The Stolen White Elephant' can be read as an allegory about
humour itself, and its uncomfortable relation to the dominant social
order. But it can also be read as a type of pointless, but comic, hoax.
Or it can be read as thematising interpretative indeterminacy itself.
But we cannot know how much of this Twain intended as he wrote.
I may be seeing here what is precisely obvious, the very point of
Twain's story, or I may be uncovering something deeply hidden,
of which he himself was unaware. His texts are marked by
undecidability.

This is again to raise the question of the hidden and the obvious.
Allegory itself, indeed, complicates the relationship between these
terms, relying on concealed meanings but also (usually) overtly
flagging their presence. For allegory implies signalled intentionality,
with explicit textual signs that trigger our awareness of a further
narrative level. When I use the term in the context of Twain's work,
I am aware, however, that the allegory may be unintentional, seen
neither by Twain nor by many of his readers, but obvious to myself
and other later readers due to the nature of the interpretive
communities to which we belong, and the critical apparatus and
frameworks we use. But the very presence of the elements that
signal such a reading raises the possibility, nonetheless, of direct
intentionity. Thus, when I discuss *Huckleberry Finn*, I sugggest – on
the basis of a certain amount of knowledge of Twain's position in
regard to post-Civil War racial debates – that his allegorical critique
of contemporary treatment of the African-American may be
deliberate, and argue that the novel is ultimately a powerful
anti-racist text. Other critics, though, disagree: reading the end of
the book as non-ironic racial and racist farce, with Jim as the
inconsequential butt of Tom and Huck's games. There is no way of
finally deciding which meaning is the more obvious one, but also if
the obvious one is the one 'authorised' by Twain.

It may be that Twain's role as a humorist, and his own ambivalent
attitude to the dominant American values of his time, led him to
write texts that move in multiple directions, and where any social
critique is placed in incongruous relation to other and contradictory
textual elements. It may be that his texts interrogate dominant
cultural assumptions despite himself: that he remained blind to
many of the incongruities, ambiguities, and disruptive elements
that, like the elephant in his story, barged their way into his
narratives. I want to keep both my critical eyes open, and to

recognise all the curious movements of his texts. Any implied authorial intention, or the lack of it, in the chapters that follow take second place to my analysis of the contradictions and divisions of Twain's writing, the shifts of perspective within it, and the 'cultural work'[39] his texts do as a result. I argue that the anxieties about fictional form, and about the status of the self, the workings of society, and the patternings of history, which his texts reveal, make his writing – and the direction it came to take – central to any consideration of his period.

2
Old World Travel:
The Innocents Abroad

> *Dan told to gather all manner of statistics, reports that brandy is 8 cents a drink, & cigars 3-pence. . . .*
> *Then came to NAZARETH, where Christ lived & carpentered till 30 year of age. . . .*
> *Got some pieces of the old Temple.*
>
> *(Mark Twain's Notebooks & Journals)*[1]

I

The Innocents Abroad, or The New Pilgrim's Progress (1869) was Twain's first full-length book. Funded by the San Francisco *Daily Alta California*, he sailed from New York in June 1867, on board the *Quaker City*, for Europe and the Holy Land. *The Innocents Abroad*, written on his return to America, was the revised and expanded version of the newspaper reports he had sent back on this 'great Pleasure Excursion'.[2]

The symbolic resonances, both of this voyage and of 'Mark Twain's' role (as the quasi-fictional narrator/protagonist'[3]) in the book that describes it, are clear. For the *Quaker City* expedition was 'the first large-scale pleasure voyage of its kind in American history',[4] and, as such, helped to usher in a new pattern of relationships between the New World and the Old. 'American travel abroad seemed to explode after 1865',[5] a result of a dramatic improvement in transatlantic transportation, and the changes in

22

both economic conditions and attitudes that followed the Civil War.[6] A new American mood of self-assertion and confidence[7] was reflected in the 'changing tone' of travel in the period. William W. Stowe suggests the different expectations of post-bellum Americans abroad to those of the early nineteenth-century travellers, who saw themselves 'primarily as learners and appreciators', when he writes that:

> By the time of Twain's Innocents . . . the chief purpose of many travelers was not to submit to Old World influences but to acquire choice bits of culture and experience at a good price. Education was all very well, and a little polish never hurt anyone, but the new American travelers . . . were not about to purchase these European commodities on any terms but their own. These successful capitalists and their wives . . . were no longer diffidently, painfully aware of their shortcomings, but proud of their own and their country's new-found economic power and eager to experience the very best that their hard-earned money could buy.[8]

I suggest, in this chapter, that Twain's attitude to his Old World materials is more complicated than Stowe implies here. But in *The Innocents Abroad* he did begin to provide the literary measure of this new American spirit. Twain's announcement of the 'purpose' of his book makes it clear that he saw himself as representative of his countrymen,[9] and of a new way of approaching Old World materials. For he wants, he says, 'to suggest to the reader how *he* would be likely to see Europe and the East if he looked at them with his own eyes instead of the eyes of those who travelled in those countries before him' (p. 3). Twain stands in for his audience in sounding 'a new American voice'.[10] And where better to sound its representative and legitimising note than on a tourist trip (for Twain, whatever his other motives, was 'willy-nilly, a tourist'[11]) back to the Old World, the traditional centre of civilisation, culture and tradition, and in the reversal of longstanding relationships of dominance and subordination which occurs there?

Travel writing tells us as much about the country travelled from as about the country travelled to. Twain, in 1867, spoke on behalf of a mass American audience, with considerable financial power, starting to redefine the Old World according to a new set of cultural needs and values. Something of this is suggested by Bruce Michelson when he writes:

> The *Quaker City* contained the vanguard of the largest and richest invasion of wandering pleasure-seekers in history. The Americans were coming to turn Europe into one vast amusement park, to transform every gallery, palace, cathedral . . . into a hometown sideshow, to gape at the 'foreigners' and have themselves a good time. The millions back home waited to hear of the great national pleasure adventure from someone who had gone along in the proper spirit. . . . Mark Twain had no better choice than to assume the role of the American gone out to play.[12]

Though *The Innocents Abroad* was not altogether original in what it did, Twain's ability to combine the themes and techniques of earlier writers, the particular voice(s) he created, and his synthesis of comedy with travel chronicle, helps to explain both its short- and long-term importance.[13] Certainly much of the book's success lies in the 'cultural comedy' it dramatises,[14] as conventional assumptions about Europe, its traditions, and the value of its artistic heritage are subjected to the apparently 'innocent' and iconoclastic eye of Mark Twain, the playful and 'free-talking American frankly sizing up the Old World'.[15]

My argument, though, is that Twain's text is not as straightforward as it may at first seem. In fact, *The Innocents Abroad* signals a recurrent pattern in his major works in the *contradictions* that it contains. The more closely the book is examined, the more apparent its complications and internal tensions are. The narrative is both a playful account of a pleasure trip *and* a more serious description of a cultural and spiritual pilgrimage,[16] and the gap between these two very different motivating impulses cannot be bridged. This helps to explain the textual swings between iconoclastic mockery and standard travelogue, and between comic irreverence and conventional piety. If Twain's task in this book is a representative one, to 'describe for a new mass audience what had been an elite-identified experience',[17] his position as a narrator and protagonist is far from unified or consistent.

This introduces another central concern, both here and in my critical study as a whole. For the interest Twain shows in *The Innocents Abroad* with the shifting, self-divided and uncertain status of the self is continued throughout his writing career. The instabilities of voice and identity in *The Innocents Abroad* do not, though, simply relate to Twain's response to his Old World subject matter. They result, also, from his divided attitude to America. Twain's humour in *The Innocents Abroad* cuts two ways as he both represents his nation and criticises it. Celebrating American innocence and frankness, he is also aware of the naivety, shallowness and blinkered nationalism that these qualities can imply. There is a further complication here, too. For Twain's text reveals that the Americans about whom, and for whom, he writes, are not a homogeneous group. As he separates American 'pilgrims' from 'sinners' in his text, so he recognises the divisions and differences that the concept of a fixed national identity disguises. In doing so, he tends to destabilise the clear-cut nature of the opposition between Old World and New on which so much of the narrative rests.

Twain's first full-length book, then, is marked by contradiction and shifts of perspective. I focus here on two other features of Twain's writing, both of which are also central to my developing analysis of his work as a whole. The first is the sense of epistemological uncertainty in *The Innocents Abroad*. For its instabilities of identity and voice indicate a deep uncertainty about the position of the subject and his ability to interpret experience in an accurate and authoritative manner. William Stowe discusses tourism as a way of 'coming to know and hence to dominate the world', with the tourist as the *sightseer* whose 'subjugating gaze reduces individuals, institutions, art-works, and landscapes to bits of knowledge and elevates the tourists and their class, race, gender, and nation to the position of the authoritative knower'.[18] If Twain, as confident American iconoclast, seems to adopt exactly this role, it is by no means on a full or permanent basis. For the very possibility of such knowledge tends to disappear in a type of 'vertigo',[19] sometimes comic, sometimes not, that repeatedly undermines any fixed and determinate reading of reality in the text. I earlier describe how the ground tends to disappear from under the reader's feet as he or she reads 'The Stolen White Elephant'. I briefly suggest, at the end of my third section, how a similar sense of unmooring inhabits this book.

I am also interested here in Twain's use of genre. As my book proceeds, I show how the thematic contradictions and instabilities in his work relate to his formal practice: the organisation of his texts and the generic shifts within and between them. *The Innocents Abroad* and *Roughing It* (1872), the next book I discuss, are travel narratives, and this form particularly suited Twain's artistic methods. For the travel book has a shape imposed on it, but one that is extremely flexible: alternating the linear description of the ongoing journey with the pauses along the way, where the writer can insert a dramatic scene,[20] a description (of people, of scenery or an event), a joke or story, a thought or associative digression.

Richard Bridgman's discussion of Twain's travel writing makes a number of perceptive remarks on the author's use of this form. He notes the way Twain's imagination was so often 'liberated' by the 'mechanisms of association': how, within the developing narrative, one subject will trigger the move to another apparently unrelated one. While such 'associative bridge[s]' often occur, both in *The Innocents Abroad* and his other travel books, the changes of topic and direction they bring are, though, by no means formally disruptive: 'for the travel account proved capable of absorbing any improvisation he might conceive'.[21] Bridgman explores the analogy between newspaper reporting, where Twain got his training as a writer, and travel narratives. 'A newspaper', he says:

provides . . . a cornucopia of facts, stories, and commentaries, minimally linked at best and without any synthesising conclusion. In a travel account, though, Twain could rely on the sequence of the journey itself to provide at least a simulacrum of coherence for his materials.[22]

If Twain is given less credit here for the consistent development of a number of themes and subject positions than he deserves, none the less, these comments on his use of the travel book genre are suggestive. For the contradictions in *The Innocents Abroad*, Twain's moves from one narrative role to another, and the shifts in attitude and perspective that accompany such moves can, despite their inconsistency, be easily contained within the baggy limits of the genre. When Twain turned to fiction, such containment would often prove rather more of a problem.

II

The Innocents Abroad can be read as a confident assertion of American nationalism.[23] I begin my analysis of the text from this perspective, putting other complications temporarily to the side. The initial popularity of *The Innocents Abroad* undoubtedly had much to do with its use of a comic irreverence and mocking wit based on an assumption of American cultural superiority. That assumption rested in turn on an American ability to spend freely on a world stage. The rapid increase in tourism to Europe – from about 30,000 a year in the 1840s to more than 100,000 by the 1890s[24] – provides one indicator of that spending power in a market where, as Twain makes clear, a favourable rate of exchange applied. Calling for 'unstinted champagne' for himself, Dan and the doctor in the Grand Casino in Marseilles, Twain comments that 'it is so easy to be bloated aristocrats where it costs nothing of consequence!' (p. 78).[25]

Financial power, of course, brings other forms of authority in its wake.[26] Twain's description, on arriving at Tangier, of 'a tribe of stalwart Moors . . . wading into the sea to carry us ashore on their backs from the small boats' (p. 60), is a pertinent example of the inequalities permeating relations between the tourist and the populations he (in this case) comes to exploit. The apparent lack of any ironic intent (though the judging of tone is often a problematic matter in this text) allows us to see economic mastery unconsciously allegorised here in terms of bodily relations, with the native Moor represented, reductively, only by his brief physical function in the travellers' onward progress. 'Drifting with the tide of a great popular movement' (p. 24), Twain, and those fellow Americans for whom he spoke, were engaged, at least in part, on a commercial mission to the Old World, to buy (if they chose) into its culture, and to spend on sightseeing, enjoyment and souvenirs: 'In Smyrna we picked up camel's hair shawls and other dressy things from Persia' (p. 517).[27] 'We came, we saw, we spent' would be one way of describing their trip. The patriotic cheer that greets the sight of the Stars and Stripes in a foreign land (p. 51) acts, moreover, as a subliminal reminder of the link between mass tourism and the quest for new and expanded markets then taking place on the part of the nation as a whole. This stress on economic power and purchase is, as I suggest in the final section of the chapter, perhaps the one unifying feature in Twain's representation of American national identity.

Robert Regan, in 'Huck Finn in the Wake of the *Quaker City*', examines the way Twain's texts invoke one another, focusing on the connections between *The Innocents Abroad* and *Huckleberry Finn*. Mark Twain and 'the boys', like Huck, 'travel light, bookless, and see and feel for themselves', casting off the 'cumbersome baggage' of prior (often genteel) 'respected author-authorities' who would 'impress free Americans into involuntary servitude'. Thus 'the "boys" of *The Innocents Abroad* defend their spontaneity by feigning ignorance of Old World culture and history, by pretending to recall no discourse anterior to their own'.[28] An alternative tactic here is to directly debunk that prior discourse, together with the piety and religious credulity that is seen to accompany it (as in the 'heart of St Philip Neri' episode – p. 234).

Alfred Kazin relates the cockiness and bumptious quality of *The Innocents Abroad* to 'the solidly good opinion that Americans held of themselves at a time when they believed themselves to have all the virtues of the English as a race and none of the defects of the English as a society'.[29] Edward Said writes that 'self-definition' is 'one of the activities practised by all cultures: it has a rhetoric, a set of occasions, and authorities (national feasts, for example, times of crisis, founding fathers, basic texts, and so on) and a familiarity all its own'.[30] Twain's book works in more than one way. In part, it questions both the unity of American culture and its absolute difference from that of Europe. Yet, contradictorily, it helped to define the distinctiveness of American identity at a time of crisis, when internal division had threatened permanently to tear the country apart.

In its account of travel abroad, *The Innocents Abroad* promotes a type of historical amnesia concerning very recent American history. The Civil War is mentioned in the section on the Azores but only as evidence of Portuguese ignorance of the larger world, when 'a Portuguese of average intelligence inquired if our civil war was over?' (p. 45). This is, significantly, immediately followed by a reference to American technological progress, a source of national pride: the completion of the Atlantic cable of 1866. Apart from descriptions of the muleteers in the Azores 'singing "John Brown's Body" in ruinous English' (p. 48),[31] and of an engraving in an American paper of Jefferson Davis 'signing a secession act or some such document', haunted by the spectre of Washington 'in warning attitude' behind (p. 154), the Civil War stands itself as a silent presence ghosting the book's strong note of national self-assertion.[32] The patriotic references that do occasionally enter the text also speak of an American unity now constructed in the face of former sectional difference. Thus, granted audience with the Emperor of Russia, Twain writes that 'our party . . . felt . . . they were representing the people of America. . . . [W]e felt a national pride in the warm cordiality of that reception' (pp. 316–17).[33]

The Innocents Abroad works in part, then, both to debunk European cultural authority and, simultaneously, to define America's own cultural identity. If such self-definitions have much to do with founding fathers and national occasions, then Twain's use of one of the most highly charged and symbolic events in the history of European–American relationships, Columbus's discovery, is of especial interest here. The influence of the European founder and father is metaphorically cast off in an episode which can be read in terms of a necessary tactical act performed as part of an explicitly nationalistic agenda. The guide in Genoa, rechristened 'Ferguson' by 'the boys' after their usual ethnocentric manner, shows mementoes of Columbus, expecting them to respond like most Americans, with 'wonder . . . sentiment and emotion' (pp. 229–30):

'Ah, genteelmen, you come wis me! I show you beautiful, O, magnificent bust Christopher Colombo! – splendid, grand, magnificent!' . . .
The doctor put up his eye-glass – procured for such occasions:
'Ah – what did you say this gentleman's name was?'
'Christopher Colombo! – ze great Christopher Colombo!'
'Christopher Colombo – the great Christopher Colombo. Well, what did *he* do?'
'Discover America! – discover America, Oh, ze devil!'
'Discover America. No – that statement will hardly wash. We are just from America ourselves. We heard nothing about it. Christopher Colombo – pleasant name – is – is he dead?'
'Oh, corpo di Baccho! – three hundred year!'
'What did he die of?'
'I do not know! – I can not tell.'
'Small-pox, think?'
'I do not know, genteelmen! – I do not know *what* he die of!'

'Measles, likely?'
'May be – may be – I do *not* know – I think he die of somethings.'
'Parents living?'
'Im-posseeble!'
'Ah – which is the bust and which is the pedestal?' (pp. 230–1)

The European discovery of America, thus implicitly the whole process of colonisation, is met with pretended ignorance. The 'is he dead?' joke (taken from Artemus Ward[34]) reinforces the fact that these 'self-reliant Americans' (p. 411), like Huck Finn, 'don't take no stock in dead people'.[35] Twain and his friends, representatives of a young and confident nation, are conspicuously *not* 'genteelmen', beholden to, and respectful of, tradition. Rather they relentlessly undercut the pious assumptions of their puzzled guide with deadpan humour and broadscale, and finally explosively absurd, jokes. Not only have these Americans got out from under the European heritage, cast off the burden of this past, but the journey of discovery itself is now reversed. Twain and the boys' discovery of Europe, their journey to see what it has to offer them and the benefits to be gained there blot out the traces of Columbus's earlier voyage.[36]

   The end of Twain's journey, here and elsewhere in the text, is a confident assertion of American 'innocence' and newness, a rejection of Old World culture as lacking interest and value to clear-sighted American eyes. Such a stance is by no means consistent. It is, however, one that informs much of the humour and best-remembered incidents in the book. This assertiveness takes a slightly different form when Twain sees the original of Da Vinci's *The Last Supper*, which fails, for him, to have that special aura associated with the authenticity and uniqueness of the great work of art. He straightaway sets his voice against the inherited weight of reverence and opinion when he says, scandalously, that the multiple reproductions of the picture he sees being painted are, to his 'inexperienced' but implicitly honest eye, 'superior . . . to the original' (pp. 150–1). He is careful to base this opinion on the poor and faded condition of Da Vinci's painting, but none the less this is, to any traditionalist, cultural heresy. Twain then repeats it shortly after when he judges the 'copies of all the celebrated sculptures in Europe' found in the shops of Florence much more 'enchanting to the eye' than 'the dingy petrified nightmares they are the portraits of' (p. 194). This partly results from Twain's role as mass tourist, doing all the things that the tourist did ('he did all these things one after another. And he did them faster and faster by aid of improving transport'[37]), and preferring, here at least, the shops to the galleries. But such responses result too from the function of the art object in the process of cultural self-definition and the question of aesthetic judgement that goes with it.[38] Twain's preference of copy to original might again be read metaphorically as an assertive gesture on the part of the formerly subservient cultural dependant. To say the copy is brighter, fresher, more lustrous and lively than the original is not, in this case, to dismiss the forming influence of the latter. It is, though, to suggest that the American nation, far from being a pale imitation of that Europe from which her customs, beliefs and settlers originally came, has come rather to outshine and better the original 'dingy' and 'petrified' place of origin.[39]

Twain evidences a combative sense of American cultural identity in such episodes. Traditional notions of a civilised Old and uncivilised New World are revised as the narrator reports back on Europe and the Near East. The Portuguese of the Azores are described as 'shiftless' and 'lazy'. That they raise their corn 'just as their great-great-great grandfathers did' (p. 44) distinguishes them from Twain's Americans who, it is implied, know when to reject the influence of the ancestor. The Moors in Tangier are 'savages' (p. 70). Italians are identified in terms of their 'garlic-exterminating mouth[s]' (p.145). 'Educated to enmity toward every thing that is Catholic' (p. 479), Twain's American Protestant consciousness has no time for an Italy 'which has groped in the midnight of priestly superstition for sixteen hundred years' (p. 201). The Arabs of the Valley of Lebanon 'never invent any thing, never learn any thing' (p. 352). The Fountain of Figia in Syria is surrounded by a 'wretched nest of human vermin' (p. 358). The Old World is repeatedly represented in terms of a type of an alien backwardness.

Indeed, as the book proceeds, and as the protagonist moves beyond European limits, so the narrator's dismissal of the representatives of other cultures becomes more hostile.[40] So too a refusal of dialogue with such people, which has appeared as an earlier textual motif, becomes increasingly rigid. As Mark Twain and his colleagues travel through this foreign world, they constantly 'translate' it into familiar conceptual and linguistic moulds, renaming their guides as 'Ferguson', an Arab village as 'Jonesborough' (p. 370). Twain describes Arab speech as a 'disagreeable

jabbering in unknown tongues' (p. 433). Jerusalem is, we are told, a
polyglot community, but the only word that Twain hears is 'the
eternal "bucksheesh"' (p. 446), just as (in a way) the only word he
speaks is 'dollar'. Mark Twain's assertive American voice drowns
out and ignores the voices of the inhabitants of the countries
through which he travels, his dollars the sign both of his authority
and his self-proclaimed superiority.

III

I start at this point to explore both the 'slipperiness'[41] of Mark
Twain's identity in *The Innocents Abroad* and the contradictory
nature of the text. Descriptions of the Old World in terms of alien
backwardness (the Portuguese in the Azores) are, as far as one can
tell, absolutely serious. The views put forward are apparently those
of the author. However, at other points, a gap appears between the
author and the fictional persona he constructs. For the ethnocentric
assumptions of the latter are, as the final examples above begin to
suggest, associated with an ignorance and a form of linguistic
arrogance that is clearly subject to satiric attack. Indeed, the claim
at the text's end that 'travel is fatal to prejudice, bigotry and
narrow-mindedness' (p. 521) is countered by the clearly xenophobic
strain that runs through the whole book.[42] The relation between the
civilised and the uncivilised gets thoroughly tangled up in the
process.

If the phrase 'soap and civilisation' denotes the bringing of
progress to primitive societies,[43] then the absence of soap in Europe
– a repeated complaint of Twain and his travelling companions –
implies a lack of civilisation too. But when this sign of backwardness
becomes a central issue (in the Milan bath-house episode), it does
not work to validate the superior nature of Twain and his fellow
Americans, but rather is used to satirise what David Sewell calls
their 'insistent monolingualism': a 'linguistic imperialism' which is
but another 'form of [their] cultural assertion'.[44]

Twain and the doctor's early attempts in Marseilles to try out their
French meet blank incomprehension, and, from that point, any effort
'the boys' make to communicate in native languages is minimal. So,
here:

After we were stripped . . . we discovered that haunting atrocity
that has embittered our lives in so many cities and villages of Italy
and France – there was no soap . . .
Dan's voice rose on the air:
   'Oh, bring some soap, why don't you?'
The reply was Italian. Dan resumed:
   'Soap, you know – soap. That is what I want – soap. S-o-a-p,
soap; s-o-p-e, soap; s-o-u-p, soap. Hurry up! I don't know how
you Irish spell it, but I want it. Spell it to suit yourself, but fetch
it. I'm freezing.'
I heard the doctor say, impressively:
   'Dan, how often have we told you that these foreigners can not
understand English? Why will you not depend upon us? Why
will you not tell *us* what you want, and let us ask for it in the
language of the country? . . . I will address this person in his
mother tongue: 'Here, cospetto! corpo di Bacco! Sacramento!
Solferino! – Soap, you son of a gun!' (pp. 147–8)

Whatever the doctor's pretensions, his ability to communicate in
Italian (or his version of it) is no better than that of Dan, who never
tries. No dialogue takes place here, only a one-way conversation
with the Americans quick to insult and xenophobically abuse those
in a relation of economic dependency to them, whose living
depends (here, at any rate) on the tourist trade. If gold is the
universal language of financial exchange,[45] then English (once the
poor attempts to speak French or Italian have failed) is the only
speech system Twain and 'the boys' will use to complete that
exchange. Dan acts on the principle that if, when you speak to a
foreigner, you repeat something often enough, spell it enough
different ways, assume idiocy on their part, and use enough forms
of command, you will get what you want. The doctor adds a
smattering of misplaced Italian and the odd inappropriate (but
Italian-sounding) word, but operates from a similar stance.
   This is the comedy of cultural aggression. Mark Twain, the tourist,
gets what he wants through his money, and refuses dialogue with
the inhabitants of the countries through which he travels.[46] Unequal
relationships of economic power are paralleled by a dismissive
impatience with the uncivilised and stereotyped foreign 'other'.
Here, however, Twain (as author rather than character) clearly holds
his naive and ignorant protagonist at an ironic remove; that

protagonist's assertive American know-nothing, monolinguistic
and ethnocentric attitudes a source of satire rather than of celebration. But the innocence of this protagonist, as I have suggested,
does not always connote ignorance. It is also associated with a
clear-eyed way of seeing, a casting-off of traditional values and
cultural reverence, with which the reader is encouraged to
empathise. The gap between the narrative persona and the authorial
voice varies as these different positions are adopted. The assertion
of American superiority is both endorsed and criticised in the text,
and a curiously unstable effect in thereby created.

Our sense of our readerly ground starts to give way here. Are we
meant to identify with the American nationalism with which the
narrator is identified or are we meant to hold it at arm's length,
seeing it as an uninformed and shallow prejudice? When do
innocence and ignorance become the same thing? There are no
simple answers to these questions. Twain shuttles his reader
between positions, makes her or him aware both of the strengths of
the way of reading the Old World of his (representative American)
narrator, and of its absurd limits. The gap between a serious
authorial voice, an adopted voice which echoes or may echo the
author's values, and an adopted voice which is the subject of satiric
undermining, but yet may or may not represent a certain element
in the authorial identity, constantly and disconcertingly opens and
closes as the text proceeds.

This is a contradictory and destabilising text in other ways too.
Certainly, the combative sense of American identity constructed in
The Innocents Abroad cannot be denied. The series of contrasts,
implicit and explicit, made between Europe and America, seem to
leave the reader clear where Twain's sympathies lie. America, unlike
the Old World, is free from aristocratic forms, every man (at least
in theory) a king. Twain describes his '*royal* summer flight across
[the American] continent in a stage-coach' (p. 87, my emphasis) – a
scenario to which he returns in *Roughing It* – and the scanning of
'the blue distances of a world that knew no lords but us' (p. 86). The
various superstitions alluded to in Europe (Galileo's scientific
discoveries judged as heresy by the Church – p. 192), and its cruel,
repressive and autocratic forms of political authority (which
underlie the descriptions of the Castle d'If, pp. 82–4; the Bastille,
p. 90; the Medicis, p. 193), also function as a reminder of American
democratic difference. Nature may imitate art in the open spaces

and grandeur of the western American landscape, with its 'mimic cities . . . pinnacled cathedrals . . . massive fortresses, counterfeited in the eternal rocks' (p. 86). As it does so, however, it implicitly provides a healthy contrast with the cultural sights of Europe, and the extremes of wealth and poverty, the aristocratic or religious privilege, associated with its real cities, cathedrals and fortresses.

But if this is so, Twain can neither celebrate his own country nor denigrate the Old World completely. Angles of vision both shift and clash in *The Innocents Abroad*, undercut each other, as Twain moves between narrative positions, and this movement renders any unitary reading of his materials impossible. Thus an attack on Rome, its lack of open government, its superstition and backwardness, from the perspective of American democratic difference, has its comparative foundation removed as Twain suddenly shifts to criticise plutocratic corruption in public life back home (pp. 210–11). Accordingly, we 'glimpse the very American face of Mark Twain, disillusioned observer of postbellum venality and future co-author of *The Gilded Age*'.[47]

Similarly, the negative picture of the Old World, and the perspective that frames it, drops away in a countering recognition of its attractions. Alfred Kazin talks of 'the sound of breathless respect for Old Europe in which so much has *happened*' that runs alongside the 'disdain for backwardness and ignorance' in the book.[48] The irreverence of Twain's narrator is matched elsewhere, in direct contrast, by cultural reverence. The 'noble' and 'beautiful' Milan cathedral, with the 'beautiful marble statues' on its roof, is described (in notably undemocratic terms) as 'surely . . . the princeliest creation that ever brain of man conceived' (pp. 136–8). To be in Venice is, attractively, to be 'in a half-waking dream . . . drifting back, back, back, into the solemn past, and looking upon the scenes and mingling with the people of a remote antiquity' (p. 186).[49]

The contradictory and clashing nature of Twain's responses to the Old World in *The Innocents Abroad* can, in part, be explained by the sense of epistemological provisionality which he explicitly dramatises in the book. For the reading of reality, and its inter-pretation, depends on the position of the subject, and this is a relative, not a fixed, thing. In the Pallavicini garden, near Genoa, Twain draws conscious attention to the problems and limits of representation, with his awareness that 'the carefully contrived accident of a framework' determines the 'entrancing beauty' of the view, excluding 'all unattractive features' from it (p. 416). The version of reality you give depends, in other words, either on the chosen or the determined point from which you give it. When Twain discusses art and its interpretation, moreover, he shows two things: one, how the nationality (subject position and ideology) of the painter affects his representation of his subject (pp. 153–4); and two, how the reading of an expression or painting varies according to the individual, and does not necessarily bear any relation to an original meaning or truth (pp. 152–3). Again, in other words, our ways of depicting reality vary according to our particular circumstances, and our ability to interpret what we see is profoundly unreliable. In this series of comments, Twain self-reflexively prepares the ground for the instabilities and shifting perspectives that all his books reveal. His subject inhabits multiple positions, and the experience he represents is multiform.

IV

The lack of respect for tradition and the exposure, both comic and serious, of Old World humbug is just one of the viewpoints Twain projects in *The Innocents Abroad*, to question the worth, and cast off the weight, of Old World cultural forms and traditions. But quite another position is taken too. For the narrator cannot ignore anterior discourses,[50] completely escape the influence of tradition, or of the guidebooks that provide the 'prior textual and cultural framework' for its reception.[51] Not only guidebooks but what we might call the huge library of Europeanism,[52] all the prior descriptions of, and attitudes to Europe, its cultural monuments and artefacts, shape, in however mediated a form, his consciousness.

This helps to account for some of the contradictions, switches of tone and perspective in *The Innocents Abroad*. The revisionary impulse operates, and can only operate, sporadically. The narrative voice may at times indulge in broad satire and burlesque at the expense of tradition, but this stance is not consistent, for preformed cultural assumptions and ways of reading Europe (and the Orient) have their effect too. The voice of the iconoclastic comic persona comes and goes, but so too does a more serious and conventional one. For this was a pilgrimage as well as a pleasure trip, and if amusement encouraged an irreverent step outside prior ways of responding to the Old World, the more established and ritualistic aspects of Twain's journey made a more conservative response to his experience inevitable.

Thus, in the Roman section of the book, the narrator finds himself unable to escape earlier established versions of, and knowledge about, the city. When he comes to St Peter's he says, 'I prefer not to describe St Peter's. It has been done before' (p. 217). Before saying this, however, he has already felt bound to give a long description of the building. His response to the Coliseum is similar. Twain commences by saying that *'every body knows* the picture of the Coliseum; *every body recognizes at once* that "looped and windowed" band-box with a side bitten out' (p. 218, my emphasis). He does what he can to get a fresh angle on this well-described material by his use here of contemporary metaphor, and, more successfully, by his 'translation' of the contests that once took place at the Coliseum, first into American play-bill (pp. 220–1), and then into journalistic, form ('the *Roman Daily Battle-Ax'* – p. 221). His earlier description, though, is one which stalely echoes any number of similar prior descriptions:

> [T]he monarch of all European ruins, the Coliseum, maintains that reserve and that royal seclusion which is proper to majesty. Weeds and flowers spring from its massive arches and its circling seats, and vines hang their fringes from its lofty walls. An impressive silence broods. . . . More vividly than all the written histories, the Coliseum tells the story of Rome's grandeur and Rome's decay. (p. 218)

The language used here and the assumptions of cultural value made are entirely conventional. Similarly, Twain's reaction to the Etruscan tear-jug (pp. 197–8) would seem to illustrate the strong influence of the sentimental tradition, and its attitude to the past, on him.[53] Different aspects of the narrator's perspective on the Old World clash more or less head-on here, with the inevitable sense of instability and contradiction that ensues.

When Twain moves beyond European boundaries, the gap between any kind of comic and irreverent response to his material and the pressure of conventional frameworks which condition the

view of the countries through which he travels becomes even more
noticeable. This might be explained partly by the fact that the earlier
lively engagement with the central paradox of the American–
European relationship (that to be an American is to be attracted to,
and to share an identity with, Europe, as well as to insist upon the
fact of cultural difference) no longer drives the text. But it is also a
result of at least three different frameworks which now limit Twain's
narrative: the general effect of Orientalist stereotypes, the prior
conventions of pilgrimage literature, and the nature of the religious
material with which he now has to deal.

For, first, when Twain writes about the 'otherness' of the East, he
does little more than repeat the stereotypes and tropes which have
conventionally been used in western descriptions of the Orient.
These, in Edward Said's words, operate around assumptions of 'the
ineradicable distinction between Western superiority and Oriental
inferiority'.[54] Thus references to Oriental timelessness and exoticism
suffuse Twain's descriptions. Constantinople has from a distance
'the quaint Oriental aspect one dreams of when he reads books of
eastern travel' (p. 283), and 'to see a camel train laden with the
spices of Arabia' coming through the narrow passages of the bazaar
in Smyrna 'is a genuine revelation of the Orient. The picture lacks
nothing. . . . [A]gain you dream over the wonders of the Arabian
Nights' (p. 326).

The 'picture' Twain gives us here is composed of a culturally
inherited discourse and set of fixed images. He gives his reader an
Arabian Nights world in terms of picturesque setting, but one which
on closer view reveals backwardness, cruelty, squalid degeneracy
and heresy. Both of these elements are different, but equally
powerful, parts of the Orientalist stereotype. Thus, when he
describes a group of 'picturesque Arabs' in the Holy Land, the initial
reference to 'a grand Oriental picture which I had worshiped [sic] a
thousand times in soft, rich steel engravings' gives way to a closer
focus on the 'desolation . . . dirt . . . rags . . . fleas' and the 'besotted
ignorance in the countenances' (p. 433). The Arab guard on the
journey onward from Galilee is described as an 'infamous star-
spangled scum of the desert' (p. 411). The narrator swings here
between two versions of a stereotype in describing these Eastern
scenes and peoples, but the same move from remote charm to direct
repulsion is recurrent.

When Twain comes to describe the sacred places on his Holy Land itinerary, he has similar difficulties in consistently avoiding the 'basic repertoire of images'[55] already associated with the region. But he is now also caught within the accepted parameters and examples of pilgrimage literature, and by the sensitive nature of his religious subject matter. He ironically recognises the former of these limits when he says of the 'pilgrims' in his party that, 'I can almost tell, in set phrase, what they will say when they see . . . Nazareth, Jericho and Jerusalem – *because I have the books they will "smouch" their ideas from'* (p. 406). The religious nature of the repertoire of images he works with, too, inhibits both spontaneity and humour. For the trajectory of the narrative (with Jerusalem as the expected climax) is fixed. And the sensibilities of his audience discourage anything but stereotyped language and reaction.

The constraints imposed on Twain by the prior conventions of pilgrimage literature are everywhere evident. The panorama visible from the high ground above Lake Galilee is 'so crowded with historical interest' that all Twain seems able to do (despite his doubts as to whether these are the actual sites of the traditions ascribed) is to list the places and their associations:

> Bethsaida; the supposed scenes of the Sermon on the Mount . . . ; the declivity down which the swine ran to the sea . . . ; part of the battle-field of Hattin, where the knightly Crusaders fought their last fight, and in a blaze of glory passed from the stage . . . ; Mount Tabor, the traditional scene of the Lord's Transfiguration.
> (p. 412)

A description of prickly pears 'like hams' (p. 413) which follows, shows Twain attempting a vernacular intervention, but he is soon back smouching *his* ideas from travel books, and consciously acknowledging the fact (see, for instance, p. 413).

Twain is trapped here, too, if not by the nature of his own religious beliefs, then certainly by the knowledge that comedy at the expense of Christianity would both risk alienating a sizeable part of his audience and prejudice his own acceptance into the more respectable American circles.[56] The irreverence of humour and hegemonic religious values are not capable of reconciliation.[57] When Twain finally reaches Jerusalem, he shows a sharp Protestant eye for the religious trappings and manufactured mementos which abound in the Church of the Holy Sepulchre. But, despite an awareness of the ironies of the religious disputes that have raged round the sacred sites, a pious reverence, similar to that of any number of pilgrims who precede and follow him, overwhelms any other response at the site of the crucifixion itself:

> I . . . looked upon the place where the true cross once stood, with a far more absorbing interest than I had ever felt in anything earthly before. . . . And so I close my chapter on the Church of the Holy Sepulchre . . . the most illustrious edifice in Christendom. With all its clap-trap side-shows and unseemly imposture of every kind, it is still grand, reverend, venerable – for a god died there; for fifteen hundred years its shrines have been wet with the tears of pilgrims. . . . History is full of this old Church of the Holy Sepulchre – full of blood that was shed because of the respect and the veneration in which men held the last resting-place of the meek and lowly, the mild and gentle, Prince of Peace! (pp. 456–7)

There are some subjects Twain finds it hard to joke about, or/and where the weight of inherited response tends to bury much of the distinctive quality of his voice and point of view.

He does, however, manage to escape this stifling reverence obliquely, when he introduces, just previously, another voice and another perspective. For he burlesques many of the qualities endorsed in the Holy Sepulchre scene – piety, the sentimental response to history and tradition, and the value and importance of cultural and spiritual places of origin – when he reaches the supposed site of Adam's tomb in Jerusalem to find it a complete fraud, and completely marginal to his own concerns or needs (pp. 451–2). The burlesque here invades, if only by suggestion, the piety of the Holy Sepulchre scene. The contradiction between iconoclastic humour and fresh response and the weight of the religious subject matter at the centre of this section of the narrative can only, though, be (partially) overcome by such indirect means. For the most part, the distinctive comic nature of Twain's voice recedes to the very fringes of the text till Jerusalem is safely passed.

V

My analysis of *The Innocents Abroad* to this point has been largely based on its opposition between America and the Old World. Much of my reading has rested on the assumption of a unitary national identity: that to be an American is to be defined in terms of New World–Old World difference. But Twain's narrative is more complicated than this, as many of my previous comments have implied. The opposition between the New and the Old World which Twain constructs is destabilised as he (also) treats his national and international materials from another perspective; as he shows the deep cultural influence Europe and the Holy Land have on American identity; and as he upsets, to a large degree, the notion that this latter identity is coherent and homogeneous.

It is Twain's exposure of cultural differences within America, as well as those between America and the foreign 'other', on which I focus here. As this occurs, so the boundaries of the New–Old World binary are inevitably complicated and blurred. Twain describes two different types of American, 'saints' and 'sinners', on the excursion. The strong nationalistic tone completely disappears when the narrator refers to the 'pilgrims' (the pious, genteel, respectable, sober and self-righteous members of the *Quaker City* company) and their abuse of the Arab mosque at Nain. Instead, a relativist cultural stance takes its place:

> We entered, and the pilgrims broke specimens from the foundation walls, though they had to touch, and even step, upon the 'praying carpets' to do it. . . . To step rudely upon the sacred praying mats, with booted feet . . . was to inflict pain upon men who had not offended us in any way. Suppose a party of armed foreigners were to enter a village church in America and break ornaments from the altar railings for curiosities. . . . (p. 432)

As the contrast between alternative types of American is developed, it is the narrator and his fellow sinners who are represented as clear-sighted, straight-speaking, companionable, non-conformist and spontaneous truth-tellers, while the pilgrims are seen as hypocrites, 'credulous and guide-book-clutching, indoctrinated with the received attitude of reverence toward the wonders of the past . . . unquestioning [in their] conformity'.[58] Twain attacks the pilgrims' lack of charity and compassion (pp. 355–6). He criticises their mean-mindedness, bickerings, hypocrisies and their desire for self-advantage (see, for instance, pp. 393–4). The 'vandalism' of the group is scorned repeatedly: 'They broke off fragments from Noah's tomb; from the exquisite sculptures of the temples of Baalbec. . . . Heaven protect the Sepulchre when this tribe invades Jerusalem!' (p. 373).[59]

Twain stresses the contrast between pilgrims and sinners much more than their shared attributes.[60] At first glance this seems to endorse the opposition between the New and the Old World in the text, for the pilgrims are generally associated with a reverence for the culture of the past and its values. In the Holy Land they borrow their words and ideas from guide books, and 'revere, almost . . . worship, the holy places' (p. 393) they see. The sense of American–Old World difference modifies here into a contrast between types of American: the genteel, pious and self-righteous (see the clearly allegorical representation of 'the "Pilgrim" bird' in Marseilles Zoo – pp. 78–9) and their opposite. The internal conflicts of the Civil War (and its South–North divide) are here drawn up along different (East–West) lines; the representatives of 'America's official culture' opposed by 'an uncouth deflating, philistine bunch of vernacular figures'.[61] The nationalistic qualities of Twain's book are, however, complicated and compromised by the fact that the Americans who *officially* represent their country are both ridiculed and closely linked to the Old World and its values.

One could argue with this conclusion, however, by suggesting that for Twain 'real' Americanism implied a necessary cultural transformation – the shucking off of the genteel and the celebration of the vernacular. But if this is the case, then the contrasts between the New and the Old World based on cultural differences that apparently *already* exist (the stress on an American rejection of past models, for instance) begin to look problematic. At the very least, they need further explanation in terms of the one particular version of American identity which is being endorsed. But I have already suggested that the narrator is himself implicated in the 'pilgrim' values he would appear, with his criticisms, to deny. Twain might set himself against his fellow American pilgrims, but in his sub-title, 'The New Pilgrim's Progress', in his description of his own 'pilgrimage' to Versailles (p. 122), in the cultural solemnities he, too, variously mouths, and in his occasional use of the first person plural, he blurs the boundaries between himself and this other group. In describing Moslems as 'trespassing on *our* holy ground' (p. 466), for instance, his narrow piety seems but a variant of theirs. When, moreover, the narrator does distance himself from the 'fantastic mob of green-spectacled Yanks' with their green cotton umbrellas, who intrude into 'the scenery of the Bible' (p. 369), his own *single* refusal to equip himself similarly collapses earlier structures of differences among the different groups of tourists (pilgrims *or* sinners). For it is Twain against the rest here. No single perspective or subject position is complete in itself in *The Innocents Abroad*. Twain's view of American identity and of Old World–New World difference lacks stability and contains contradictions.

The various Americans (pilgrims and sinners) of *The Innocents Abroad* do, however, have one thing in common. I have described the American economic power of the period, and the confident sense of national self-assertion as the 'invasion' of the Old World took place. I quoted, too, William W. Stowe, who linked travel abroad in Twain's period with American capitalist enterprise and expectation. When Twain describes the 'vandalism' of the invading tribe of pilgrims in the Holy Land, he conveniently omits the fact that he himself was not above such vandalism. The editors of his *Notebooks* mention 'a small marble head' taken on his trip to the Acropolis,[62] while Twain's own reference to getting 'pieces of the old Temple' (see the prefacing quotes to this chapter) comes as he describes the Mosque of Omar in his journal. For there is *one* constant in American identity as Twain represents it; one important connection between these sheep and goats (saints and sinners). For both are linked in their expansionist and acquisitive drive. It is in this, and this alone, that the word 'American' comes to take on a unified meaning. Twain may downplay, foreground only sporadically, the economic power of a fast developing capitalist society and its influence on the events, places and people he describes. But that influence haunts this text, as it did the majority of Twain's works. In *Roughing It*, the theme of capitalist expansionism makes its strong return, this time, though, in the geographical and historical context of the American westward movement.

3

Roughing It and the American West

It's a Great Country, Ma.

(*Mark Twain's Letters*)[1]

This perennial rebirth, this fluidity of American life, this expansion westward . . . furnish the forces dominating American character. . . . The frontier is the line of most rapid and effective Americanization. . . . The fact is, that here is a new product that is American.

(Frederick Jackson Turner)[2]

I

The West that Mark Twain described in *Roughing It* (1872) was a confused and confusing region. In a letter to his mother from Carson City, written on 25 October 1861, he spoke of the country as:

fabulously rich in gold, silver, copper, lead, coal, iron, quicksilver, marble, granite, chalk, plaster of Paris, (gypsum,) thieves, murderers, desperadoes, ladies, children, lawyers, Christians, Indians, Chinamen, Spaniards, gamblers, sharpers, cuyotes (pronounced ki-yo-ties,) . . . poets, preachers, and jackass rabbits.[3]

Stephen Fender notes the 'jumbling of categories' here, and comments, more generally, that the letters of this period 'bristled with unresolved contrasts'.[4] Such an analysis can be usefully extended and applied to the version of the West represented in *Roughing It.*

The historian Frederick Jackson Turner, in 1893, famously located American cultural rebirth in the 'new field of opportunity' offered by the western 'wilderness'. The contrasts, evolutionary discourse and metaphors of rebirth and 'steady growth' under frontier conditions, which Turner used to support his argument[5] had, though, already been deconstructed twenty years earlier by Twain. They appear one-dimensional and reductive in comparison to Twain's account of the chaotic aspects of western life in *Roughing It.* If Twain seems at first to tell a similar story to Turner, he quickly complicates and undermines it.

The description of the 'practical joke' played by the inhabitants of Carson City on the newly arrived US Attorney, General Buncombe, suggests something of what I mean. Buncombe is duped into involvement in 'The Great Landslide Case'. Accordingly, he agrees to represent the interests of a local rancher, Dick Hyde, against Tom Morgan, who owns the land on the mountainside immediately above:

> the trouble was, that one of those hated and dreaded land-slides had come and slid Morgan's ranch, fences, cabins, cattle, barns and everything down on *his* [Hyde's] ranch and exactly covered up every single vestige of his property, to a depth of about thirty-eight feet. Morgan was in possession and refused to vacate the premises – said he was occupying his own cabin and not interfering with anybody else's – and said the cabin was standing on the same dirt and the same ranch it had always stood on.
>
> (p. 253)

Buncombe's spirited defence of his client fails, but, on personal appeal, ex-Governor Roop, who is hearing the case, modifies his verdict:

> at last his face lit up happily and he told Buncombe it had occurred to him that the ranch underneath the new Morgan ranch still belonged to Hyde, that his title to the ground was just as good as it had been, and therefore he was of opinion that Hyde had a right to dig it out from under there and – (p. 257)

This, of course, is a hoax, one of the favourite forms of western humour.[6] It operates round a repeated motif in the book: the taking in of the eastern greenhorn by the western community. But the content of the episode has additional interest. The conflicts over property and title described, the social and legal confusion that occurs as one layer of land covers up another, and the comic chaos suggested in the idea of digging one ranch out from beneath the other, implicitly interrogates the neat and ordered process Turner implied in the 'law of continuity and development' he proposed for western history.[7]

The idea of an evolutionary shape to history can accommodate temporary confusion along its way. Twain, however, unlike Turner, consistently and repeatedly focuses on the unresolved contradictions and multiplicities of the West. He stresses, too, the difficulty of interpreting this disorienting western world; of gaining any firm and reliable knowledge about it. For the sense of epistemological uncertainty identified in *The Innocents Abroad* recurs here, but with greater emphasis. Any authoritative reading of this ever-shifting reality proves unattainable. Twain uses the motif of the 'blind lead' recurrently in *Roughing It*. The career his protagonist takes, and the narrative he tells, keep running into dead ends. The form of the book is meandering and digressive, with 'bizarre jump[s] from one narrative stance into another'.[8] A repeated sense of instability and inconclusiveness defines the text.

Twain does, however, suggest one source of continuity and shape, not just to western American history, but to the history of the nation as a whole. The focus on the regional myths of the West, and its representation as a place of conflicting accounts and indeterminate meanings, runs alongside – and is in tension with – a larger theme. Martha Banta, in a revealing phrase, refers to Twain's work as a whole in terms of a 'capitalist historiography'.[9] In my final comments on *The Innocents Abroad*, I suggested that the one thing linking the different types of Americans he depicts is the way they are jointly identified with the expansive and acquisitive drives of an emergent capitalism. In *Roughing It*, the stress on western distinctiveness exists alongside another story which undermines, and replaces it. Twain identifies a constant element to American historical development as a whole: the driving force of commerce, business and the market, which erases regional difference in its path, and affects every stage of national expansion in the period of which he writes. This problematises any reading of the westward move that sees it, as Turner does, as a journey into the 'wilderness'; as a healthy regression 'into the simplicity of primitive conditions'.[10] For heterogeneity and difference (all that makes the West what it is) and homogeneity (the development of a national economic system, and the uniform effects of this process) exist – and especially in this place and at this time – in considerable tension with one another.

Twain's focus on the western education (or lack of it) of his first-person protagonist, on regional conflict, and on the anecdotes, persons and incidents that exemplify the unique features of the West, tends to cut against his other, and larger national, story of the inevitable spread of capitalist enterprise and its values. The western characteristics Twain identifies cannot, in the long term, co-exist with the capitalist expansionism which he also describes.

Roughing It, then, is marked by a sense of narrative tension and ambiguity which results from the shifts of focus and perspective in the text. As my study continues, I draw increasing attention to Twain's unease about the direction of American history and the dominant values of his time. These are already beginning to be apparent in this book. Twain, though, neither consistently foregrounds, nor explicitly comments on, the incompatibilities between the two (regional and national) stories he tells here. His stress on immediate experience (much of it comic) filtered through the first person voice, tends to resist serious and sustained historical analysis. As in *The Innocents Abroad*, his use of the travel narrative allows him to shift narrative direction and to change tone and register almost at will. The associative method Twain developed[11] works against tight textual unity. Indeed, in a book where the author admits openly that 'I digress constantly anyhow' (p. 359), the sense of internal contradiction and of jumbled categories becomes – as I suggest in my final section – no artistic disadvantage, but rather part of the very fabric of what is an accomplished comic textual performance.

II

At first glance, Twain's language and the shape he gives his narrative in *Roughing It*, would both seem to confirm, rather than contradict, Turner's frontier thesis and its description of significant western difference. The 'exhilarating sense of emancipation' the narrator and his fellow travellers feel as they leave 'the States' behind them[12] mirrors Turner's description of the 'buoyancy and exuberance which comes with freedom' on the frontier.[13] The historian's celebration of 'perennial rebirth' in the move west, similarly, is suggested in Twain's use of metaphor: the overland coach in which his protagonist travels is described as 'an imposing cradle on wheels' (p. 54). The figurative link is then reinforced as he strips to his underclothes, not quite naked but nearly so, to increase comfort in the womb-like interior of the vehicle: 'as "dark as the inside of a cow," as the conductor phrased it in his picturesque way' (pp. 65–6).

Roughing It, then, initially appears to be structured round the idea of the restorative return to the primitive. Jeffrey Steinbrink, accordingly, describes the first stages of the trip West as 'a flight from civilization to conditions more . . . rudimentary, . . . from the rules of decorum and the forms of polite address to the unrestraint of practical usage and the vigor of colloquial language, from the tame to the wild'.[14] The clothing (swallow-tail coats and white kid gloves) of genteel respectability is discarded with other 'baggage' at St Joseph to conform with the weight restrictions on the overland coach (p. 52). New modes of dress take its place, and by the time the narrator has reached Carson City he has 'grown well accustomed to wearing a damaged slouch hat, blue woolen shirt, and pants crammed into boot-tops', glories 'in the absence of coat, vest and braces', and feels 'rowdyish and bully' (p. 186) as a consequence. These are not quite the 'hunting shirt and the moccasin' Turner associates with effective Americanisation on the frontier. But certainly 'the garments of civilization', the styles of dress and customs identified with effete European influence, are here also, to use the historian's trope, stripped off by the wilderness.[15]

The 'freshness' and 'breeziness' of the new frontier landscape entered by Twain's protagonist and the sense of emancipation associated with it (p. 54) are initially reflected by a narrative that fairly rattles along. Twain's growth in literary confidence since *The Innocents Abroad* is seen in his increased technical command: the gap he establishes between the 'young and ignorant' (p. 49) first person semi-fictional[16] narrator-protagonist and a more experienced, and retrospective, narrative voice, both shapes the text and allows a dual perspective on its materials from the first.[17] It soon becomes apparent, however, that Twain's representation of the West is by no means as straightforward as the above parallels with Turner might suggest. The West, for Twain, is a place of contradictions. *Roughing It* tells a more complex story than anyone versed in the historian's later narrative of the rise of individual liberty and democracy on the frontier, and aware of the clear oppositions which structure that narrative, might expect.

Twain's attitude to the American Indian is a case in point. For Turner, the Indian and the untamed wilderness stand in one-to-one relationship to each other, joint components of a 'savage' West which the frontiersman (the bringer of a 'new order of Americanism') will civilise and settle.[18] It is, indeed, exactly such a view of the Indian, depending on a clear savage–civilised binary, which informs Twain's description of the Goshoot (a pun on Gosiute) Indian. A repeated pattern in the book is replayed here as the naive and romantic expectations of the greenhorn protagonist are shown to be illusions. Cooper's 'Noble Red Men' turn out 'paint and tinsel' creations, a product of 'the mellow moonshine of romance'. Twain uses evolutionary discourse (on which Turner, too, will rely) to claim that the members of 'this silent, sneaking, treacherous-looking race' are descended from 'the self-same gorilla, or kangeroo, or Norway rat, whichever animal-Adam the Darwinians trace them to' (pp. 166–8).[19] He launches a swingeing attack on the Gosiutes as 'the wretchedest type of mankind I have ever seen' (p. 166), equating their particular tribe with every other Indian as he does so.[20]

But the opposition between savage and civilised is far from stable in the book. Twain's earlier story of the 'town-dog' futilely chasing the despised 'spiritless and cowardly' coyote and being taken in by the deceptive speed of this swindling stranger (pp. 75–8) has conventionally been read as an allegory of the tenderfoot gaining knowledge from the western veteran, as he works his way through his various humiliations toward 'the superior maturity and sophistication of the old-timer'. As such, it has been taken as a paradigm for one of the narrative's basic patterns.[21] But Twain repeatedly (three times) links the coyote to the Indian as he tells this story, and says that they are connected in 'blood kinship' (p. 79). And Coyote is, of course, the Indian trickster, an intelligent but duplicitous shape-changer and prankster, 'perhaps the most conspicuous figure in the oral literature of the Native American peoples' in the western United States.[22] Turner's narrative of 'the disintegration of savagery'[23] takes an unexpected twist as a note of relativistic uncertainty appears here. For the 'title' (to return to the Buncombe case) to superior knowledge, if we are to read the episode allegorically, is held not by the western veteran but by the supposedly 'savage' – but in fact culturally different – Indian. It is the Indian too who knows more than the white inhabitants of the region when the flash flood descends; who has that gift of prophecy that the narrator never gains (p. 317).

The frontier in *Roughing It* becomes, in other words, not a place of clear meanings and well-structured contrasts, but of instability and complexity. This can be seen, too, in Twain's representation of the opposition between eastern genteel and western vernacular forms of language, and the social difference it signifies. For any tendency to endorse 'the vigor of colloquial language' and to consequently dismiss eastern 'forms of polite address' is, similarly, undermined in Twain's description of Buck Fanshawe's funeral.

The battle over language enacted here is foreshadowed in the early symbolic emphasis Twain places on the weight of the Unabridged Dictionary which (together with the United States statutes) he and his brother carry West. This 'uneasy Dictionary' is thrown about as the stagecoach passes through the new and hilly landscape, and 'assault[s]' and 'damage[s]' the passengers within (p. 66). On reaching Carson City, it is placed in the 'government fire-proof safe' in the narrator's room (p. 180). Just what worth this linguistic tool will have for Twain, the apprentice westerner and apprentice writer, remains (as in the case of the law book as legal tool) ambiguous. Its value, indeed, is almost at once put in question with the introduction, via 'the Sphinx', of vernacular and regional forms of speech – 'danged', 'sot', 'a-bust'n' – which appear in no dictionary of the time, and which correspond to no written grammatical rules (p. 56).[24]

In the chapter on Buck Fanshawe's funeral, Twain directly contrasts vernacular and genteel forms of language. The meeting between Scotty Briggs, the 'stalwart rough' with 'flaming red flannel shirt, patent leather belt with spanner and revolver attached, . . . and pants stuffed into boot tops', and the minister, 'a fragile, gentle, spirituel [*sic*] new fledgling from an Eastern theological seminary . . . unacquainted with the ways of the mines' (pp. 337–8) repeats a recurrent textual motif: the encounter of, and difference between, old-timer and tenderfoot. It does not, though, bring the usual result. Briggs and the parson (whom Briggs wants to conduct Fanshawe's funeral service) represent for Kenneth Lynn 'two utterly different conceptions of what American life should be'[25] and speak two utterly different languages. However, no one form of speech (and way of thought) triumphs here. Rather a thoroughgoing relativisation of discourse occurs as the two languages engage with one another on different, but intersecting, planes.

David Sewell describes Twain's representation of Briggs's voice as creating 'a tour de force of Western slang'.[26] Briggs's attempt at dialogue with the representative of a genteel and decorous culture is initially jammed by the difference in register of their different forms of speech. Scotty uses a predominantly 'low' discourse, informed by experiences of the gambling table, the mining camp and popular forms of entertainment. The minister, in contrast, uses the 'high' language appropriate to his religious sensibility and membership of an educated élite: one of considerable grammatical and verbal sophistication and complexity. So a sample of their interchange, starting with Scotty's words, runs as follows:

'Why you see we are in a bit of trouble, and the boys thought maybe you would give us a lift, if we'd tackle you – that is, if I've got the rights of it and you are the head clerk of the doxology-works next door.'

'I am the shepherd in charge of the flock whose fold is next door.'

'The which?'

'The spiritual adviser of the little company of believers whose sanctuary adjoins these premises.'

'You ruther hold over me, pard. I reckon I can't call that hand. Ante and pass the buck.'

'How? I beg pardon. What did I understand you to say?'

'Well, you've ruther got the bulge on me. Or maybe we've both got the bulge, somehow. You don't smoke me and I don't smoke you. You see, one of the boys has passed in his checks and we want to give him a good send-off, and so the thing I'm on now is to roust out somebody to jerk a little chin-music for us and waltz him through handsome.'

'My friend, I seem to grow more and more bewildered. Your

observations are wholly incomprehensible to me. Cannot you not
simplify them in some way? At first I thought perhaps I
understood you, but I grope now. Would it not expedite matters
if you restricted yourself to categorical statements of fact
unencumbered with obstructing accumulations of metaphor and
allegory?'
Another pause, and more reflection. Then, said Scotty:
  'I'll have to pass, I judge.'
  'How?'
  'You've raised me out, pard.'
  'I still fail to catch your meaning.'
  'Why, that last lead of yourn is too many for me – that's the idea.
I can't neither trump nor follow suit.'
The clergyman sank back in his chair perplexed. (p. 339)

Two 'complete and separate ways of knowing the world'[27] collide
here. Class, regional and experiential difference is reflected in the
instability of language, as meaning fails to emerge in what Bakhtin
calls 'a single intentional whole'.[28] Eventually the two men start, if
only briefly, to understand each other, as the parson is able to
'translate' – an activity which itself points to the provisional nature,
and competing claims, of differing idiolects – Scotty's 'kicked the
bucket' as 'departed to that mysterious country from whose bourne
no traveler returns', and as Scotty, still trying to make linguistic
contact, answers 'why pard, he's *dead*'. The parson can then, for
once in the whole episode, reply that 'Yes, I understand' (p. 340).
The narrative voice seems to act as a neutral medium once the
dialogue between the two men has started, thus illustrating the
more effectively the 'outright impasse' that, for the most part,
occurs.[29]
    There is no favouring of western language and value here. A
rejection of genteel forms of language is implied in the failure of its
rhetorical forms and elaborate but well-worn turns of phrase
adequately to connect with the facts of western life.[30] But vernacular
forms of language are not thereby rendered fully admirable. Scotty
Briggs asserts his liking for the minister by saying, 'I think you're
white', and closes the funeral sermon with the words, 'AMEN. No
Irish need apply' (p. 344). The limited register of his discourse, and
its xenophobic, racist and violent aspects, prevent the reader from
taking such a language (and ideology) as a preferred model.

III

Twain's attitude to his western materials, then, is complex and contradictory. He endorses a celebratory version of frontier experience – the evolutionary replacement of a worthless and depraved savagery, and the triumph of untamed and exuberant vernacular values over inherited formal and genteel cultural patterns – only also to undermine it. Moreover, the sense of buoyant adventure and emancipation repeatedly associated with the West in *Roughing It* is countered by the unmooring of the narrator: his confusion at the lack of sense to be made of his experiences there.

This confusion relates both to the dislocating paradoxes of the region and to the repeated dead-ends that mark the protagonist's experience there. These go together with, and in part explain, the sense of epistemological uncertainty in the text: the difficulty the narrator has finding his bearings in this alien western world. The West is represented as a place of illogical and conflicting detail, as the account of the outlaw Slade (a figure who fascinates the narrator) suggests. Slade is the epitome of the 'Rocky Mountain desperado' (p. 104), an 'actual ogre who, in fights and brawls and various ways, *had taken the lives of twenty-six human beings*' (p. 110). He is a man marked by his savagery, cutting the ears from one of his slaughtered enemies and carrying them 'in his vest pocket . . . with great satisfaction' (p. 110). But he is also associated with the efficiencies and rationalisations of western development. A division agent for the Overland stage company, it is his 'energetic administration [that] had restored peace and order to one of the worst divisions of the road'. In an area with 'absolutely no semblance of the law' (p. 106), Slade acts as 'supreme judge . . . jury and executioner' (p. 107), protecting the private property both of his employers and of passing emigrants. Twain, stopping at a stage post, finds himself sitting down to breakfast with Slade, whose 'quiet and affable' behaviour just cannot square with the 'raw-head-and-bloody-bones the nursing mothers of the mountains terrified their children with' (p. 110). A vigilante hanged by a vigilance committee, 'an outlaw among outlaws and yet their relentless scourge . . . at once the most bloody, the most dangerous and the most valuable citizen' (p. 103) of the area, Slade does not, for Twain, add up. As Lee Clark Mitchell puts it, 'with Slade as with so much else in the West, all that remains are conflicting accounts'.[31]

A number of critics have focused on the metaphoric qualities of the 'blind lead' episode in *Roughing It* (pp. 286–99). Thus John E. Bassett, for instance, examines the book's gaps and contradictions to argue that 'Twain provides as many false leads and missed leads as do the silver mines' themselves.[32] The narrative itself, and the life of the protagonist it describes, keep running into dead ends. They (both) then start up again up in new, but generally unsatisfactory, directions. The narrator's early occupational moves (private secretary, miner, mill operative) only raise the question of 'what to do next?' (p. 300). His stint as a journalist in Virginia City is followed by restlessness and dissatisfaction (p. 398).[33] The moves to San Francisco, to and from the Tuolomne mining camps, seem yet another series of false leads. The logic of the narrator's life, and of the narrative itself, repeatedly stalls.

One of Twain's repeated tactics as a writer, and a distinguishing mark of his humour, is the plumbing of misleading, and usually romantic, surface to reveal its illusory quality. Thus the naive narrator's 'unmarred ecstasy' at apparently discovering a gold mine is undercut by the experienced Mr Ballou, who informs him that the 'deposit of shining yellow scales' he sees is no more than 'nasty glittering mica' (pp. 222–4).[34] Such a stripping away of romantic veneer is typical of a realist aesthetic. Right from the start of Twain's career, though, the epistemological confidence conventionally associated with this aesthetic – a privileged access to the nature of the real – is denied. Though the stripping away of false surface can reveal essential truth (as in the fool's gold incident), it is as often as not a negative one; that what was thought valuable has no worth. More commonly, all such unmaskings (and other such explorations of reality) reveal is a sense of bewilderment, an awareness that our readings and constructions of the world are both partial and unsatisfactory.

This bewilderment results from the puzzling aspects both of the western materials which the narrator attempts to interpret, and of the resources available to help him. The phrase 'Three Sides to all Questions' (p. 38), which refers to Twain's chapter about the 'Mountain Meadows Massacre', suggests the impossibility of discovering any clear interpretive way through the varying accounts of the West he is given. For the increasing amount of information Twain gains about the Mormons and their activities is matched by an accompanying inability to know 'what portion of it was reliable and what was not' (p. 157). Thus one version of the story has the Indians bearing major responsibility for the massacre in question; another blames the Mormons; yet another shares responsibility between both parties. And even when the narrator finds out that the Mormons *'were* the assassins' (p. 157), this still does not allow him a unified perspective on Mormonism as a larger whole: in the first two appendices to the book – one 'essentially sympathetic' to Mormon history and achievement; the other, in its immediate focus on Mountain Meadows, not – Twain conveys 'ambiguous feelings about the Mormons, which he could not otherwise synthesize into a single characterization'.[35] He both starts and ends here stuck between conflicting versions of the truth, his excavation of it – at least in part – stalled. Again, the metaphor of the blind lead seems an appropriate one.

The sense of uncertainty and provisionality in *Roughing It* also comes from the unstable and problematic nature of the relationship between the individual figure (the narrating subject) and the ground he explores. As the narrator keeps, literally and metaphorically, losing his bearings, so the possibility of his giving any firm or authoritative reading of reality is interrogated. Any such reading, given by a subject positioned *within* the disorienting world he describes, can only be relative, provisional and unreliable. The loss of bearings acts as a repeated motif in the text, and works to self-reflexive and allegorical ends. The Overland stage loses its way in the rainy midnight gloom, 'wandering about a plain with gaping gullies in it' (p. 126), missing disaster by inches. Lost in a snowstorm, Twain and two companions circle round in their own tracks, the 'mental compass' of their leader awry, the search for a known, familiar and well-marked path frustrated by the 'white oblivion' (p. 242) all around. Such episodes take on clear figurative significance. The regular patterns of the sage bushes convey an impression of 'a distinctly defined avenue' leading 'in *any* direction that you proceeded' (p. 243). This means that, once the snow has fallen and the men, individually, attempt to find 'proof' that they are on the right track (the road that leads to safety), the regularity of the landscape convinces each 'that *he* had found the true road, and that the others had found only false ones' (p. 244). Knowledge is relative and unreliable here, a product of the relationship between the individual subject and the reading he constructs of the confusing reality around him, with no guarantee of truth or coherence available.

Relativistic uncertainty about the position of the subject, as he attempts to negotiate a confusing and pathless (or many-pathed) ground, is resolved comically here. The three men renounce their vices, respectively throw away whisky bottle, playing cards and pipe, to accept the inevitability of freezing to death. They wake the next morning, though, to find themselves safe beside a stage station, shamefacedly seek out their discarded possessions, and abandon their various reforms. The 'painfully ridiculous and humiliating' nature of all this is acknowledged, but it is the clownish aspect of the men's behaviour that is foregrounded. Thus Ballou openly acknowledges his foolishness by saying, 'Will some gentleman be so good as to kick me behind?' (p. 249). A parable of epistemological uncertainty – and of the self-deluding attempts of the human subject to understand his own motivations, to respond rationally to surrounding events, and to control in any but the most minimal way the patterns of those events – has, accordingly, its most serious implications deflected in the move to farce that occurs.[36]

But any such deflection can only be temporary, for the incident fits, too, in the larger context of the narrative's overall pattern. Twain's protagonist is continually, literally and metaphorically, losing his way, but the fundamental structure of *Roughing It* remains fixed: that of the continuing journey West, and the sense of adventure and possibility associated with it. This is the path repeatedly recovered. In the last analysis, though, the whole shape and point of this underlying process is put in doubt. Twain replays his earlier representation of the westward move in the Sandwich Isles section of the book. Critics have tended to dismiss this whole late sequence as 'detachable',[37] but to do so is to miss the underlying thematic unity of the text.[38]

If Hawaii is the last stage of the westward move of the protagonist, the utopian connotations of the journey – the promise of freedom and rebirth – continue to be presented in a highly ambivalent way. When (earlier) the narrator first heads West, he finds 'happiness' (p. 161), and then, in Nevada, an emotion close to 'unmarred ecstasy' (p. 221) as his fortune seems to beckon. San Francisco is then, though, described as 'Paradise' in contrast to the Washoe alkali deserts and sage brush (p. 418).[39] But Honolulu, in its turn, has 'a Summer calm as tranquil as dawn in the Garden of

Eden', and is explicitly contrasted with San Francisco's 'noisy confusion' (p. 454). This last dreamy climax is then, itself, immediately interrupted by a scorpion bite. Before this happens, and completely unexpectedly, the narrator has praised the rich and varied *eastern* American landscape, when compared to California, as 'a vision of Paradise itself' (p. 408). The utopian quest, in other words, is continually displaced and decentred. Twain ends up, in at least one stage of his narrative, desiring the place he first left. The westward movement which structures the whole book turns out itself to be something of a blind lead.

IV

Twain starts *Roughing It* by 'tapping into and . . . extending the myth of the West'.[40] But the independence, and the move back into nature and beyond civilising restraints, associated with that myth prove half-truths at best. I have focused until now on the contradictory aspects of Twain's representation of the West as he both acknowledges the distinctive qualities of the region, but undermines any unified or simple (mythic) reading of it. I have shown, too, the interpretative indeterminacy that confronts the narrator as he tries to make sense of this western world. But there is a different, and contrasting, strand to Twain's book – a clear sense of history, unmuddied by any sense of interpretive disablement – in the story of American capitalist development it tells. This story both threatens to displace the (alternative) stress on the conflicting aspects of the West, and to collapse the contrast between regions on which the book is structured. The full implications of this element in the text, and its uneasy relation to the material around it, however, go relatively unexplored, and are developed in an inconsistent way. It may be, indeed, that Twain was not aware, or only half-aware, of them.

Alan Trachtenberg shows the effect that 'the script of industrial progress' was to have on America in the post Civil-War period, saying that:

the logic of events in the 1870's and 1880's disclosed . . . not an agrarian but an industrial capitalist scenario. Penetrating the West with government encouragement, the railroad and the telegraph opened the vast spaces to production. Following the lead of the railroads, commercial and industrial businesses conceived of themselves as having the entire national space at their disposal: from raw materials for processing to goods for marketing.[41]

Twain, writing in the 1870s, is aware of the shift in temporal–spatial coordinates that modernisation (here taking the shape of railroad penetration of the West) has brought. The three hundred mile journey from Omaha to the North Platte crossing, he reports, now takes just fifteen hours and forty minutes, in luxurious circumstances. Thus the time of the overland coach journey – the only practical mode of travel available to the protagonist of *Roughing It* – is cut by almost two complete days (pp. 73–4). But other references, to the laying of the telegraph for example (p. 135), illustrate that the type of incorporation Trachtenberg describes was already well under way in the 1860s too.[42] No space exists beyond business and the marketplace in the West that Twain describes.

It is this underlying historical process – toward advanced capitalism[43] – which silently undermines, but at the same time explains, many of the contradictions in the West that Twain represents in *Roughing It*. Howard Horwitz's analysis of *Life on the Mississippi* (1883) deconstructs the opposition Twain established between the romantic independence of riverboat piloting and the institutional hierarchies and economic constraints of a developing corporate system. Horwitz comments, revealingly, that what ended with the Civil War was not, as Twain suggested, the glory days of steamboating. Its decline had in fact started earlier with the growth of the railroads. Rather, what had died was 'in fact, only the mythological independent self, a notion already an exercise in nostalgia in the 1850s'.[44] This is entirely relevant to *Roughing It*. For Twain's romantic celebration of individual autonomy and of the majesty of an untamed nature, both synonymous with the mythic idea of the West, exists in uneasy and contradictory relation with the historical awareness that the region is already no separate space, and that the idea of independent selfhood is fast under erasure. In the 1860s, the practices of industrial capitalism were already and inevitably, as Twain's book reveals, part and parcel of westward expansionism.

Thus the idea of individual retreat from the complexities of civilisation toward a pure space of nature (a standard part of the western myth) is replayed in Twain's book, but also interrogated, in the ambiguities of his representations of Lake Tahoe. Twain's admiration for the lake's beauty was often repeated, both in his books and in his private correspondence. He speaks of it in the language of regressive wonder, stressing its distance from the world of men and action. Tahoe becomes variously 'the Fountain of Youth' and the 'beautiful relic of fairy-land forgotten and left asleep in the snowy Sierras when the little elves fled from their ancient haunts and quitted the earth'.[45] In *Roughing It*, Twain and his companion breathe the air 'angels breathe' (p. 188) at Tahoe. In a landscape subject to 'Nature's mood' (p. 191) and away from all other human presence, their main 'business' is 'drifting around in the boat', enjoying 'the luxurious rest and indolence' (p. 192) found there.

The conversion of the language of the work ethic to playful ends, and the idyllic mood and Edenic aspects of the scene, however, cannot hide the fact that no pure retreat from culture into nature exists.[46] The interrelated quality of these terms is suggested as Twain moves from the Carson City world to this apparently untainted space, only immediately and destructively to affect it. The ordinary domestic routine with which man announces his presence (lighting a fire to cook) brings 'devastation' as the dry lakeside mountain is transformed into 'a tossing, blinding tempest of flame' (p. 194).[47]

The impossibility of separating out wilderness world from historical event (in the form of commercial enterprise) has been solidly established earlier in the sequence. For Twain has other 'business' here, and now the word is used in its normative sense. He wants to become a 'land-owner' (p. 190), to fence in the wilderness, establish a timber ranch, and 'become wealthy' (p. 187).[48] The hum of similar enterprise is already evident even as the two men enter what appears to be this natural paradise, with the sawmill and workmen only three miles away (p. 188). Twain's references, following the forest fire, to the fact that he and his companion carried 'no insurance' (p. 195), and to the 'payment of damages' (p. 196) for their raid on the provisions of others, reinforces the fact that there is no move available here beyond the market; beyond the institutional matrices and contractual codes of (national) business practice.

Ideas of autonomy, emancipation and unspoiled nature are, then, in paradoxical relationship here to capitalist processes and assumptions. That the latter, in historical fact, provide the dominant ongoing narrative of the West is clear in *The Big Bonanza* (1876), the story of the Comstock Load written by Dan de Quille (William Wright), Twain's colleague on the Virginia City *Territorial Enterprise*. Just fourteen years after Twain's first trip to Tahoe and four years after his writing of *Roughing It*, De Quille would report how the mining industry, with its incessant need for timber, had made Tahoe a primary resource for its industrial needs and, in doing so, had wrought considerable environmental damage:

> The Comstock lode may truthfully be said to be the tomb of the forests of the Sierras. Millions on millions of feet of lumber are annually buried in the mines. . . . For a distance of fifty or sixty miles all the hills of the eastern slope of the Sierras have been to a great extent denuded of trees of every kind . . . Yerington, Bliss, & Co., one of the heaviest lumbering firms in the Sierra Nevada Mountains, have built a narrow-gauge railroad from their sawmills on the shore of Lake Tahoe. . . . Logs are rafted across Lake Tahoe to the mills from all points . . . This is all very well for the company . . . but it is going to make sad work, ere long, of the picturesque hills surrounding Lake Tahoe . . . But timber and lumber are imperatively demanded.[49]

Twain's own entry to Tahoe's lakeside paradise was part and parcel of its swift commercial development and despoilation. Natural resources, on the mining frontier, were subject to the 'imperative demands' of an emergent capitalist economy, and seen in 'business' terms from the moment of the mines' first discovery.

Twain's narrative again moves in several and contradictory ways in his descriptions of his Nevada experiences. The hum of commercial enterprise provides the continuing background noise against which a more romantic story of the West (of uniqueness, adventure and individualism) is told.[50] It is this noise, too, which is in the process of rendering that latter story defunct. Twain's realisation of the impact of economics on western history does not mean that he abandons an (alternative) representation of the region based on individualism, freedom, male camaraderie and the possibility of fresh starts. But the stress on money-making in the book undermines the notion of any escape from what Banta calls 'late capitalist procedures'.[51] If the unresolved contrasts of Twain's narrative are a sign of his own ambiguous attitudes and responses to such issues, they could only, historically, be resolved in one way. The Tahoe trip, then, describes incompatible activities, for the retreat to nature is, at the same time, the beginning of a commercial enterprise. So, too, do analogous contradictions appear in Twain's other descriptions of the silver- and gold-rush West. Thus mining is associated, in its earlier Californian gold-rush phase, with:

> a driving, vigorous, restless population . . . stalwart, muscular, dauntless young braves . . . royally endowed with every attribute that goes up to make a peerless and magnificent manhood . . . – none but erect, bright-eyed, quick-moving, strong-handed young giants. . . . It was a wild, free, disorderly, grotesque society!
>
> (pp. 414–15)

The move into a new western community is defined here by its freedom of opportunity and assertive, even anarchic, individualism (images recurrently endorsed by Twain in his text, not just in this nostalgic note). Again, though, the history of mining, at least in the period when Twain was in the West, tells an increasingly different story. In actuality, and as Twain sporadically suggests, East and West, metropolis and frontier, were symbiotically bound together. Nevada mining practices, in Twain's account of them, come almost to parody the speculative enterprises of the wider commercial market and of the commodities exchanges (developing rapidly in the post-Civil War years).[52] The type of futures trading he describes – the salting of mines, the shady assaying practices, the feverish buying and exchange of stock – mirrors the activity in the nation's financial capitals. Walter Benn Michaels describes the 'fictitious dealings' of the commodities markets in terms that fit Twain's mining context equally well: 'the mechanism of the futures contract was simple: it allowed the producer of a commodity to sell the commodity on an exchange for future delivery; it allowed him, in other words, to sell a product that he did not yet have'.[53]

East and West, city and country, in other words, could not in economic terms be separated in an incorporated age. The opening and exploitation of the Comstock Lode 'gave renewed impetus to the growth of San Francisco as a financial and industrial center, stimulated the development of new mining and metallurgical technologies, and elevated mining into the company of America's biggest businesses'.[54] Twain refers in *Roughing It* to the 'energetic San Francisco capitalists' who run the Sheba mine (p. 213), and to the 'New York capital' enlisted for further mining development (p. 424). As the silver rush continued, the Nevada mines were increasingly controlled by 'capitalists in San Francisco, Portland and the East'.[55]

Mining in Nevada was, in Earl Pomeroy's words, 'unmistakeably an industry rather than a treasure hunt', with the miners coming 'less as refugees from advancing urbanism than as its exponents'.[56] Twain's dream of 'pick[ing] up . . . nuggets of gold and silver on the hill-side' (p. 49) bore little relation to actual mining conditions, with the complicated technology and considerable finance needed to reach, refine and process the majority of the ore. Some fortunes were made, and the 'blind lead' incident Twain reports (when 'I was absolutely and unquestionably worth a million dollars . . . for ten days' – p. 299) did evidently have its basis in truth.[57] For the most part, though, the hierarchies of labour and capital in Nevada mining reflected those elsewhere. The description of Virginia City and the other 'busy city under it, down in the bowels of the earth', with the superintendents above ground conveying orders by signal bells to the population working in the 'dismal drifts and tunnels' beneath (pp. 380–1), reads like an allegory of relationships between management and production in the broader industrial economy. Twain's account of his own 'dreary and laborious' (p. 262) work in the quartz mill, and its 'exceeding hardness' (p. 267) is another reminder that 'on the Comstock Lode free-lance prospectors disappeared quickly and were replaced by thousands of wage laborers employed by corporations with headquarters in San Francisco and New York'.[58]

As Twain, then, describes the difference between the East and 'the curious new world' (p. 49) of the West, and illustrates the specific regional traits of the latter (its geography, its social forms, its humour), so at the same time the reader comes to realise that the two regions are impenetrably connected: that western difference can only remain an eccentric or marginal exception to dominant national business practice, and cannot be described outside its parameters. Twain travels to a West associated with manly independence and freedom, and such notions are not altogether disappointed. But he also finds himself working (however briefly) as a wage slave in a mining industry which itself underpins the monetary base on which the national economy rests. And it is this part of the present that points the way to the American future.

Twain's remark, concerning difficulties in establishing the new Territorial government in Carson City, that 'greenbacks had gone down to forty cents on the dollar' (p. 206), and the statement that 'paper money has never come into use on the Pacific coast' (p. 313), act as a reminder of the importance of gold and silver (until the latter's demonetarisation in 1871) to the entire American financial system at the time. The belief in the 'intrinsic' value of money, and the corresponding distrust of 'paper money' (greenbacks) then prevalent, are evident in Twain's words. Confidence in the gold and silver standard, and the corresponding trust in the 'natural' value of such metals (that the face value of the coin was equal to its actual and 'universal purchasing power'), meant accordingly that the more such metal in circulation, the more wealthy the nation.[59] The workings of the Nevada mines and the financial health of the nation were thus, for many of Twain's contemporaries, directly linked. Again, Twain writes his way into the West, only to reveal (in however partial a manner) that he has written himself back into the economic and social complexities that his younger self had thought to escape. For the West is already incorporated, or fast becoming incorporated, part and parcel of an emergent capitalist nation

V

Roughing It ends with Twain's return from the Sandwich Isles, where he found the same contradictions and unresolved contrasts he discovered elsewhere in the West. When he gets back to California, it is to start his career as a successful comic lecturer. In terms of its account of the narrator's changes of profession, this is how the book ends. Lecturing, here, can be taken as a symbolic displacement for writing. Despite their difference, both activities mark Twain's own recognition, as a businessman *and* artist, of the way that the multiplicities, comedies and contradictions of his own western experience could be reshaped artistically and used to entertain a wider audience.[60] Twain's first lecture was first given in San Francisco, but soon he would be lecturing countrywide. And it is clear that his written text, *Roughing It*, was directed to a national audience from the first.[61]

The importance and centrality of this national market is a theme of *Roughing It*, but it is also what motivated Twain as he wrote. He used the flexible formal structure of the travel narrative (which paralleled the baggy quality of his lectures) successfully to contain all the various and inconclusive aspects of his western subject matter. From one point of view, *Roughing It* seems little more than a bricolage. Its episodic structure is predicated on the basis of the repeated dead end rather than that of evolutionary growth and gradual education. It represents the experience of the West as a loose rag-bag of different materials, filtered through a variety of tones,[62] which continually escape the confines of a single narrative position or perspective. But, from another angle, what Twain does here is to mine literary gold from such heterogeneity.

Lee Clark Mitchell points out the analogy between Twain's description of 'pocket mining' (the sporadic discovery of small nests of gold), and his techniques in *Roughing It*, similarly scattering 'tall tales and humorous anecdotes . . . amid long stretches of dull facts and boring details extracted from scholarly sources'.[63] Twain represents the random and paradoxical qualities of western experience, accepts the wandering and diverse quality of his text as apposite to such material, and gives his America readers gold (as well as garners it) in the clusters of jokes, descriptions and comic stories he tells. As a businessman as well as an artist, he makes his own success out of the contrasts, blind leads, misdirected dreams and failed enterprises that he describes.

4

Tom Sawyer and American Cultural Life: Anxieties and Accommodations

What's the politically correct term for whitewash?

(*Time* review of *Panther*)[1]

I

It seems, in retrospect, no coincidence that *The Adventures of Tom Sawyer* was published in 1876, the year the United States celebrated the centennial of its nationhood. For the book 'lays claim to being America's most popular novel', and its title character has the status of a 'national icon'[2] – pictured (along with whitewashed fence) on bicentennial stamps, recalled in Disneyland at Tom Sawyer's Island,[3] the repeated subject of films, musicals and other representations. If Tom Sawyer occupies 'the perfect place . . . in our national literature and consciousness',[4] the boy cannot be divorced from his background. For Twain's book has come to stand for a wider 'glorification of life in small-town America',[5] an expression of longing for an earlier time and a simpler society, when the tensions that marked Twain's own period, and – in more extreme form – our own, did not exist. 'Twain', in Louis J. Budd's words, 'charms millions as the magic flutist of nostalgia for childhood in a simpler, nicer time'.[6]

Such forms of cultural nostalgia generally cover over the fact that authenticity, wholeness, innocence and security retreat endlessly before the search for them. Twain knew this, and, as Cynthia Griffin Wolff points out in referring to the 'darker side' of the novel (the 'ominous air of violence' that suffuses it), 'every one of [the] sentimental evocations' of *Tom Sawyer* as 'exuding the security of childhood-as-it-ought-to-be in small-town America . . . is false to the original'.[7] Twain's reconstruction of community life in a Missouri riverbank town of the 1830s or 1840s ('thirty or forty years ago'[8]) is not the simple exercise in antimodernism for which it is so often taken. Rather, the ambiguities and contradictions of the book reveal cultural tensions both of the time of the novel's setting and of its writing.

Tom Sawyer relates both to Twain's American present and its past. It was just one of a spate of 'boy books' written in the period between the end of the Civil War and the early twentieth century, but set in the ante-bellum period. The long period of the genre's popularity testifies, for Marcia Jacobson, 'to the fact that it spoke to persistent and apparently insoluble needs on the part of Americans' in a period of 'massive, disruptive social change'. Jacobson sees the boy book as offering a 'vicarious escape from . . . the culture that produced it'.[9] The vicarious escape offered by Twain's novel, however, is not into a world which differs completely from that of the 1870s. Undoubtedly the social patterns, forms of economic activity and institutional frameworks represented in his fictional St Petersburg are simpler, and allow room for the type of individual freedom of action and movement that would later disappear. The nostalgic quality of the book stems in part from this. But though modernisation increased remarkably in speed and intensity in the post-bellum period, what occurred was a series of developments *within* an existing process, and no sudden transformation. The social critique in *Tom Sawyer* is directed not just at Gilded Age America but at the conditions of Jacksonian America too. The escape that it offers has more to do with the *boy* than the place: one who functions at the margins of the normal social rules and constraints, and who is associated with charisma, heroic individualism and the spirit of play.

But the forms of escape associated with Tom are always, in turn, compromised by pressures toward cultural conformity. There is a peculiar double movement to Twain's text that has already been prefigured in *Roughing It*, and on which I focus in this chapter.

Tom Sawyer is both a rebellious *and* a socially respectable, even representative, figure. He is given the authority and agency of the free individual *and* made subject to the pressures of a determining environment. Twain both resists and accepts the historical logic of American capitalism; of American cultural life. His novel reveals anxieties about the direction and development of that culture, and the tensions it contains, but also acts to suppress them – acts, to paraphrase Jacobson, to further its dominant ends.[10] In the matter of race relations, in particular, Twain whitewashes the uncomfortable socio-historical facts of American life to massage (however unconsciously) the sensibilities of his audience. The reasons for the novel's enduring popularity may lie not just in its nostalgic appeal, but in its very ambiguities and paradoxes: the way it both resists and accommodates itself to changing American social and economic patterns.[11] It is this double process I examine here.

Ante-bellum St Petersburg is the fictional equivalent of Hannibal, Missouri,[12] the small town on the Mississippi where Twain spent most of his childhood. The reasons for Twain's turn to fiction, and to the time and region that was to serve as the subject matter for some of his best known and most accomplished writing – *Life on the Mississippi*, *The Adventures of Huckleberry Finn* and *Puddn'head Wilson* all return to this setting – must remain a matter for speculation.[13] One explanation, though, might be found in the influence and impact of the other boy books appearing at the time, and especially Thomas Bailey Aldrich's *The Story of a Bad Boy* (1869). For it was his reading of the latter which, according to Alan Gribben, 'apparently prompted Mark Twain to value at last the wealth of literary materials lying unclaimed in the recollections of prewar Hannibal'. Such influence may also have prompted the change in narrative mode from the earlier travel books. *Tom Sawyer* (and particularly its early stages) shares the same flexible move between autobiography and fiction of those prior narratives. But its fictional form and reliance on an omniscient and retrospective narrative voice may have been triggered both by the reading Twain was doing and the stimulus to his own memory it spurred.[14]

Twain's turn to the novel, however, did not bring taut formal unity with it. For here, too, Twain contains his various materials only loosely. The developing narrative of Tom's boyhood life, which gives its own shape to the narrative, proceeds far from consistently.[15] Twain's use of satire, burlesque and sentimentality often run in uneasy relationship to one another.[16] There is a logic to the book's ending, shaped both by the melodramic plot of Tom, 'Injun Joe' and the buried treasure, and the success narrative it climaxes. Twain's formal unease is, though, even then textually overt: 'So endeth this chronicle. . . . When one writes . . . of juveniles, he must stop where he best can' (p. 221). I do not concentrate on literary structure in this chapter. It is worth noting in the light of my later argument, however, that Twain is here able to contain the various thematic tensions and ambiguities of his book within the one formal frame. The cultural anxieties he traces are always kept in textual check: apparent here, but balanced by the social accommodations made; partly covered over by the use of conventions of mystery, adventure and romance (formulating Tom's financial and community success within these generic bounds); and disguised in the return to an apparently unproblematic boyhood world. As Twain's writing career progressed, his doubts both about the status of the individual and the direction of the society in which he or she lived increased. So, accordingly, did his problems in containing conflicting themes within a unified narrative form. The developing story of my book lies, in part, in the tracing of these doubts and problems.

II

The moves between boyhood and adulthood, and between a pre- and post-Civil War world, which *Tom Sawyer* makes, and the complex and ambiguous attitude to the developing patterns of American cultural life the novel reveals, are the immediate focus of my analysis. I begin with the whitewashing episode, for if there is one scene that most readers remember from the book, and which has gathered considerable iconographic significance, it is this. The whitewashed fence was illustrated by True Williams in the first edition as having four horizontal boards with equally wide gaps between, supported by well spaced-out vertical posts of approxi- mately Tom's shoulder height. That fence has come, nostalgically, to signify the securities and clean orderliness of small-town America, even despite the problematic nature of Twain's representation of that locale. We are, though, immediately aware of boundaries being staked out here (and the boundary metaphor is a repeated one in the novel). Wayne Fields puts it rather nicely:

[Tom Sawyer's] nightly forays and adventures depend upon the St Petersburg fences. In climbing over them, as he presumes to leave the commonplace behind and imagines himself escaping all the constraints of authority while playing at the lawlessness of pirate and outlaw, the fences serve as tangible – though ironic – evidence that he has 'gotten away,' crossed some significant boundary, in a necessary prerequisite for adventure. But just as important is the return in which the enclosures [of orderliness, parental and civil authority], no longer cause for claustrophobia, provide respite and security. Without fences there would be no appropriate barriers over which adventurous boys could crawl. Without fences there would be no safe retreats when the adventure is over or when it threatens to become too real.[17]

Williams's depiction of the fence (repeated in similar form in other representations of the scene) departs considerably from Twain's original description. The fence is not nearly as easy to cross as the illustration suggests. The barrier between what is kept in and kept out is a significant 'thirty yards of broad fence nine feet high' (p. 15). In Neil Schmitz's words, 'the fence, after all, is a brutal affair, almost a wall, so long and so high you can't see over it or around it'.[18]

The conventional (*OED*) definition of 'whitewash' in the context used here is of a 'solution of . . . whiting and size for brushing over walls . . . etc., to give clean appearance'. But it can also mean 'to cover up, conceal, or gloss over the faults and blemishes of'. It is easy for the reader to gloss over Tom's faults and blemishes, the ambiguities in his presentation, in this scene. For the initial motive behind his actions is undoubtedly attractive, as he looks for spontaneity, play and 'pure freedom' (p. 16) rather than 'the misery of profitless convict labor, the end of which is a vast thirty yards distant'.[19] Tom is identified with the play principle, as he is so often throughout the novel,[20] always seen yearning for 'seductive outside summer scenes' (p. 37) rather than domestic or institutional confinement. Here, he is already outside, but the idea of seduction has been cancelled out, his 'captivity at hard labor' (p. 14) a result of Aunt Polly's domestic disciplines (he is being punished for playing 'hookey,' p. 8). Cardiff Hill, 'a Delectable Land, dreamy, reposeful and inviting' (p. 15), lies close to the village boundaries, but the invitation is closed to Tom. 'When all the boys is having holiday' (p. 8)[21] and 'skylarking' (p. 15), he is tied to his set work, and work is something 'he hates . . . more than he hates anything else' (p. 8).

The reader is encouraged to empathise with Tom and his commitment to childhood play. He manages his escape ('Mayn't I go and play now, Aunt?' – p. 20), is 'over the fence and gone' beyond the reach of 'capture and punishment' (p. 21), through his own imaginative ability to convert work to play for his fellow boys. The fence metaphorically separates the arena of social discipline from that of adventure and romance. Thus a make-believe battle, and then the first sight of Becky Thatcher, follows Tom's move beyond his aunt's domestic enclosure. Tom, at the spatial point where these two sets of values intersect, manages to fudge their difference. For though Ben Rogers and the other boys 'fagged themselves out' as they 'worked and sweated in the sun' (p. 19), Tom has succeeded in transforming their perception of this activity, in whitewashing hard labour into apparent play. As the narrator comments, naming the principle that Tom exploits, 'work consists of whatever a body is obliged to do, and . . . play consists of whatever a body is not obliged to do' (pp. 19–20).

Before commenting further on Tom's role here, I focus on the opposition between work and play which is constructed; one already, in fact, partially undone by the verbs used to describe the boys' activity as they paint. Play, in other words, is highly contaminated by work here. The relation between these two terms, and the way it was culturally understood at the time of Twain's writing, can be analysed to show both the impact of modern disciplinary practices[22] (with leisure and playfulness rationed out according to the primary needs of a workplace world) and, further, to illustrate how Tom Sawyer himself – contrary to initial impressions – is deeply implicated in the capitalist system he would seem to reject.

This is complicated material, and I proceed slowly. At the time Twain wrote *Tom Sawyer*, the cultural perception of the relation between play and work (like that between the savage and the civilised) was rooted in the idea of a child–man divide. This perception was, indeed, already becoming established in the pre-war

period of the novel's setting. Michael Oriard looks back to 1830s
America to see the start of a pattern that became more evident as
the Industrial Revolution advanced: the 'uncomfortable awareness
that perhaps leisure, not labor, offered the best possibilities for
human fulfilment'. He shows how the play impulse was harnessed
to the new industrial order as the nineteenth century progressed.
Recognising the 'labor/leisure dualism at the heart of industrial
capitalism', and its corollary, that 'play embodied a countercultural
desire for work-oriented men' in Gilded Age America, Oriard shows
how the boy (and girl) book provided a way of containing and
disguising such tensions.[23] These books helped to smooth over the
divide between labour and leisure in their celebration of 'work and
play as two halves of the ideal life', with childhood represented as
'the time for play'. This allowed for the creation of a series of
'idealized figures on whom middle-class America projected its
desires and fantasies, but without jeopardising its ultimate commitment to work'.[24]

Twain's book, however, complicates this pattern. For *Tom Sawyer*
never quite works as the story of a merely playful boy. Rather, Twain
implicates Tom in the business ethic from which childhood,
supposedly, provided an alternative and escape. The partial
unravelling of the work–play opposition in the whitewashing scene,
as the play of childhood overlaps with work, points to the
ambiguities in Tom's representation in the novel. He is associated
both with 'boyhood's free spirit'[25] and with proto-capitalist attitudes
and practices.[26] He is nostalgically linked throughout the novel with
adventure, imagination and the escape from the responsible adult
world, but also depicted as an entrepreneur, an emergent
businessman, finally rewarded by the status, praise and fortune
which symbolise complete social acceptance and success. The
peculiar double effects here do not add up. The gap between labour
and leisure differs from the model Oriard suggests,[27] for Tom is
simultaneously both playful boy and apprentice businessman.
Twain appears, moreover, to criticise capitalist attitudes and values
in his description of the methods Tom uses to achieve his profitable
ends, and his suggestion of what is being sacrificed in the process.
But if ambivalences appear here about the values associated with
the world of labour which are, in the boy book, normally covered
over, Twain has his own way of (partially) disguising them. The
criticism of business values remains implicit rather than overt;

suppressed, to considerable degree, by the *confusion* of work and play, by the nostalgic tone of the book, and by Tom's central, and often heroic, role in the success story it enacts. To start to unpack the contradictions in Tom's representation and the divisions in his performance is, though, to suggest the cultural tensions it masks. A strong note of ambiguity concerning his activities runs right the way through the novel.

Tom's first fortune results from his whitewashing scam, which leaves him 'literally rolling in wealth' (p. 19). If to whitewash is to 'cover up and conceal', Tom conceals rather a lot in the victory he wins at the expense both of Aunt Polly and his friends. Later, when Becky is threatened with punishment following her accidental tearing of the schoolteacher's *Anatomy* book, Tom says that 'girls' faces always tell on them' (p. 132). Here, he disguises his intentions behind a false face, 'took up his brush and went tranquilly to work' (p. 16) once he decides on his plan to whitewash his friends; to con them out of their possessions. For Jesse Bier is not alone in seeing Tom as a 'con man'.[28] Tom tricks his friends into doing his work for him, and relieves them of their wealth, whatever its form ('twelve marbles . . . a tin soldier . . . a kitten with only one eye' – p. 19) into the bargain. Unearned increment is too modest a term to describe the capital Tom accumulates out of nothing but Aunt Polly's raw materials and his wits alone.

In *Confidence Men and Painted Women: A Study of Middle-class Culture in America, 1830–1870*, Karen Halttunen identifies the figure of the confidence man as standing at 'the center of anxieties that advice manuals expressed about American youth' in the period. These anxieties focused on the move, on the part of young men in particular, 'far beyond the surveillance of their families, their towns, and their churches' as they responded to ante-bellum social change and sought work 'in the booming cities of industrializing America'. The confidence man, she continues, became a figure representing all that was threatening in 'the growing confusion and anonymity of urban living'. Charisma was likely to replace established social authority in such conditions, and 'fluid self-aggrandisement' easily resulted from the hypocrisy and duplicity – beneath the mask of perfect sincerity – of such trickster figures.[29]

This fearful scenario was already becoming established in the Jacksonian period about which Twain wrote. In one very obvious sense, however, Tom Sawyer cannot be associated with such anxieties, firmly bound as he is to the relatively self-contained small-town world of St Petersburg (referred to variously as both town and village). One might, however, see here both a hint of the fears of that period, and an anxiety about the types of changes (and the figures who would symbolise them) altering America, both before and after the Civil War.[30] For the processes of social transformation in the period were continuous ones. Twain represents Tom not only as a proto-capitalist but as a confidence man into the bargain. In doing so he taps into anxieties not only about business values but about social status too: anxieties first apparent in Jacksonian times but present in more persistent and stronger form in Gilded Age America.[31]

Tom Sawyer is a junior version of the confidence man or 'man of confidence', the 'man-on-the make' adept at 'manipulating surface impressions for selfish gain'. His 'highly theatrical attention to the presentation of self' is, by and large, extremely effective in this village society and prefigures forms of behaviour that would flourish in a rapidly changing Jacksonian (and post-Jacksonian) America, when 'everything [was] up for grabs: wealth and status to be won by enterprise not birth, an entire social order to be decided by wit and opportunism'.[32] Tom consistently turns traditional forms of social power upside down. He directs the pirate play world on Jackson's Island beyond the scan of family authority. He disrupts the rituals of both church and school. These 'rebellions' are, though, ultimately safely contained within the fabric of ongoing village life, and the sentimental frame of the boy book which represents it.

But there are signs of a more fundamental change in the social order here, too. Tom is associated, as these occur, not with a childhood disruption of established authority, but with the establishment of new patterns of social authority and success. Here, in other words (and in contrast to his former role), he actually represents the dominant values of an emergent capitalist culture. The tensions within the book are clear as such a representation clashes with Tom's position as a figure of anti-modernist wish-fulfilment: the playful child who cannot be pinned down by society's fixed routines and disciplines, and who can temporarily escape its authority adventuring on Jackson's Island or Cardiff Hill.

Tom can certainly be read in terms of an emerging enterprise culture. In *Tom Sawyer: A Play* (commenced in 1875–6, finished in 1883–4), Tom's business acumen in the whitewash scene becomes even more obvious, as he tells the other boys, 'Come, pay in *advance*! We don't *trust*, here. Pay up, pay up before you *begin*.'[33] A confidence man who has no confidence in others, Tom trades his way to the prizes available in St Petersburg by duplicitous means.[34] 'A wily fraud', Tom none the less has 'the certified checks' to gain possession of the forty-cent Bible at Sunday school: the tickets that vouch for the 'industry and . . . application' (p. 30) needed to memorise two thousand of its verses. These checks, too, are 'good for their face' (p. 34), despite the lack of knowledge, on Tom's part, normally expected to underwrite them.

Such forms of language repeatedly suggest the connection between Tom's dealings and the financial market. Worldly wealth, security and profitable exchange certainly consume Tom's interest. Almost straightaway, in the sequence when he sees Huck's captured tick, Tom will ask, 'What'll you take for him?' (p. 49). And while Huck plans to spend his share of any discovered treasure on 'a pie and a glass of soda every day, and [a trip] to every circus that comes along', Tom, as his dialogue with Huck indicates, has more serious things in mind:

'Well, ain't you going to save any of it?'
'Save it? What for?'
'Why, so as to have something to live on by-and-by.' (p. 155)

When Indian Joe discovers the buried fortune in the haunted house, Tom's response is to 'Find him! Track the money!' (p. 169) and plan to 'snatch that box' (p. 173) containing it. This, one might argue, would constitute theft, as opposed to Indian Joe's act of legitimate discovery. When the boys do eventually get the treasure, any attention to their ethical position conveniently dissipates due to Joe's prior death. But this death is a direct result, however unintentional, of Tom's actions: all that leads to the boy's entomb-ment in the cave; and its sealing following his escape.

The use of the resurrection motif is recurrent in *Tom Sawyer*. It commences with two 'resurrectionists' (for so nineteenth-century grave-robbers were known) raising the dead for medical purposes. It concludes with Tom and Becky's return to the daylight world, and to the community, after three days and nights buried in the cave. Joe, the socially terrifying figure whose initial transgression of Christian ritual started this cycle, ends symbolically buried in place of the children. There is a peculiar twinning between Joe and Tom here,[35] and one that again partly works to suggest something rather dubious about Tom's financial activities. Scott Michaelsen, in fact, notes Tom's linked association with both robber and entrepreneur as conforming to a standard trope in the representation of the capitalist in Gilded Age literature.[36]

As *Tom Sawyer* ends, Tom's money is out 'at six-per-cent' and his income is 'prodigious' (p. 216). He is, then, certainly shown as, in some degree, an apprentice version of the 'man-on-the-make' whose charisma, enterprise and eye for the main chance together bring him success. This script addresses (in however veiled a manner) anxieties about social and economic change in the Jacksonian period about which Twain was writing, but also in Gilded Age America too. The social order Twain describes in the novel is one in transition, with (or so it is implied) the introduction of new patterns of wealth based on enterprise[37] rather than birth. The final sequences of *Tom Sawyer* indicate a dramatic change in social and status hierarchies that complements Tom and Huck's new wealth: the two boys earn as much hard cash, in interest on their money, as the minister gets in a good week, and their twelve thousand dollars 'was more than anyone present [at its counting] had ever seen at one time before, though several persons were there who were worth considerable more than that in property' (p. 216). New ways of measuring wealth, and of determining social hierarchy and authority, are readily apparent here.

This, though, is a lop-sided reading of the novel. Undoubtedly anxieties about money, class and social change, and their effect (both before and after the Civil War) on American culture are evident in *Tom Sawyer*. But it is easy to read the book, as I did at the start of this section, as about childhood skylarking and adventure, and the escape from the adult world of responsibility and business success, rather than seeing the representation of Tom as a site for social critique. Indeed, to recognise Tom's business side is not necessarily to see Twain as attacking capitalist values; for his enterprise and material gain, both legitimised by the traditional American success ethos, are expected components of the popular genres (adventure and romance) on which Twain relies. Moreover, though the narrating voice might at times adopt a tone open to ironic interpretation in describing the way Tom accrues wealth, and his accompanying actions, it would be difficult to read the novel (and especially its final sequences) consistently in terms of such a deliberate intent. If the boy book genre generally recalled past cultural vitality and authenticity,[38] then it is Tom's opposition to the 'frowsy hum of study' (p. 50) in the schoolplace, his subversion of day-to-day institutional and social rituals, and his imaginative efforts to escape these boundaries into a world of heroic individualism and romantic adventure which undoubtedly helped (and helps) to account for *Tom Sawyer*'s success. In other words, and again, cultural tensions are both revealed and masked here. Tom is shown both as boy businessman (the child as father of the man) and as romantic rebel at one and the same time. Anxieties about the growth and direction of an entrepreneurial and materialist society are balanced, on one side, by an implied acceptance of its norms, on the other, by a return to an apparently unproblematic ante-bellum world of childhood play.

III

Anxieties about the direction of American cultural life in *Tom Sawyer* are also evident in its representation of the individual subject: Tom's freedom of action and romantic self-expression are contrasted with, and run alongside, a quite different type of passive determinism. The resulting tension indicates a concern with the question of subjective agency which was to haunt Twain throughout his career, and especially in the major novels following *Tom Sawyer*. The relationship between individual autonomy and the effect of social conditioning became, increasingly, a crucial area of debate for nineteenth-century Americans. Twain joins that debate here, but tends finally to evade its more disconcerting aspects.

It is clear that on the most obvious textual level, Tom Sawyer acts as the hero in a romance. He is a central character, and leading actor, in the life of St Petersburg, dominating the various spaces he inhabits. An early review indicated that the appeal of the book lay (and still lies) in its story of 'certain bold and restless youths who, finding every-day life very monotonous, went in for living like outlaws in the woods, exploring for hidden treasures, and other romantic adventures'.[39] The whole village is composed of performance artists: 'Mr Walters fell to "showing off". . . . The

librarian "showed off".... The young lady teachers "showed off"'
(p. 33). But it is Tom, with his quick imagination, leadership and
flair for adventure, who is the figure centre stage. 'Theatrical
gorgeousness' appeals 'strongly to his nature' (p. 104), and Tom is
nowhere happier than when he can indulge his flair for the
dramatic, whether in arranging to attend his own funeral service
(p. 118) or in pouring gold coins in a heap before a startled audience
(p. 215). His success is measured in terms of the role of 'glittering
hero' (p. 151) he assumes, 'thronged' by an excited population
'roaring huzza after huzza!' (p. 200). For Tom, nothing could be
better than making, over and over again, 'a mighty stir' (p. 216).

Tom Sawyer, then, is the charismatic centre of the novel.
Adventure, mystery and romance dominate his life, and in all three
realms he plays the lead part, whether as 'Tom Sawyer the Pirate!
The Black Avenger of the Spanish Main!' (p. 61), the detective who
tracks down the dangerous Injun Joe's money, or as the lover
'swimming in bliss' as he sweet-talks Becky Thatcher ('Do you love
rats?', p. 56) into becoming his fiancée. He sets up performances
which rival and outdo those available from more traditional sources,
and exposes the boredoms and familiarities of the minister's Sunday
sermon in the alternative entertainment which he (in this case,
unintentionally) instigates, when a poodle sits on the pinch-bug he
has released:

> Then there was a wild yelp of agony, and the poodle went sailing
> up the aisle; the yelps continued, and so did the dog. . . . By this
> time the whole church was red-faced and suffocating with
> suppressed laughter, and the sermon had come to a dead
> standstill. (pp. 41–2)

Jackson Lears discusses the late-Victorian image of the innocent
child in the context of 'a world where selfhood had become
problematic'.[40] Twain's return to ante-bellum boyhood in *Tom
Sawyer*, and the active and heroic nature of the main protagonist's
role, implies similar anxieties even in the mid-1870s. Indeed, Eric
Sundquist looks further back, to the ante-bellum period, to discover
concerns which were to become more and more prominent as the
century progressed. He sees even then, in *Moby Dick* (1851) and *Life
in the Iron Mills* (1861), a focus on 'the material and technological
details of American life' and a measuring of 'the distance between

the sovereign territory of the individual self and the powers of social
or political community that surround and create individual des-
tiny'.[41] It is exactly this same tension between different conceptions
of the self that is an underlying motif in Twain's novel. For, as Fred
G. See says, putting this in a slightly altered way:

> There is a contradiction in Clemens' work between the self caught
> in sequence and measurement and the self freely expressed in
> fantasy and play. These are the two linked and opposing ways of
> ordering reality that lay claim to Tom Sawyer, and he is the border
> between them.[42]

We can start to see this tension between the free expression of the
self and the determining influence of environmental forces in the
repeated use of insect metaphors in the novel. Tom Sawyer is given
a type of god-like authority, not only in his ability to loose the
pinch-bug from 'the percussion-cap box' (p. 40) in which he keeps
it, but also in his later control over the tick that takes its place as
captive there. Tom releases the tick onto his school desk, and Joe
joins him in 'exercising the prisoner' (p. 54). The boys use pins to
direct the insect, playing a game of 'crossing the equator'[43] as each
tries to keep it on his side of the desk:

> At last luck seemed to settle and abide with Joe. The tick tried
> this, that, and the other course, and got as excited and anxious
> as the boys themselves, but time and again, just as he would have
> victory in his very grasp so to speak, and Tom's fingers would
> be twitching to begin, Joe's pin would deftly head him off and
> keep possession. At last Tom could stand it no longer. The
> temptation was too strong. So he reached out and lent a hand
> with his pin. (p. 55).

The stress on power and manipulation, on anxious but unsuccessful
attempts to escape their limits, and on boundaries being crossed,
prepares us for the shift in perspective and position which then
occurs. For the schoolteacher comes down with 'a tremendous
whack . . . on Tom's shoulders, and its duplicate on Joe's' (p. 55), to
remind the boys both of his superior power and of their relative
lack of autonomy in his presence.

This metaphoric shift where Tom becomes the captive insect, and the relativising of the relation between authority and subjection that it enacts, is repeated and played out in different ways throughout *Tom Sawyer*. The book starts with Aunt Polly turning around 'just in time to seize a small boy [Tom] by the slack of his roundabout and arrest his flight' (p. 7). Tom is repeatedly, too, subject to switchings and floggings by Mr. Dobbins, 'the potency of the masculine "muscle" . . . used with . . . consistent vindictiveness and violence'[44] to keep the mischievous boy in check. The town librarian is associated with 'insect authority' (p. 33), a phrase which cuts two ways in suggesting both the further levels of authority which lie beyond his own, but also in implying the low and powerless status of those in his charge. When Tom, burdened by his secret knowledge of Joe's crime, hears a great storm at night, he takes it as a direct response by 'the powers above', and sees 'nothing incongruous about the getting up of such an expensive storm as this to knock the turf from under an insect like himself' (p. 144). If Tom continually 'insists on the exciting apparatus of action,' there is a constant awareness of the social and institutional forces which restrain and hold him in check: that 'another authority always comes first, whatever he is doing'.[45] Elizabeth G. Peck, in fact, goes so far as to suggest that, in this respect, Tom's characterisation foreshadows 'the environmental determinism of *The Tragedy of Pudd'nhead Wilson*'.[46]

The impact of the determining forces – social, religious, legal and moral – on Tom's development and the way in which they compromise a sense of his autonomy can, however, easily be overlooked in the novel. Tom's fracturings of the social rules are always temporary and *depend* on the safe return to society. His 'play' ultimately conforms to the values of respectable society; all his effects are finally predicated on the approval and indulgence of his elders. His 'rebellions' are sanctioned ones.[47] Joe's words, when Tom describes the delights of swimming on Jackson's Island, are no more than an overt admission of Tom's own underlying attitudes: 'swimming's no good; I don't seem to care for it, somehow, when there ain't anybody to say I shan't go in. I mean to go home' (p. 108). Individual expression and social conformity are variously represented *both* as oppositional and as complementary in this novel. If Tom's final actions are heroic, they work to the benefit of the community. He ends up fully contained within its boundaries, the protector both of justice (that is, as this community recognises

it) and of weak womanhood, his social success assured. The
opposition between subjective desire and social regulation and
convention is covered over. The whitewashing that is being done
here, concerning the nature of individual agency and its limits is,
however, implicit in the description of Huck Finn's initial separation
from the community, and in his status as 'forbidden society'. For he
does what Tom will never want – or be allowed – to do:[48]

> Huckleberry came and went at his own free will . . . ; he did not
> have to go to school or to church, or call any being master, or obey
> anybody. . . . In a word, everything that goes to make life
> precious, that boy had. . . . Tom hailed the romantic outcast.
>
> (p. 46)

Full self-expression is described, in Huck's case, as entirely at odds
with community membership, and the social conditioning that
accompanies it. Though Twain fails to develop the implications of
this in any depth, and indeed ends the novel by pulling Huck
(uneasily) into the community alongside Tom, such a tension would
not, in his work, stay buried for very long. Indeed, as *Tom Sawyer*
comes to its close, so the alternative possibilities contained in
Huck's person and voice start, disruptively, to emerge.[49]

IV

Tom Sawyer's representation, as I have shown, is complex and
ambiguous. He ends up socially successful, contained (symbolically)
by the whitewashed fence, within the boundaries of what,
nostalgically, can be constructed as the attractive, peaceful and
well-ordered haven of American small-town life. But his position
here is at odds with other aspects of his characterisation. Cynthia
Griffin Wolff points out that Tom has common traits, too, with the
most aggressively antisocial figure in the novel, Injun Joe, whom
she sees as his 'shadow self'.[50] She suggests that the 'carefully
constructed rituals of devastation' in which Tom participates in the
safety of his 'own fictional world' are sublimated versions of 'the
rebellion and rage that never fully surface in his dealings with Aunt
Polly and the other figures of authority in this matriarchal world',

a rebellion and rage that Joe overtly represents. For Wolff, the death of the 'ruthless predator', Joe's 'summary banishment', is 'an ending with no resolution at all'. For he is banished from sight, mind and text, as 'all too dangerous to traffic with'.[51] Tom's resurrection from the underground cave (with all its symbolic connotations) is consequently presented as prelude to the start of a useful adult career, all fears about his antisocial impulses carefully put below ground with Joe's dead body. Judge Thatcher then pronounces on Tom's socialised future, saying 'he meant to look to it that Tom should be admitted to the National Military Academy, and afterward trained in the best law-school in the country' (p. 217).

The anxieties evident here, and the textual patterns of threat and containment revealed, can be taken, though, in a rather different direction. For what *Tom Sawyer* reveals, but only in turn firmly to suppress, is a highly uncomfortable attitude to the history of American race relations. In the matter of race particularly, the reader of Twain's boy book is finally left with a whitewashed version of Mississippi village life, all anxieties about its prejudices and injustices pushed firmly, but not completely, under cover. The novel hints at this subject, only then *almost* wholly to conceal ugly social and political realities pertaining both to the time when the book is set, and when it is being written. Part of the book's cultural significance may lie in the readiness of its (adult) audience to collude in such a whitewash.

First, to connect with Wolff's argument, it is noticeable how sexual anxieties in the novel are, by and large, taken beyond the borders of St Petersburg village life to settle on the figure of Joe, the social and racial outsider. If the innocent patterns of Tom and Becky's pre-adolescent romance reflect the genteel courtship rituals and conventional gender relations of their immediate community, their behaviour is directly contrasted with (and yet peculiarly linked to) the sexual threat contained in Injun Joe. For, as John Seelye suggests, there are sexual undercurrents to Joe's plan to 'tie the widow to her bed' and then 'slit her nostrils . . . notch her ears like a sow's' (p. 180).[52] Tom generally seems pre-sexual, but he is associated with a type of 'secret sexual knowledge'[53] in the Anatomy book incident, where he first surprises Becky as she looks at the 'handsomely engraved and coloured frontispiece – a human figure, stark naked',[54] then takes the punishment for the torn page that results. Forrest Robinson suggests the implicit connections being made in a Tom–Becky–Joe triangle, as he discusses Becky's failure to face Joe in the cave sequence. Saying that 'as Tom well knows, Injun Joe is quite literally beyond Becky's ken', he continues:

> Becky's carefully guarded ignorance about Joe's appearance in the cave is culturally of a piece with her carefully preserved ignorance in the matter of the anatomy book. Tom knows immediately and for a certainty that knowledge about Indian Joe, in anything like its full range of implication, is incompatible with Becky's culturally defined 'innocence'.[55]

Joe appears as Tom's shadow self here too, his sexual presence and threat testifying to a quality necessarily repressed on the boy hero's part. The racial and social outcast is identified with a violent and dangerous sexuality that cannot be contained by normal village life. Anxieties about adult sexuality, and the social violence it can wreak, are here dumped on Joe's symbolic figure.

One last meaning of whitewash (for my purposes here) is that given in *Webster's Dictionary* (1858 edition): 'a wash for making the skin fair'. Certainly, the notion of 'community' in St Petersburg takes on a distinctively European-American cast. Twain is writing in the Reconstruction period about an ante-bellum slave-holding society, but little hint of social criticism concerning the subject of race enters his text. Slavery appears not to be an issue, and the stable and fixed nature of racial hierarchies is repeatedly confirmed. This American small town is run for, and by, its white citizenry. No sign of racial tension between white and black is apparent here.

Jim, in *Tom Sawyer*, is a 'small coloured boy' (pp. 8–9). Thus, by necessity, the metaphorical equation of slave with child that characterised the Southern family romance,[56] and which *Huckleberry Finn* would shortly challenge, cannot be subjected to critical interrogation. No African-American is seen – and this is only to be expected given the social world Twain describes – in church, school or at formal social occasions. There are, however, occasional textual signs, if very quickly passed over, of the racial problems which were, in fact, so crucially to alter the shape of Southern (and American) history. Indian Joe puts himself ahead of the African-American in the social hierarchy when he says that the Widow Douglas's former husband had him 'horse-whipped . . . like a nigger' (p. 180). The hint here is of 'white injustice and mistreatment',[57] not just toward

Joe, but also toward the slaves with whom he compares himself; of a brutal treatment of those who are considered social and racial inferiors. If this theme remains undeveloped, it certainly briefly disturbs the surface of the text, and serves to indicate a shadow on, or stain beneath, the St Petersburg whitewash.

A similar brief disturbance occurs in the footnote pointing to the shades of difference in this community between the ownership of a slave and a dog. Thus the naming of a dog, Bull Harbison, is followed by the note that 'if Mr. Harbison had owned a slave named Bull, Tom would have spoken of him as "Harbison's Bull"; but a son or dog of that name was "Bull Harbison"' (p. 75). This analogy, and marginal distinction, between slave and dog, foreshadows a central motif of *Puddn'head Wilson*. There is no sign here, however, of the irony of the later text. The very presence of this apparently uninflected note (one of only two footnotes in the whole book) does, though, stop the reader short; make her or him wonder if the contemporary critics who saw Twain's naming of St Petersburg as a deliberate reference to a 'Republican freedom from class prejudices' lacking in its Russian counterpart,[58] had read the novel entirely correctly. St Petersburg can pass for an easygoing, free and equal society, a model of the American democratic ideal, but only by ignoring *racial* difference. The very few references to black–white relations that can be considered troubling, and the complete lack of their development, can (to speculate) suggest one reason for *Tom Sawyer*'s long-term popularity. On the surface, at any rate, it nostalgically projects an idyllic version of white (whitewashed?) small-town America, where the racial issues that were to plague the country both before and after the Civil War are unproblematised, pushed to the margins of the text. In this respect, Twain's boy book looks back, as the genre so often encouraged, to a trouble-free world, and one all the more attractive to its audience for so being. It is just the odd passage in the book which suggests something different; reveals anxieties that never completely disappear beneath the textual surface.

A related argument can be made about Injun Joe's role in the book. Injun Joe, unlike his fellow marginal man, the African-American slave, does unsettle the community of St Petersburg. But, positioned so clearly within a melodramatic frame, and defined so overtly as racial and moral 'other', the threat he poses is always subject to his expected final textual containment (indeed obliteration). Joe's half-breed status is repeatedly foregrounded, and this accordingly raises the threat of racial contamination. If Twain is writing about a period when Andrew Jackson 'as the President of the United States responsible for Indian removal . . . developed a philosophical explanation which transformed Indian deaths into moral inevitability',[59] he is writing in a period of continued hostilities between the US Government and the Indian (Custer's Last Stand took place in the centennial year too) which were only to close, much later in 1890, with 'the symbolic end of Indian freedom'[60] at Wounded Knee.

Injun Joe is, in *Tom Sawyer*, unmistakably other, the repository of all the traits that St Petersburg and its dominant white citizenry would deny and reject. His spring from the courtroom window, tearing 'his way through all opposers' (p. 151), shows him violently breaking the boundaries that limit small-town life (Tom, too, repeatedly crosses the symbolic boundary of the window; one more thing they have in common). Sexually cruel, criminally and unnecessarily violent, and powerfully and antisocially disruptive, Injun Joe is a demonic figure, described variously as 'that murderin' half-breed' (even before he kills Dr Robinson – p. 68), 'Injun devil' (p. 73), a 'stony-hearted liar [who] had sold himself to Satan' (p. 81), and as 'half-breed devil' (p. 147). Joe himself puts his own desire for vengeance on Dr. Robinson down to his 'Injun blood' (p. 69). Twain's story dramatically projects the extinction of this savage and racially different other as necessary for the continued safety and good order of small-town life. As Robert Tracy puts it, Joe is:

> in Whitman's phrase a 'dusky demon and brother,' whose brotherhood is denied and whose demonhood is exaggerated. . . . [At the novel's end] the Indian dies and the treasure disappears into a bank – a neat and accurate symbol of the fate of the trans-Mississippi frontier. Civilization's progress exorcises the devils, exterminates the Indians, and banks the proceeds.[61]

Anxieties about racial injustice are raised in *Tom Sawyer*, and the oblique suggestion is made that Joe 'was the victim of white society before he was its villain'.[62] Such anxieties have their base, if we take Joe's case as paradigmatic, in historical fact: the whitewashing of America, in the case of white–Indian relations, covered up considerable injustice and violence by the dominant racial group.

But these textual tensions are undeveloped, the cultural uncertainties they indicate suppressed almost as soon as raised. The demonisation and extermination of Joe, and his role as melodramatic agent of evil, suggest how firmly – hysterically, one might almost say – uncomfortable socio-historical facts are being covered up as they appear in this fictional form.

The Adventures of Tom Sawyer, then, presents us with an American village world[63] where divergent racial elements (and the cultural heterogeneity they might suggest) are, for the most part, marginalised or suppressed.[64] If metaphorically, 'all those buckets of whitewash [are necessary] to St Petersburg's security and self-confidence',[65] perhaps they have been necessary to the security and self-confidence of many of the readers of Twain's book too. For one *can* read this fictional world as one where the pressures of modernisation do not apply, where boys (tolerated by adults) can play their pranks and indulge in antisocial behaviour with no lasting effects,[66] and where social hierarchies (and especially those constructed on the basis of race) are, finally, entirely stable. To do so would not be entirely inaccurate, but would deny the complexities and ambiguities which closer study of the novel reveals.

5

Racial Politics in
Huckleberry Finn

---

*'Now, old Jim, you're a free man again, and I bet you won't
ever be a slave no more.'*

(*The Adventures of Huckleberry Finn*)[1]

I

Adventures of Huckleberry Finn (1884–5) is the best-known novel in
America's literary history. Sales figures have been estimated at over
20 million worldwide.[2] Hemingway said that 'All modern American
literature comes from . . . *Huckleberry Finn*'. T. S. Eliot called it a
masterpiece.[3] It is one of the few American novels where new
academic scholarship or dispute consistently stimulates wider
public interest, as in the case of the 1991 discovery of the first
two-fifths of the handwritten manuscript of the novel. 'Jim and the
Dead Man', a previously unknown passage found here (edited out
prior to the book's original publication), received considerable
attention when it appeared in the *New Yorker* in 1995, placed alongside the comments of five contemporary American writers reflecting
on 'Twain's novel and our most persistent moral dilemma'. The
exact nature of this dilemma is not specified. William Styron,
though, indicates its implied grounds in writing that Huck and Jim,
'with their confused and incalculable feelings for each other, remain
symbols of our racial confusion'.[4]

In this chapter, my focus too is on race. I thus necessarily downplay other important aspects of the book that stands as a 'vital critical centre'[5] in any discussion of the American literary tradition. Thus, for instance, the importance of Twain's use of the vernacular voice, a type of 'verbal outlawry',[6] cannot be overestimated. In having Huck tell his own story, he overturned all the novelistic conventions of his time concerning the use of formal or standard English, and set the American novel on a new course. Twain also interrogates the whole nineteenth-century sentimental tradition here. If right action is grounded, as Huck's is, in feeling alone, the issue that remains is what authority one person's right feeling has over anyone else's, and how such judgements are made.[7] I sideline, too, the important question of individual agency and identity and their relation to the social and institutional environment, to nature and to political belief (a democratic ideology). *Huckleberry Finn* works, first and foremost, as a comic novel, but I do not examine Twain's use of different forms of humour, and I only touch on his use of genre in the text. These are just some of the issues which have made the book such a rich arena for critical explication and debate, and have helped to contribute to its status as an American 'classic'. The production of books and articles on *Huckleberry Finn* is so profuse that the reader who wishes to explore in more detail its other aspects will have no difficulty in finding a series of excellent critical guides available.[8]

The subject of race is generally muted in *Tom Sawyer*. In *Huckleberry Finn*, though, it becomes a matter of central concern. I use Huck and Jim's conflict over the meaning of the word 'freedom' to illustrate how their two stories diverge, and how the marginalisation of Jim's voice affects our readerly knowledge of his role and status. I then argue that *despite* the differences between Huck and Jim, Twain also (and alternatively) shows how their stories come together to complement one another, and represents their relationship on the raft as idyllic. In doing so, his novel enters, however indirectly, into the public debate about race in 1880s' America, and suggests a new model of interracial relationships. This idyll necessarily comes to nothing within the narrative frame within which Twain works, but nonetheless gives the book a powerful and polemic social and political charge which the frustrating nature of its ending (for this is how I read it here) cannot entirely defuse.

I suggest that, like *Tom Sawyer*, *Huckleberry Finn* is not just about the ante-bellum past in which it is set, but also reveals anxieties about social problems in Twain's contemporary America. In the former novel, Twain's use of the boy book provides him with a generic form[9] which helps to disguise ambiguous attitudes to American social and historical development. So too, here, the particular setting of the novel, its different narrative strands, its use of a child protagonist, and of the comic mode, make for a text that can be read in a number of different ways: as one which both responds critically to immediate social issues but also diverts attention from them. In this chapter, and exceptionally in my book, I focus on the former process alone – to stress how the novel can be read as an allegorical commentary on, and positive response to, discriminatory racial practice in a post-Reconstruction America.

This is not, however, to deny the way *Huckleberry Finn* disguises its engagement with Twain's American present, nor that it contains ambiguous and contradictory elements. It is perfectly possible to read the book, as others have and still do, as both racist, in its representation of Jim, and disappointingly conservative, in its return to comedy and to a modified version of the social status quo at the story's end. Twain's use of the first person voice and of the picaresque hold his novel together in formal terms, but there are clear hints of the type of narrative tensions that would become more evident in later works. The novel pulls in two directions. In the late evasion sequence (when Tom Sawyer reappears to help 'free' Jim), an extravagant and farcical humour clashes with what (on another level) is a serious and contentious social theme. One narrative sequence and literary mode – Jim and Huck's raft journey as idyll – is abandoned, or rather, left incomplete, as another story of boyish excitement, high jinks, and convenient plot resolution finally replaces it. But while I recognise the various formal and generic manoeuvres of *Huckleberry Finn*, and the strains and cracks in artistic vision which they signify, I choose here to emphasise a dimension of Twain's book which has been unrecognised, despite the textual indicators, until quite recently: the challenge it offered to the racial assumptions of its time.

If modern readers recognise race as a (perhaps the) central subject of *Huckleberry Finn*, what now seems extraordinary is that Twain's contemporaries, as far as we can tell, did not read the book in those terms. Steven Mailloux speaks of the 'perplexing silence on the novel's attitude toward racism' at its time of publication. This may have been because a more obvious cultural debate concerning juvenile delinquency and 'the bad-boy boom'[10] engaged the audience's attention; one certainly less disturbing in terms of its moral and intellectual self-regard.

Race did, however, figure strongly in the twentieth-century critical reception of the novel, and, by 1950, T. S. Eliot's comment on the 'kinship of mind and the sympathy between the boy outcast from society and the negro fugitive from the injustice of society'[11] reads as a commonplace. While the majority of critics of that time focused on the moral abuses of slavery and the failures of Southern society in the ante-bellum years of the novel's setting, very few saw something more pressing and barbed in the satiric attack it contained on post-bellum racial practice. Thus the novel still had some of its sharpest historical teeth drawn. From a present-day perspective we might reformulate Huck's resonant question about why Tom Sawyer should 'bother to set a free nigger free' (p. 366) to interrogate Twain's artistic intentions: why should he write about slavery, and the moral and social anxieties that went with it, when it was over and done with? Any answer to this question must remain provisional, and it may be that Twain was unaware, or only part aware, of the contemporary relevance of his narrative (though there is some evidence to suggest otherwise). But, whatever the authorial intention, to read *Huckleberry Finn* with the racial circumstances of its time of writing in critical mind, is to discover how clearly it engages such a social and historical context. Indeed, to read it as a straightforward representation of pre-Civil War America is to wipe the novel of much of its significance; to divert from ongoing historical process (the war is over and the slave is free at the time that Twain writes) and to focus instead on personality: Huck's bonding with Jim, his struggle with his conscience, his conflict with the surrounding public world. This easily slips into an ahistorical and mythic opposition between innate goodness, good heart and free self, and the corrupt society against which they together stand. Such versions of the novel became normal, particularly in the 1950s and 1960s.[12]

Recent years, though, have seen increasing critical emphasis on how Twain's book is involved in the debate over racial status in post-Reconstruction America. This coincides with a developing historicist critical turn, and an interest in the way that literature engages in the cultural dialogues of its day. The ending of *Huckleberry Finn* (the evasion sequence and its conclusion) offers a bleak, if indirect, commentary on the compromised nature not just of Jim's final 'freedom' but of that of the recently emancipated slave in the 1880s' South. When Jim is re-enslaved at the Phelps's,[13] Twain's use of apparently comic incident has a disturbing effect. Thus Tom, at one point, plans to saw Jim's leg off, only abandoning the idea because 'Jim's a nigger and wouldn't understand the reasons for it' (p. 312). Jim is returned to the category of imbecile here as Tom, however briefly, threatens his selfhood with literal deconstruction. The play between history (the failure of Reconstruction signalled by the 1876 election and the collapse of the Republican party) and fiction (Jim's projected *de*construction; his role as passive African-American victim of white authority) is more than coincidental. And Twain may well have known exactly what he was doing here. Shelley Fisher Fishkin notes that from the early 1870s onward he was collecting press clippings concerning Klan activities and other brutal treatment of the African-American in the South.[14] R. J. Ellis, too, notes the recurrent 'unease about the situation of the post-bellum Southern African-American' in *Life on the Mississippi* (1883), the travel book intimately related to, and (partly) written alongside, *Huckleberry Finn*.[15]

Most critics now agree that *Huckleberry Finn* engages the explosive question of race relations in post-Reconstruction America, but in an indirect and ironic way. Twain's contemporary audience, and later ones, may not have read the text from this perspective, but the question then raised is of artistic method and interpretative community quite as much as whether Twain had 'a sharp sense of history' or not.[16] Steven Mailloux, discussing Twain's contemporary readership, points out that George W. Cable set *The Grandissimes*, written in 1880, among Louisiana Creoles in 1804 but that reviewers still 'easily interpreted the novel as a parable of 1880's race problems'. Twain was publicly associated with Cable on lecture tour in the winter of 1884–5. *Huckleberry Finn* came out then, and so did Cable's 'The Freedman's Case in Equity': a 'polemical attempt to reopen the debate on the race question' published in *Century Magazine*. The passages from his novel that Twain most often read on this tour were, too, 'those that most directly involved his humorous critique of white supremacist ideology'.[17] If this provides further evidence of Twain's intentions, certainly his reading audience appear not to have put two and two together, and to have identified his novel with that same contemporary debate.

II

Toni Morrison argues that a 'dark, abiding, signing Africanist presence' haunts the 'hearts and texts of American literature'.[18] This idea of a black ghost in the American literary machine (part of a more general reaccentuation of the literary landscape in the direction of cultural heterogeneity) directly informs Shelley Fisher Fishkin's *Was Huck Black?*. Fishkin contends that Twain owed a profound debt to African-American cultural forms in his writing of *Huckleberry Finn*; that the novel was a product of 'mixed literary bloodlines', and that Huck's own distinctive voice may well have been modelled, in actuality, on an African-American source. She traces the possible genesis of this voice to a short newspaper piece, 'Sociable Jimmy', where an African-American child – in Twain's words, 'the most artless, sociable, and exhaustless talker I ever came across' – takes charge of the brief narrative. This, Fishkin suggests, was 'a model for the voice with which Twain would change the shape of American literature'.[19] In other words, the book that has been celebrated for its representation of a distinctively American colloquial style has, both in terms of its general content and its particular syntax, African-American roots.

Fishkin argues, valuably and convincingly, for 'cultural syncretism', seeing American lives and literature as a 'tissue of cross-cultural influences'.[20] Her central thesis, however, might be modified by putting more stress on the code-switching that went on at an everyday level between Black English and both standard American English and other non-standard dialects[21] in the South that Twain knew, and less on the 'Sociable Jimmy' piece. What remains unresolved, though, is the nature of the relationship between Huck's voice and Jim's. For if Huck's speech is influenced by, and borrows from, African-American syntax and forms of expression,[22] it is none the less clearly differentiated from that of the black man, Jim. They just do not speak in the same way. This can be seen when, for example, Huck's 'But hang it, Jim, you've clean missed the point – blame it, you've missed it a thousand mile' is answered by Jim's 'Who? Me? Go 'long. Doan' talk to *me* 'bout yo' pints. I reck'n I knows sense when I sees it; en dey ain' no sense in sich doin's as dat' (p. 134).

Indeed, for much of the early sections of the novel focusing on Huck's relation with Jim, their voices and stories diverge from one another, are in strong competition. Fishkin tends to play down this divergence in her analysis, though she does show Jim's voice to be a 'diminished' one.[23] Huck's voice may contain black elements, but Jim (who *is* black) clashes with Huck in terms of his role, his use of language and his values; is clearly marked off from Huck in his African-American distinctiveness and difference.

Huck's voice contains Jim's in the literal sense that Huck chooses when and how (directly or indirectly) to report his companion's words, but his control over Jim is often precarious. According to Mikhail Bakhtin, language is the site of 'opposition and struggle',[24] a register of social and historical diversity, of power relations and hierarchies, in any given culture. To focus on the competing nature of Huck and Jim's languages and stories in *Huckleberry Finn* is, almost automatically, to call attention to their different uses of the word 'freedom', a heavily overdetermined word both in the text and in American political culture generally.[25] My analysis of the use of this term serves as paradigm of the textual conflict between Huck and Jim. It also, though, prepares the way for the later stage in my argument when I examine how their two voices and narratives overlap and *complement* each other as well as differ.

'Freedom' signifies differently for Huck than it does for Jim. On the raft Huck speaks as one who is 'free and easy and comfortable' (p. 176), words shot through with a specific set of meanings: the product of his situation now in comparison to his former one. He is comfortable because he can laze about all day. He is free of Pap's violence, of Tom's games which never quite make sense to him, of a hierarchical and repressive social structure personified by the Widow Douglas and Miss Watson. He is easy since he has no firm plans for the future. The three words – free, easy, comfortable – act synonymously for Huck since, on the raft, desire is no longer displaced. The language (and values) of Southern riverbank society are challenged by his stress on drift, nakedness and ease rather then decency, regularity and respectability. As Neil Schmitz comments: 'the raft is for Huck the end of his journey, the place where his "free and easy" river world is regained'.[26] Huck's description of the way he and Jim run the raft, 'we let her alone, and let her float wherever the current wanted her to' (p. 178), is suggestive of his own unforced and relaxed preferred mode of behaviour.

Huck's needs and interests are restricted at every turn by dominant social codes and those who would enforce them. Desire and social pressure are generally at odds. Huck is floating on the fringes of the body politic, the body social. Freedom for Huck lies outside the normal boundaries of society, and indeed what he would call freedom, society would call license, moral irresponsibility, a fracture of the social charter. Huck is thus left necessarily compromised, even divided, able to function only by siting himself within the social (and ideological) networks available to him, but needing at the same time to reject, as far as he is able, such networks; finding them oppressive and diminishing in terms of his sense – one he could never put into words – of mental, physical and moral agency. Huck, in other words, cannot escape the language and values of the surrounding society, even as they stick in his craw. His voice and value scheme, to put this very differently, can never, in this Southern world, be entirely congruent with Jim's.

The word 'freedom' certainly has a different meaning for Jim than it does for Huck: it signifies the removal of the internal and external oppressions associated with the institution of slavery.[27] The change in Jim, once he has run off, is first measured on Jackson's Island, where he tells Huck, 'I owns mysef, en I's wuth eight hund'd dollars' (p. 100). This is a fascinating sentence. Jim judges his own worth as property in the dehumanising terms of economic exchange. In doing so, he shows how far the language and values of the white masters of this society have influenced his own way of thinking and speaking; he is unable to break fully free from his slave self. Yet, if he remains (to use Harriet Jacobs's term) 'human stock' in his own mind, he also becomes, as he asserts self-ownership, master of his own fate with 'the right to do what he likes with his own property', his own body. If 'according to Southern laws, a slave, *being* property, can *hold* no property',[28] Jim starts to change his sense of self in closing the gap between possession and possessor.[29] The right to autonomy he expresses signals a profound mental shift from his prior status as owned slave.

At this stage in the novel it is clear what Jim is escaping *from*, but no clear statement has been made as to what he is running *toward*. When Jim does come to speak more directly of his intended actions, it is noticeable that his words are given in indirect discourse, with Huck acting as the mediating narrator. It is also noticeable that a gap between Huck and Jim's joint interests, and Jim's self-interest, is being drawn. It is Huck who first spells out the plans that will take Jim north to 'freedom' (now clearly positioned as a positive other to slavery) when he says that 'what we was after' was to get to Cairo,[30] the point where the Ohio and the Mississippi rivers join, for then 'we would sell the raft and get on a steamboat and go way up the Ohio among the free States, and then be out of trouble' (p. 137). Jim echoes this sense of shared narrative intention when he interprets his 'dream' of fog and tow-heads: 'he said . . . if we minded our business . . . we would pull through and get out . . . into the clear river, which was the free States, and wouldn't have no trouble' (p. 142). Huck and Jim's plans are mutually identified here, as their use of pronouns shows.

As Cairo comes close, the relation between the two voices becomes more problematic. I focus on the pronoun activity that occurs in the text at this point to suggest the developing sense of conflict between them. Jim has not been associated with the plain use of the word 'free' until Chapter 15 of the novel, when Cairo is near, and, for the first time, escape to the north opens up as a practical possibility. In the following chapter, with Cairo apparently directly at hand, Jim's excitement, as he literally dances around, is accompanied by a sudden increase in his sounding of the words 'free' and 'freedom' – six times in the first three pages (pp. 144–6). Now, for the first time, the full extent of Jim's plans become known: to get to a free State, save up money, buy his wife and then buy (or steal) his children out of slavery. It is here, too, that pronouns start shifting about as Jim starts to distance himself from Huck. First the 'we' that Jim has used earlier modulates, as Huck reports his speech, to the singular 'he': 'Jim said . . . he'd be a free man the minute he seen [Cairo]' (p. 144). Then that third person singular gives way, not to the first person plural, but to its third person variant as Huck begins to disappear from Jim's picture of the future. A gap appears between Huck and Jim's joint plan, formulated earlier, of going 'way up [together] . . . among the free States' (p. 137), and the further plans now revealed. For once '*he* got to a free State' and had earned enough to buy his wife, Jim intends that '*they* [he and his wife] would both work' to buy their children's liberty, and 'if their master wouldn't sell them, *they*'d get an Ab'litionist to go and steal them' (p. 146, my emphases). Huck becomes here a friend and companion in the present, or at least one who is treated as such (the implications of this phrase become clear shortly), but one who has no future role. When Jim's voice is then heard speaking directly, later in this same sequence, he swiftly jumps from the remaking of a plural identification of interest with Huck ('We's safe, Huck, we's safe!') to the first-person expression of self-assertion: 'I'm a free man' (p. 146).[31]

Two related issues emerge in the way the relationship between Huck and Jim is represented in the novel. The first is the dynamic tension of Jim's 'freedom-talk'[32] with Huck's own interests, and accordingly with Huck's narrative freedom of expression; his textual power. One story cuts against the other here. Huck's narrative of 'freedom', leisure and good companionship on the raft (one which depends on Jim for its value) conflicts with Jim's slave narrative. For the latter contains a version of freedom which is, in Laurence B. Holland's words, 'antithetical' to Huck's, centring as it does on Jim's desire 'to escape from slavery and enter *into* the civilization that chafes Huck'.[33] Huck and Jim's languages, their words and plans, to varying degree, conflict. Freedom for Jim means, to borrow from Frederick Douglass, to 'clear himself from the chains and fetters of slavery'.[34] When Jim says that a raft 'doan' *make* no track' (p. 97), he is thinking of how best to evade the dogs and men who would hunt him down as a fugitive slave. When Cairo approaches and Huck is faced with Jim's words running in a direction counter to his own, is threatened with what amounts to abandonment, he immediately slips back into the language of the dominant culture. This is his way of retaining a measure of control over the situation. Now, instead of mutually (and mistakenly) identifying himself with Jim as an escapee ('Git up and hump yourself Jim! . . . They're after *us!*' – p. 117, my emphasis), he reconstructs Jim as property, '[Miss Watson's] nigger' and one who has run off from his 'rightful owner' (p. 145). And he responds to Jim's escape plans in a way fully sanctioned by the slave-holding culture of his region – with racist slur: 'give a nigger an inch and he'll take an ell' (p. 146). Huck reacts exasperatedly to Jim ruining his narrative, disrupting his script.[35] He takes over the hegemonic language as a way of gaining power over Jim; denying the validity of, and the needs revealed in, his words. He reduces him to a stereotype who, if he will not go easily along with Huck's definitions of freedom, with Huck's words and Huck's plot, can simply be handed back to his former 'owners'.[36]

Huck would much prefer to stay on the raft while Jim wants to get off it. For Huck, the very meaning of the raft – freedom, ease, safety, 'home' – is conditional on Jim's presence. The 'we're all right, now' that Huck sings out with 'joy' (p. 279), when he reaches the

raft after escaping from the King and the Duke in Pikesville, gives
way to tears when he discovers that Jim is gone. His use of the
first-person plural carries the implication that Huck (first-person
singular) will be far from 'all right' if he continues his journey alone.
Huck gets 'sort of lonesome' (p. 91) or 'mournful' (p. 288) very
quickly by himself. He survives, but without much 'joy'. The worth
of Huck's river story depends on Jim being there to share it.

It is noticeable that once Cairo is passed, Jim's voice is
increasingly silenced in all but its most passive aspects. Any
practical way for Jim to escape slavery has by now faded as an
option, and, what is more, both his and Huck's plans are
increasingly disrupted by circumstance or co-opted by others. The
notion of Jim as *agent* of his own liberation fades from view.
The 'determined and clear-headed adult'[37] in him is killed off as his
status changes: as he becomes subject to the King and the Duke's
authority on board the raft, and then to Tom Sawyer's command[38]
(with Huck acting as his subordinate double) on the shore. Jim's
voice ends up marginalised, almost unheard. Following the Cairo
episode, there is just one brief scene on the raft (pp. 177–80) where
Huck and Jim are shown in harmonious relation to each other before
the King and the Duke take over. Attention then switches to the
latter pair, the meanwhile Jim is first tied 'hand and foot with a rope'
(p. 195), and then made up to impersonate a 'sick Arab'; looking,
with his face painted blue, not 'only . . . like he was dead . . . [but]
considerable more than that' (pp. 220–1).[39] If Jim is subject, to
borrow a later linked word, to 'mortification' (p. 291), with its
twinned meaning of humiliation and devitalisation, on the raft,
things are not much better, with Tom and Huck, on shore. Again,
he ends up as a passive target for the thoughtless manipulation of
others, his 'linguistic agency . . . a major part of the novel's verbal
wealth' now thoroughly sapped.[40]

There is sharp irony in the evasion sequence in the correspondence between play and selfish and gratuitous abuse, as Jim's
position is re-established as 'socially constituted fiction': the black
man as docile, unintelligent and subhuman inferior.[41] Jim, in alien
territory, imprisoned, in trouble, now falls back into the habitual
responses of an earlier stage in the text. Twain unsettles his reader
as he links his series of what are, superficially, comic effects, to the
dehumanisation of Jim that now occurs. For Jim acts the largely
silent butt to Tom and Huck's new plot: 'he couldn't see no sense

in the most of it, but he allowed we was white folks and knowed better then him' (p. 321). His status becomes that of victim for practices that verge on the sadistic: 'Tom shoved a piece of candlestick into the middle of a corn-pone . . . and it worked just noble; when Jim bit into it it most mashed all his teeth out' (p. 322). His role now is that of the preposterous black body shaped at will to the humorous pleasure of the white manipulator, spectator and superior.[42] Twain takes us back, perhaps inevitably given the social situation he describes, to a Jim pinioned firmly within stereotyped representations, and able to do little more than to accept them: his voice and narrative more or less effectively silenced once the brief interlude alone with Huck is ended.

A second issue emerges from my analysis of Huck and Jim's relationship. This concerns Jim's overall role in the novel and how Twain represents him. Huck's textual freedom of speech directly counters his social powerlessness.[43] Jim though remains doubly constrained, not just by the social (his lack of civil rights[44]) but also by the textual, for this is someone else's narrative. His voice sounds powerfully and independently (in direct discourse) only fitfully. Indeed, this containment of Jim's voice – the fact that his story is necessarily placed in the context of, and subordinate to, Huck's own[45] – can account for many of the critical debates over his characterisation.

Commentators have argued over the text's racial discourse as a whole. Thus, for instance, while John H. Wallace calls the book 'racist trash', David L. Smith argues that it takes an 'explicitly anti-racist stance'.[46] Similar problems surface in discussion of Jim's characterisation, for while some critics see him as 'frozen within the conventions of the minstrel darky', others would agree with Smith in describing him as 'an intelligent, sensitive, wily, and considerate individual' who shows in his behaviour that 'race provides no useful index of character'.[47] What is at issue here is our knowledge (and ignorance) of Jim's *consciousness*. For though we are often given Jim's words, we are never allowed direct access to his thoughts. Even my earlier reading, which would see Jim's actions and motives in terms of the traditional slave narrative, must remain a partial and conditional one, because of that lack.

To be sure, Jim's words do at times clearly speak his intentions: to get freedom for himself and his family. But W. E. DuBois contends that the black man approaches the dominant white world from behind a 'vast veil', and shares with his fellow African-Americans that double consciousness resulting from his participation in two social systems.[48] If this is so, then we must ask how one who is a slave (Jim) can ever be known from the outside: by Huck or the reader? When Jim says, more than half to himself, 'Dog my cats ef I didn' hear sumf'n' (p. 53) as Huck and Tom disturb him on their midnight escapade, is this his natural mode of speech and part of his deepest being, or is it a highly artificial mode of discourse in a context where he never knows who might be listening: the only kind of (comic and non-threatening) talk available in a society where any note of black self-assertion is taboo? Equally, when Huck paddles off from the raft and Jim calls, 'Dah you goes, de ole true Huck; de on'y white genlman dat ever kep' his promise to ole Jim' (p. 147), is Jim showing his true face (as a trusting and humbly naive black man expressing grateful appreciation for a white superior's kindness) or is he speaking from behind a mask, constructing a 'simulated identity [as] his best defence against white cruelty and infidelity',[49] cleverly playing on Huck's emotions to preserve his own freedom intact?

To read Jim in one way, as a shallow-headed 'minstrel darky', or in another, as a shrewd and self-interested dissimulator, is to impose, I would suggest, a determinate reading on a character who is textually represented in an indeterminate way.[50] Jim's freedom-talk, and the thoughts and actions that give it substance, remain undeveloped in the novel (and especially at its conclusion). It may be that an agenda of cultural pluralism has led some critics to place more stress on the determinate nature of his role than the text justifies. This is not to downplay his importance nor that of the subject of race in the novel. It is, though, to serve as a reminder that the book starts, 'You don't know about me . . . ' (p. 49), with Huck engaging us in direct readerly contact and contract. Huck's voice controls this narrative. It is his story, not Jim's, that is being told.

However it is the authority of Huck's voice and the shape of his narrative that does, *despite* what I have said about the tensions between him and Jim, finally allow the story of race in *Huckleberry Finn* to retain its positive potential. Jim's narrative is taken over, and his thoughts and feelings fade from view. His role in the novel, too, is concluded with a series of anticlimactic and in many ways unsatisfactory turns in the plot. But this ending is balanced, and in many ways countered, by the other, disrupted, narrative that Huck has told: of companionship and equality on the raft. For the raft is not only a place where Huck and Jim engage in a form of dialogic contest. There is a different story told here too, as Huck describes what the raft means to him; and one in which Jim does, provisionally, take on a positive and equal role. It is this other story, when juxtaposed with the change in Jim's status as the novel draws to its end, that has lingered so insistently in the American collective mind.

III

However we reconstruct Jim's character and motives in the novel, it is clear that by its end any measure of autonomy, self-determination and self-respect potentially available to him, once he has made his initial escape from his slave condition, has been pretty well obliterated. The evasion routine reduces Jim to a dehumanised and reified level. He is not even present when Tom reveals he is in fact 'free', but is chained, hands and legs, in a cabin. Jim's brief speaking part in the last chapter focuses on his new financial status, the forty dollars Tom has given him that 'pleased [him] most to death' (p. 368). There is no hint of resentment here at Tom's exploitative behaviour, the way he has been used as a puppet to the latter's (corrupt) imaginative needs.[51] One of the main ironies of the ending, in terms of the discourse of freedom that the text has engaged, is that Jim's own agency counts for nothing in terms of his eventual change in status. The lack of any real final sense of celebration is suggested in William L. Andrews' comment that 'the fugitive slave has got his freedom, but lost his manhood'.[52]

The negative connotations of the ending of the novel are, I would suggest, a product of historical circumstance. For whether we consider the novel in terms of its fictional chronology or in terms of its time of writing, the position of Jim as representative African-American (if this is how we can take him) was bleak. The final sections of the novel implicitly ask questions concerning the nature of 'freedom' for an African-American male in both periods. Jim might be legally free with the forty dollars in his pocket (about two-fifths of per capita income in 1840[53]), but he is left alone, eleven hundred miles from home, and apparently 'all but forgotten by

Huck'.[54] The limits of his freedom are apparent with any knowledge
of the status of the free slave in the region at the time. Victor Doyno
summarises:

> A manumitted Black would certainly not enjoy genuine freedom
> in 1845. . . . The likelihood of Jim earning enough money to
> purchase his wife and children is close to zero. . . . [A]nyone
> could contest the freed status of a Black such as Jim by claiming
> that he was not in Missouri when Miss Watson died. In the 1845–
> 1850 era, Jim could very easily be re-enslaved in Arkansas. . . . If
> a freedman stayed in Arkansas longer than 180 days, he could be
> imprisoned for a year.[55]

More crucially for the final stages of my argument, freedom was
also a highly problematic term as it applied to black lives in the
South after the War. The 'web of constraints',[56] in terms of both
institutions and attitudes, that bound the free black before the
War came, before long, also to characterise race relations in the
post-bellum period. The freedom granted by the Thirteenth
Amendment signified, for African-Americans, the end of oppressive
and dehumanising white authority and a chance for new forms of
self-development; was to mean autonomy and equal rights. Such
hopes quickly evaporated, together with the first promises of
Reconstruction. As W. E. B. DuBois wrote: 'the slave went free; stood
a brief moment in the sun; then moved back again toward slavery'.[57]
White Southerners (with the implicit and sometimes explicit
support of the national political system) gradually re-established
authority and control over the African-American population, and
enmeshed them, in Eric Foner's words, 'in a seamless web of oppression, whose interwoven economic, political, and social strands all
reinforced one another'.[58]

Jim's powerlessness and victimisation as he undergoes renewed
imprisonment and a set of imposed discomforts frequently
bordering on a form of torture, the meanwhile two members of the
dominant white race slowly prepare to liberate his already legally
free self, clearly parallels such a historical context. Fishkin sums up
what has now become the critical consensus when she says that
'scholars are increasingly coming to understand the evasion as a
satire on the way the United States botched the enterprise of freeing
its slaves'.[59]

To return to Twain's treatment of Huck and Jim's relationship is not only, however, to justify the artistic logic of the evasion scenes.[60] It is also to suggest that the earlier sequences on the raft work, despite the thrust of my earlier argument, to fuse, as well as to oppose, Jim and Huck's voices and stories. This needs fuller explanation. I have shown that Huck's version of freedom, a relaxed drifting on the margins of the dominant society, differs from Jim's. Huck has, throughout the novel, a divided response to Jim, seeing him as friend, companion and equal, but also (quite otherwise), in socially constructed terms, as 'nigger'. For the catch-22 which limits Huck's 'freedom' at almost every turn is that he gives allegiance to the social charter; mouths the words and shares the values of the dominant culture even as he would (sometimes) resist them. He accepts the language, and thus the institutional and moral assumptions, of the society around him, never questions the validity of slavery as a system, nor its opinions concerning black status (as property). That is why, when Aunt Sally asks 'Anybody hurt?' on the steamboat cylinder head blow out, he can come out with the chilling answer, 'No'm. Killed a nigger' (p. 291). That is why, too, when Huck speculates on the response of his home village community if he were to write Miss Watson a letter telling her of Jim's whereabouts, he says: 'everybody *naturally* despises an ungrateful nigger, and they'd make Jim feel it all the time, and so he'd feel ornery and disgraced' (p. 281, my emphasis). Huck is unable to distinguish culture from nature here; to see Jim's position as enslaved, diminished and rebellious black subject as justifiably different from his 'natural' position – in Southern eyes and mind – as a humble and submissive servant to the requirements of his 'kind' mistress. Huck also accepts those religious values which, hand in glove, accompany the political. His fear 'that people that acts as I'd been acting about that nigger goes to everlasting fire' (p. 282) again marks his acceptance of dominant systems of belief.

Huck's attitude to Jim, though, is split. For at the same time that he accepts such systems, he knows they cannot satisfy his needs on the raft and (often) cannot serve to categorise his relation with Jim. When it comes to immediate action and pragmatic response, he fails, consequently, to share the definitions that he mouths. That is why, for instance, Huck can bring himself both to 'humble myself to a nigger' (p. 143), something his Southern society would consider unthinkable, and later decide to 'steal Jim out of slavery again'

(p. 283) despite the admonitions of his social conscience. This does not mean, though, that Huck rejects the value of conventional belief, but rather that he sees his lack of it as a sign of his own inadequacy as one who is 'ignorant and . . . low-down and ornery' (p. 61).

As Huck comes to know Jim (and vice versa) through their day-to-day comradeship, in a way that escapes the boundaries and norms of the surrounding community, so he becomes a strongly positive presence in Huck's raft narrative. Indeed on the raft, while – however temporarily – their two stories overlap, Huck is at times able to escape his conditioned response to racial difference. This coming together, as the tensions between Huck and Jim disappear, does depend on a certain pause in the action of Jim's narrative: a leaving of his own plans in abeyance as the raft drifts further downstream. For Jim, this is not necessarily a problem. He may want to head north and intend to rebuild his family and re-enter society on a new basis, but, before Cairo, he can share his means (travelling on the raft) with Huck even if their ends (to leave the raft, or stay on it) are different. Huck's version of freedom on the raft is not in the short term, but only ultimately, antithetical to Jim's interests. Even once Cairo is past, and Jim's interests become, in textual terms at least, subordinate (we hear little more of his plans), the raft can still become a place apart where racial tension can disappear. In fact the shelving of Jim's immediate plans contribute to this effect.

When, though, the textual return is made to the matter of Jim's freedom, its thematic centrality is subsumed in the focus on Tom's romantic plots. The evasion sequence, as I have suggested, is a fictional echo of a bleak historical reality: 'an unsatisfying farce that reflected the travesty that "freedom" had become for African Americans in the post-Reconstruction era'.[61] Jim's final manu- mission, too, brings no suggestion of a radical change in his status (if we know anything about ante-bellum Southern history). The effect of this is that, if the reader is looking for a positive version of race relations in the novel, he or she must go back to the sequences on the raft, both before and after Cairo, when Huck and Jim are at ease and at one with each other. It must immediately be recognised that it is Huck who voices this unity. He is the one, after all, who passes such comments as 'we judged that we was free and safe. . . . We said there warn't no home like a raft' (p. 176). But this is consonant with Jim's direct words and actions as they are represented; appropriate to the relationship he has been establishing with Huck, and to a situation where he is back in a kind of limbo (as far as the development of his own slave narrative goes).

Despite the indeterminate representation of Jim's character, then, and despite the fact that his and Huck's needs and narratives tend to run off, when they are most clearly specified, in different directions, there is a powerfully positive (if necessarily undeveloped) social and political charge in the sections of the novel, on the raft, where their two stories do temporarily elide. A positive version of 'freedom' does appear, however hedged in by internal and external circumstance, and whatever the unanswered questions it raises. The form it takes is that of Huck and Jim alone together, naked, talking 'about all kind of things' on the raft, and letting 'her float wherever the current wanted her to' (pp. 178–9). Relaxed and at ease with one another, all tension and competition can and does drop, for the moment, away. Their relationship of two becomes, for one critic at least, a version of 'that redemptive American community which the shore has betrayed'.[62] These moments of social harmony on the raft, and the frustration of what follows, function (I would contend) as a form of narrative incompletion. Such incompletion connects up with an ongoing debate on race in America which had reached a particular crisis point as Twain wrote. The free and equal relation Huck and Jim manage to have – despite all the previously made provisos – acts as a political stimulus, in however loose a sense. It offers, and offered Twain's contemporaries, a model of social possibility which, once depicted, cannot easily be put out of cultural mind.

IV

To present Huck and Jim's relationship on the raft in this way is to modify traditional readings of the novel. These have tended to see the raft as a type of pure space unaffected by the larger social world, and to distinguish between the notion of idyll, which occurs on the raft, and the historical. I would contend that the boundary between the idyllic and the historical is not watertight, and neither (to add a corollary) is that between indirect and explicit forms of social and political comment. Race is a central component in the depiction of

Huck and Jim's relationship in *Huckleberry Finn*. Twain, thus, necessarily engages the wider social and political context of his America. The best version of such racial interaction may be utopian (only possible on the raft) given a set of historical circumstances – in the 1830s–1840s, and in the 1880s – which make a mockery of African-American freedom. It can, though, function to suggest, however tentatively, that rigid current social practice is open to future positive change. On the raft, Twain gives his fellow Americans a different and more progressive version (that is, from a liberal pluralist standpoint where black and white stories can be constructed as potentially running together) of what 'freedom' in the area of racial politics might start to mean than is offered elsewhere in the novel, or in the post-Reconstruction America with which it is in dialogue.

Jonathan Arac argues in a recent influential essay that Twain's novel is 'antihistorical', that 'the form and fable of *Huckleberry Finn* reject the very possibility of public debate'.[63] Richard C. Moreland's analysis of Huck's role, and his tendency to reject the influence of any 'natural, social, or certainly psychological limitations on his own freedom and will', complements that analysis. Referring to the plan 'fixed up' (p. 283) by Huck, following his 'heroic, private moral decision to help Jim escape', Moreland says that:

> The last part of Twain's novel demonstrates in intensely tedious and frustrating detail the inadequacy and ineffectiveness of Huck's unmediated private act of will to set Jim free. . . . Such acts of will prove inadequate and ineffective unless they are also followed up with the positive and specific 'plans' and narrative plots that would articulate and negotiate Huck and Jim's desires in a relationship and a course of action that would resist and counter Tom Sawyer's cultural powers, rather than allow him to write Huck and Jim into his own . . . series of romances into which other stories and plans too often seem to disappear.[64]

Twain's novel, and its frustrating ending, *can* be seen to engage the 'contingencies of history'[65] if we take a different approach. For could Twain imagine (can we imagine) any other ending to *Huckleberry Finn*, given both the status of its narrator and central protagonist and the structures of social and cultural power which

bind him?[66] Arac distinguishes between an allegorical interpretation
of Twain's text and its direct entry into the field of 'public debate'.[67]
In fact, the lines between direct and indirect methods are almost
always blurred when fiction, not history, is being written, and an
entry into public debate does not necessarily have to be openly
announced – especially for a humorist (which Twain was), and
especially in difficult political times (which these were).

However intentional the allegorical resonances of *Huckleberry Finn*
may be, it is difficult to know, given the historical circumstances in
which Twain wrote, and the chosen boundaries of his narrative, how
he might otherwise have addressed national political concerns.
Oblique and indirect tactics are necessary in a social world which
offers no space of freedom for political or collective action,[68] and it
is exactly such a world which Twain represents. Moreland speaks
of the 'positive and specific "plans"' by which Huck might further
his relationship with Jim, and instigate an ongoing 'course of action'.
The lack of specificity in these words may mask the historical fact
that, for a young, ill-educated and low-class social misfit in the
South circa 1840, the likelihood of acting against the socially
reinforced authorities, and of helping to right the injustices of
slavery (if he were indeed capable of so recognising them), was nil.
So read, the temporary merger of Huck and Jim's stories on the raft
and the type of freedom found there, come to function, in their very
fragility and precariousness, as that form of narrative incompletion
previously claimed. Their joint story of (temporary) autonomy,
companionship, safety and even equality, reflexively relates to, and
interacts with, the larger, more complex and unresolved narrative
of American race relations: one that cannot be settled in so relatively
easy or exceptional a manner.

The representation of Huck and Jim's relationship on the raft and
the frustration that follows can, then, be turned by the cooperative
reader into historical engagement: into what Moreland calls
'ongoing cultural work in progress'. That work would explore how
black and white stories might begin to be reconciled, put together,
reconstituted on a different racial and social basis.[69] Twain's
depiction of Huck and Jim points to this historical lack, but also to
its possibility. The rhythm of the novel shows Huck moving from
various forms of isolation to that 'embryonic model of community'[70]
with Jim, on the raft. The undeveloped quality of this model is clear,
both in its homosocial nature and the rudimentary form of its

two-person base (the minimum for social existence). It is, though, what might grow from this embryo that merits cultural attention. This may sound like a reworking of Leslie Fiedler, who famously proposed a Whitmanesque and homoerotic harmony between Huck and Jim as 'nearly coeval loving pair' on the river. My reading borders on, but also significantly departs from, his. For Fiedler's main concern is for the personal and not the political, a separation which is enforced by the opposition between nature and culture central to his analysis. The river is thus seen as a 'place out of time and history . . . beyond the bounds of society', while nature itself is described 'as Eden'.⁷¹ I, too, see the idyllic aspects of (some of) the river sequences as central to Huck and Jim's relation. I would, however, keep the link intact between idyll and the social and political; between Huck and Jim's (sometimes) desegregated lives and post-emancipation racial inequities. Indeed, it is the political implication of this relationship I would stress.

Huck's relation to the dominant Southern social order is charac-terised by repression. The terms used to describe this order, if we see Widow Douglas as its early representative, are introduced at the very start of the book: 'dismal regular and decent' (p. 49). It is associated with both temporal and spatial constraint: 'it was rough living in the house all the time. . . . The widow rang a bell for supper, and you had to come to time' (pp. 49–50). Despite the distractions of Tom Sawyer's games, Huck is a passive and often withdrawn figure within this social world, subject to the discourses of mastery of all those – Pap, the Widow, Tom, the Grangerfords, and the King and the Duke – who assume authority over him.

With Jim on the raft, *despite* the fluctuations in their relationship and the battles for power engaged, things can be different. In many ways the raft functions as an estranged or alienated social world where Huck and Jim depart from the accepted norms of interracial behaviour: strip off their clothes; share food; enjoy 'talking, and singing, and laughing' (p. 283) together; rebuke and apologise to each other, as and if the occasion demands. On the raft, not all, but some of the time, the interaction of black and white without fear, prejudice or constraint can be accommodated. In the idyll, for this is what it is, 'all temporal boundaries are blurred and the rhythm of human life is in harmony with the rhythm of nature'.⁷²

Mikhail Bakhtin associates the idyll with the restoration of 'folkloric time'. He does not, however, see this as regressive, but rather focuses on its positive and political implications, with the folk figured as the 'untamable, rebellious, and regenerative force that will destroy the status quo', 'newer and finer worlds' rising from the ashes of the old order.[73] The idealising tendencies implicit here, and the revolutionary politics accompanying them, can be modified if we refigure this argument in terms of race not class, and in the American context of Twain's writing. To do so is to look forward to what, with difficulty, might be a future possibility, rather than to trust in a past, and still available, socio-political model (the folkloric) on which one can build.

Approached in this way, Huck and Jim's relationship can be seen in terms of the political and the social, as well as the natural (the idyll). River and riverbank are never, in Twain's novel, neatly containable terms. And if the language and personnel of the riverbank can spill into the river world, then, too, what is established on the raft – the utopian form, however fragile and intermittent, of Huck and Jim's union – can have implications for, potentially spill into, the larger social world. At one remove from the larger social order and its immediate pressures, Huck and Jim's relationship nonetheless reflects back on that order. What is presented as historically rigid, the politics of race relations in the South, is always open to change. The idyllic and utopian (or the indirect, in Arac's terms) are necessarily defined by their opposites, the practical and realisable (the direct), and always call in their direction.

The relaxed discussions Jim and Huck eventually come to have (about, for instance, the origin of the stars – p. 179) and their unpressured togetherness (lying on their backs, legs dangling in the water, talking) democratise the narrative, and realign the boundaries of pleasure and possibility. Though dispute occurs on the raft,[74] the equality of voice also found in their relationship subverts a larger social system which has only one definition of racial interaction. The mutual generosity and potential for harmony realised within the limits of this embryonic interracial community provides a defusing of the accepted power relations and a promise of a new racial dynamic. The celebration of Jim and Huck's bodies on the raft, and their sharing of a language, potentially calls into being a democratic society in which black and white can operate as joint constituents.

The eventual defeat of that community can be read as a sign of incompletion. For its possible rebuilding and re-creation, in the future and in whatever form, necessarily operates to unsettle the resolution of the novel's plot; to resist its final machinations, explanations and closure. The text's balance tilts unavoidably, following the facts of Southern history, back toward authoritarian control, repression and racial inequality, and away from equality, easy companionship and generosity of spirit. As it does, however, so is the remembrance of this latter potential for interracial harmony and community guaranteed; so is the promise of its fuller realisation at some future stage put on the historical agenda.

There are still unresolved issues here. The distance between the model of social possibility the novel offers, operating on a microcosmic level and in limited spatial confines, and its realisation as concrete political, economic and social practice, is considerable. The question as to exactly *how* the relationship on the raft might function, when then projected into the wider social world, in terms of any 'positive and specific "plans"', remains unanswered. The historical relevance of Twain's novel lies in its representation of, and challenge to, white supremacist thought and social practice at a time when race relations were rapidly worsening; when, in Christine MacLeod's words:

> what with Northern indifference and the emerging Black Codes in the South – with vagrancy and curfew laws, the sharecropping system, white monopoly of credit, widespread vigilante intimidation and endemic racism – the average freedman had about as much chance as Jim has at the Phelps Farm of realizing any practical distinction between his current situation and his previous condition of servitude.[75]

The indirect manner in which such a challenge is made, however, necessarily means that the terms I have used to describe Huck and Jim's relationship on the raft and Twain's positive representation of interracial compact – democracy, equality, community, even freedom – must remain abstract signifiers, from a historicist point of view. All language is subject to contested meaning. Harriet Jacobs, in her *Incidents in the Life of a Slave Girl* (1861), would meet ante-bellum celebrations of a polished Southern 'civilisation' head on with her brief words on the punishments meted out to slaves in the region: 'cruelty is contagious in uncivilized communities'.[76] Similarly, words like democracy and equality can carry simple meanings in a

two-person relation on a raft, but once a larger and more complex
social fabric is re-engaged, any consensus definition of the terms
soon disappears. There are only practices of freedom, and those
practices are defined differently according to the interests of
particular social groups, and in particular historical circumstances.
After all, the freedom Jim gets from Miss Watson at the end of the
novel is of a different kind than that (outside the normal social
boundaries) Huck already has; is a version of that freedom which
Huck claims, while in the Widow Douglas's care, to lack. The
relative nature of the word in political terms can, moreover, be
measured by the fact that Martin Luther King would still yearn,
speaking on behalf of his race in the 1963 March on Washington
speech, to be 'Free at last!' – to gain the freedom that the emancipation proclamation had supposedly handed over a hundred years
before.

To put this in another way, *Huckleberry Finn* does address, though
in an indirect manner, the debate about the race question of the
1880s.[77] The evasion sequence functions as 'displaced polemic',[78]
serving ironically to critique regional and national political actions
and racial ideology in the period following the collapse of
Reconstruction. Novels engage with history in a variety of ways,
and to approach it 'by de back' (to use Jim's words – p. 134) is as
valid a tactic as any. In doing this, questions are left unanswered,
not only about the level of authorial intent, but particularly as to
just how the forms of freedom found, and built, on the raft might
translate to larger, and more complex, social actuality. The problems
involved in such a process are indicated in the temporary and
provisional nature of the harmony Huck and Jim do find, and the
diverging aspects of their stories which continually threaten it. But
one might say that the business of the novel is not to suggest
concrete and detailed solutions to intractable social problems.
Twain's representation of black and white co-operation may not, in
terms of text and story time, last long, and might be flying in the
face of contemporary historical fact. It does however offer an
embryonic model of social (and thus political) possibility – of unity
despite difference; of equality and empathy – which has remained
in the arena of public debate, however muted that debate may at
times have become, from his time to the present.

6

Fantasy and *A Connecticut Yankee in King Arthur's Court*

It is said [that] if you ask a Connecticut Yankee in any part of
the world how he is, he will, if not 'sick,' answer 'moving, Sir,'
equivalent to saying 'well'; for, if well, he is sure to be on the
move.

(Lady Emmeline Stuart Wortley)[1]

Up to this time there had been absolutely <u>no</u> system. Everything was done by guess; nothing was <u>calculated</u>.
(Twain's notebook entry on Webster & Company,
the publishing house he had established)[2]

'There,' exclaimed Dr Southwick. 'There is the culmination of
ten years' work and study. We live in a higher civilization from
this day.'
(On the apparently successful completion of the first legal
electrocution in America, 6 August 1890)[3]

I

Hank Morgan, Twain's Connecticut Yankee, is certainly a man on
the move. Hit on the head by a crowbar, he 'momentarily tears the
fabric of time'[4] as he travels in an instant from the Colt Arms

110

Factory in nineteenth-century Connecticut to sixth-century Arthurian England. Twain himself is on the artistic move here, too. His turn from the ante-bellum Mississippi setting of *Tom Sawyer* and *Huckleberry Finn* to the England of a much earlier period is accompanied by the shift to fantasy as a literary mode.

Twain constantly experimented with literary genre. In *Tom Sawyer* and *Huckleberry Finn*, his step to an ante-bellum American past allowed him both to engage, but also to evade, his anxieties about the direction of his contemporary American society. As I have suggested, this formal tactic, in the boy book *Tom Sawyer*, provided an effective way of representing ambivalent attitudes both about the past and the present. His use of the retrospective travel narrative in *Roughing It* served parallel ends.

Huckleberry Finn works similarly, though the contentious nature of its central subject makes it an altogether more troubling book. I have used the allegorical fit between the evasion sequence and post-Reconstruction events to suggest that the novel can be read as a criticism of post-bellum American racial practice. The book's peculiar generic mix, though – and quite possibly the unwillingness of its first audience to hear something it preferred not to hear, especially when it came in apparently comic guise – allowed its full implications to pass unnoticed, until (indeed) very recently. This may have entirely suited Twain, or may, indeed, have passed him by. For where I refer to Twain's authorial intentions in my last chapter, this is very much a provisional act: done in the knowledge that the text carries conflicting meanings, *can* be read in quite another way, and that such intentions – allegorical or otherwise – cannot be guaranteed.

Indeed, I would argue that many of the social criticisms I have already identified (and will identify) in Twain's texts, and the doubts about the status and limits of the individual subject that run alongside them, may well not have been deliberately thematised. As I suggest in my first chapter, in the end this is for me beside the point. For it is in the work that Twain's texts do as they engage the cultural dialogues of their times that my main interest lies. Twain was a comic writer dependent on entertaining his audience for his continued financial and literary success. He was also a businessman and a member of respectable society, identified as often with conservative values as with radical ones, at least till the end of his career. Even his attitude to racial issues was not entirely unambiguous.[5]

We repeatedly see in his work both challenges to the assumptions of the dominant culture, and endorsements of them, as his texts move in quite contradictory directions. *A Connecticut Yankee* is no exception to this rule.

Firm definition of literary genres is a difficult matter, and particularly in Twain's case. *Huckleberry Finn* is based, as Harold Beaver points out, on at least four models, 'the picaresque, the epistolary, the autobiographical, and the adventure story'.[6] This, though, is not what causes problems in terms of interpretation and audience response. These come about, I would suggest, as a result of the gap between a number of different perspectives that both control the text and are (potentially) made available as we read it. I have said that the novel works as allegory. To interpret it in terms of American racial issues in the post-Reconstruction era is, though, to see through Huck's voice to a second narrative position: that of the author who writes from the perspective of the 1880s. The possibility of allegory then opens up. But it is very easy to read the novel in another way, as realist literature. To read on this level alone is to remain unaware of the full nature of its racial critique. For the realist techniques Twain uses pull the reader into a direct engagement with his central protagonist and narrator, and the ante-bellum world in which he moves, and work to counter an allegorical alternative.

Realism, of course, is itself a slippery and highly problematic term, and whether the novel fits this category or not is a matter of considerable critical dispute.[7] It is, however, generally associated with an unproblematic rendering of accepted social norms. If there is a gap between an allegorical and realistic reading of *Huckleberry Finn*, I would also argue that, taken at the latter (realistic) level alone, another type of gap – and one this time which has nothing to do with historical periodisation – opens up. This happens as the first-person narrator's account of his own experience is placed beside the different assessment of that experience which his words and actions allow. I point here to the role of the author in manipulating his marginal, naive and alienated protagonist, but I also suggest that Huck's words may tell us (the readers) more than that author intends. For it is in the margin between the recounting of Huck's direct experiences, and the realisation by the reader of their larger implications, that the conventional assumptions associated with realism – assumptions concerning the nature of the self, the values of the social order in which that self moves, and the balance between the individual and his surrounding society – are interrogated. In other words, I see in *Huckleberry Finn* an endorsement of accepted norms and a critique of them running side by side. And though all but the most literal of readers engage at some level with the latter challenge, the extent to which they do so depends on how far they are able to see the fullest implications of Huck's narrative, and to acknowledge the further perspective available (to see meanings in Huck's story that he himself cannot see). This needs further explanation.

The techniques and attitudes in *Huckleberry Finn* in many ways conform to generally accepted definitions of realism. Realism as a term asserts a claim to transparency: what June Howard calls a 'privileged relationship to [the] assumed extra-textual world, invoking an ability to embody "reality" . . . as constitutive of the genre itself'.[8] Twain uses Huck to provide a 'translucent window'[9] on to the immediate world. Huck's vernacular voice leads us into a solidly framed historical context, the small-town ante-bellum Southwest. This is the 'reality' we are asked to take for granted, with all its social practices, its racial distinctions, its cultural codes. Such dominant social assumptions are the given which holds the whole novel in place. Realism firmly embeds individual character in its surrounding environment, focusing on dress, manners, social connections and occupations. This provides a way of exploring the relationship between the individual and his (in Huck's case) environment at a time when prior romantic beliefs in 'the sovereign territory of the individual self'[10] were no longer tenable.

The realistic text, none the less, does generally assume the essential wholeness and coherence of the subject: what Rosemary Jackson calls 'the unity of "character" . . . – that definition of the self as a coherent, indivisible and continuous whole which has dominated Western thought for centuries'.[11] It also binds character and reader within a fixed social framework, the world as it exists. Indeed, the genre is perhaps most often described in terms of the *balance* it depicts between the individual and the social world. Thus Lee Clark Mitchell, loosely bunching Twain, Henry James and William Dean Howells as realists, identifies a shared key concern in the fact that:

they all presented characters as 'subjective selves' who possessed clear capacities for restraint and responsibility. . . . Realist authors enforced a moral perspective on narrative action, a perspective involving the same considerations of intention and responsibility we habitually project on each other (and onto fictional characters as well).[12]

Huckleberry Finn works as a realist text, according to these criteria. Huck can be read as a unified character, a sympathetic and free-speaking (in a sense, he speaks the text) young boy making his way in a difficult Southern world, but responding to it with a clear seeing and pragmatic eye. However, Huck offers no real challenge to the dominant norms of the Southern social order. Though he resists those norms, he sees this as a sign of his own marginality rather than of their inadequacy. An established and unchanging social fabric provides the backdrop against which all Huck's dodgings and weavings occur, and the failings of that order to meet both his and Jim's needs are, to a degree, forgotten, as they are safely (if provisionally) reconciled with Aunt Sally and her world at the finish. We can identify a realist agenda, too, to one of the climactic scenes of the novel where Huck decides to '*go* to hell'[13] (p. 283) rather than letting Jim back into Miss Watson's hands: this can be constructed as an act of individual moral responsibility that counters the 'outer force'[14] of a determining social environment.

There are, however, other ways of reading all of the above. Critics usually argue that the realistic novel upholds 'bourgeois ideology'.[15] But realistic fiction can interrogate social rules and conventions, and the unproblematic nature of subjectivity; does not necessarily take them for granted. And this is what happens in Twain's text. Thus the possibility of escaping social determinants in independent moral action in Huck's decision not to tell on Jim is deeply undermined by Miss Watson's prior actions (for she has already, in fact, set Jim free), by the negative quality of Huck's choice, and by his own consequent position as Tom Sawyer's minion. Equally, the very idea of the intending 'subjective self' is, to a degree, questionned by the extent to which Huck's own language and thoughts are unconscious products of his larger society, and by a textual play on disguise and the slippage of identity (foregrounded, for instance, in Jim's question 'Is I *me*, or who *is* I?[16]) which tends to subvert any notion of fixed selfhood. Finally, though Huck may be a marginal social figure, Twain none the less does use him to launch a penetrating interrogation of the nature of the real. He uses the device of the alienated and uncomprehendingly naive first person narrator and protagonist to mount a serious challenge to the dominant cultural order (though, certainly, the setting of the novel in a prior historical period eases such a task). Bakhtin sees one function of the fool in literature as 'by his very uncomprehending presence . . . mak[ing] strange the world of social conventionality'.[17] Tony Bennett spells out some of the effects of this in Twain's novel when he says that the character of Huck 'functions as a formal device whereby the ideological forms upholding the institution of slavery are turned inside out, made to appear strange and, in the process, called into question'.[18]

In *Huckleberry Finn*, to sum up, both the gap between American present and American past, and that between the naive narrative voice and an informed authorial and readerly presence, establish a number of double effects. The allegorical shift to the racial politics of the 1880s depends on the recognition that the novel need not necessarily be read in terms of realism alone. The critique of dominant values that I identify above, and which does occur within a realistic frame, is both readily available for the reader to see in the text, and yet is possible – at a number of levels – to overlook. Twain's own intentions, as far as this latter critique goes, cannot be entirely determined here. For while the authorial position he constructs is clearly meant to challenge southern social and ideological values, we have no way of going further, and knowing to what degree he was aware of the various questions about subjectivity and moral agency the text also raises. What happens here, where an interrogation of dominant values (which works on a number of different levels) is both conducted and disguised at one and the same time, and where the intentions of the author are unclear, is entirely in line with the patterns of Twain's writing as a whole.

In *Connecticut Yankee*, the type of gaps and distances Twain exploits in his fiction widens. For, if a similar shift occurs between authorial voice, readerly perspective and fictional narrator, Twain now moves the setting of his novel way back in time, and uses fantasy as his fictional mode, to create a whole series of disjunctive effects. As I argue in the rest of this chapter, this latter genre is particularly suitable to Twain's continued critical interrogation of the directions and developments and values of his own America. As I also argue, though, Twain himself remained, at the very most, ambivalent (and even perhaps unconscious) as to the full extent of such a process. Moreover, the very displacements of the novel, its comic effects, and its contradictory thematic elements, mean that it remained (and remains) entirely possible to pass over the criticisms of American culture that the book contains.

In the move to fantasy, however, I see the introduction of a mode that would become increasingly useful to Twain. For fantasy potentially challenges conventional assumptions and norms by moving away from realist forms completely. It turns everyday reality upside down by introducing another *obviously* unreal scenario; an alternative and different world to set against the everyday one. Such generic effects would increasingly meet Twain's artistic needs as his career progressed, and as his unease with American 'realities' (as measured in terms of everyday conceptions of selfhood, value systems and beliefs) became more pressing. And everything in his fiction suggests that this indeed was the case.

II

My placing *A Connecticut Yankee* in the category of the fantastic is not entirely unproblematic. One might choose to describe the novel otherwise, as medieval romance, for example, or as a coming together, and conflict between, romance or sentimentalism and realism, or as a dystopian novel, as burlesque and satire, as displaced western, or science fiction.[19] Rather than giving a detailed analysis of the ways in which *A Connecticut Yankee* conforms to the conventions of fantasy, I follow generally accepted critical opinion here in taking its generic categorisation for granted.[20] Rosemary Jackson's comment on the relation between the mimetic and the marvellous in fantasy is, though, worth recalling, given the particular relation between realism and its opposite in Twain's text:

> Fantastic narratives confound elements of both the marvellous and the mimetic. They assert that what they are telling is real – rely on the conventions of realistic fiction to do so – and then they proceed to break that assumption of realism by introducing what – within those terms – is manifestly unreal.[21]

For Jackson, fantasy is 'the inside, or underside, of realism. . . .
It is all that is not said, all that is unsayable, through realistic
forms.' In Todorov's words, it is 'nothing more than the uneasy
conscience of the positivist nineteenth century'. Such definitions
ignore realism's own ability to challenge dominant values, and to
dislocate what is conventionally taken for granted. But they
nevertheless suggest what fantasy can do: violating and upsetting
the real, 'opening spaces where unity had been assumed'.[22] In taking
his modern American man, Hank Morgan, 'a Yankee of the
Yankees',[23] and transporting him to Arthurian England (or at
least a fabular version, via Malory, of that England[24]), Twain
defamiliarises and questions everyday American assumptions and
values. He does so by setting them, through the figure of Hank, in
an alien context, alongside a culture which is resistant to them, and
which operates on a completely other mental and ideological basis.
Nineteenth-century positivist notions are (literally) exploded in
the process.

This is, however, only half the story, for again the novel covers
up the criticisms of American culture it has to make quite as much
as it reveals them. My main interest here is in suggesting the dis-ease
with contemporary America which the novel illustrates.[25] But I
would not underestimate the extent to which this is masked in *A
Connecticut Yankee*; indeed the extent to which it may have been
masked to Twain himself. Everett Carter has made a strong case for
identifying Hank's values, at least as regards the worth of science,
republicanism and technology, with Twain's own while he was
writing the book (and before his investments in the Paige typesetter
had proved to be the disaster they later turned out to be).[26] And it
is certainly clear that most contemporary reviewers focused on the
celebration of democratic values, and the defence of 'basic human
rights . . . fundamental equalities' represented in the novel.[27] I
would argue that the book contains contradictory thematic
elements, and that it can be interpreted as a satiric attack on the
established church and aristocratic ways of late nineteenth-century
British society and a celebration of democracy, just as easily as it can
be taken as a critique of Hank's own values and behaviour. It is also
easy to forget, in either case, that this is a genuinely funny novel,
and that this is the level on which many readers take it. Thus one
can, for instance, identify (in a po-faced manner) Hank's lack of
humanity in such jokes as the one when he gives Morgan le Fay the

go-ahead to 'hang the whole band' (p. 155) after the 'agony' (p. 152) of their performance. But it is equally easy to see the scene as Twain having, and giving his audience, fun, with no regard to thematic consistency. If I am aware my own analysis errs continually in too straight-faced a direction, this does not mean that I am unaware of Twain's comic effects, but that I would concentrate, none the less, on the cultural anxieties I discover here.

Carter marshalls his evidence to say that:

> the meaning of *A Connecticut Yankee* is, as the author repeatedly said it was, that the American nineteenth century, devoted to political and religious liberalism and to technology, was better than the traditional past. The efforts of modern men to continue a progress towards a fulfilment of material goals is shown to be a worthy mission of man.[28]

This may be true. It is clear, however, that there are contrary, and quite possibly unintended, meanings loosed in the novel too. Thus a number of critics, of whom Mark Seltzer, Martha Banta, Ronald Takaki and Cindy Weinstein can be taken as representative, focus on the ways in which *A Connecticut Yankee* fictionally represents the problems facing an American society in the process of rapid and disorienting change as Twain was writing.[29] For these critics, it is modernisation, and the fears, pressures and disruptions that accompanied it, which provide the informing context for analysis of the novel. Thus, Takaki, for instance, reads the text as one in which:

> Twain traveled back in time to assess his own age and its Yankee enterprise and technology . . . offer[ing] a diagnosis of American civilization and its nervousness. . . . His 'Connecticut Yankee' . . . is the modernizer of a feudal society. What he scatters, however, are the seeds of destruction. . . . [Hank is] a scientific manager [who] establishes a centralized bureaucracy to increase efficiency and productivity. Ultimately, however, his aim is not production or profits but control for the sake of control. Here . . . in Twain's novel, we have a condemnation of arrogant Yankee misuse of technology, and a frightening fable which exposed what was actually happening in nineteenth-century American society. . . . As [the 'enterprising' men of white America] built their 'America by design,' they were employing technology as a mode of

production as well as an instrument for the domination and reinforcement of social relations in a capitalist society. Like Hank Morgan, they were creating centralized bureaucracies and placing society under the direction of professionals and scientific managers. They were substituting technology for the body and also channelling men, women, and children into factories and reducing them to machine attendants.[30]

My own reading of the novel runs along similar lines. Carter may be correct in his analysis of authorial intent. Twain's anxieties about the direction of post-Civil War American society (however unconscious or partially formulated they might have been) are, though, as I have shown, consistently evident in both the themes and forms of his work from an early stage of his career. His texts necessarily connect up with the cultural conversations of their times. All Twain's fiction before *A Connecticut Yankee* reveals doubts and ambiguities about both the direction of American history and the shaping of American cultural values. His use of fantasy in this novel significantly extends any prior use of estrangement and dislocation devices. In the manifestly unreal transfer of a type of American everyman into an earlier Arthurian world, and the type of comparisons and disjunctions it allows, Twain releases (despite all the countervailing effects) a more wide-ranging critique of dominant American social assumptions than in any of his work to that point.

III

Recent critical work on late nineteenth-century literature (prompted especially by Walter Benn Michaels's *The Gold Standard and the Logic of Naturalism*[31]) focuses recurrently on the question of individual agency, and how it functions or fails to function within the context of what Martha Banta calls a 'capitalist historiography'.[32] Cindy Weinstein traces such concern over the status of the individual in a modernising economy back to mid-century. She follows Foucault in looking at the way the human body is 'imprinted by history', and illustrates how the literature of that period 'registered a critical cultural moment in which relations between labor, bodies, and agency, were being (re) invented, renegotiated'.[33] Mark Seltzer examines this same cluster of anxieties concerning the boundaries between 'interior states and external systems, and between bodies and persons and machines', with particular reference to the later years of the century, relating such anxieties to what he calls the 'psychotopography of machine culture'.[34] One explanation for the recent revival of critical interest in this latter period is the direct relevance of such concerns to our contemporary awareness (post Foucault) of the relation between the status of the human subject and the politics of the body: that body punished and corrected, supervised and controlled, regulated by the various systems of power and forms of discourse by which a modern bourgeois system, to echo his terms, disciplines its subjects. In this, novels written at the end of the nineteenth century appear increasingly to foreshadow contemporary and even postmodernist concerns.

Twain's interest in the question of agency and identity has been a subject of extended critical enquiry. There is a well-known passage from *A Connecticut Yankee* which serves as an obvious stimulus for discussion of the types of bodily discipline and body–machine interactions described above. Hank's role here is as one who reduces one particular man to a machine, in his drive for both efficiency and profit. The passage comes in Hank Morgan's description of his visit to the Valley of Holiness and his account of one of the 'supremely great' hermits who lives there, one whose 'mighty celebrity' had 'penetrated all Christendom':

> His stand was a pillar sixty feet high, with a broad platform on the top of it. He was now doing what he had been doing every day for twenty years up there – bowing his body ceaselessly and rapidly almost to his feet. It was his way of praying. I timed him with a stop-watch, and he made 1,244 revolutions in 24 minutes and 46 seconds. It seemed a pity to have all this power going to waste. It was one of the most useful motions in mechanics, the pedal movement; so I made a note in my memorandum book, purposing some day to apply a system of elastic cords to him and run a sewing-machine with it. I afterwards carried out that scheme, and got five years' good service out of him; in which time he turned out upwards of eighteen thousand first-rate tow-linen shirts, which was ten a day. I worked him Sundays and all; he was going, Sundays, the same as week-days, and it was no use

to waste the power. These shirts cost me nothing but just the mere trifle for the materials – I furnished those myself, it would not have been right to make him do that – and they sold like smoke to pilgrims at a dollar and a half apiece, which was the price of fifty cows or a blooded race-horse in Arthurdom. They were regarded as a perfect protection against sin, and advertised as such by my knights everywhere, with the paint-pot and stencil-plate; insomuch that there was not a cliff or a boulder or a dead-wall in England but you could read on it at a mile distance:

> '*Buy the only genuine St Stylite; patronized by the Nobility. Patent applied for.*'

There was more money in the business than one knew what to do with. As it extended, I brought out a line of goods suitable for kings. . . .

But about that time I noticed that the motive power had taken to standing on one leg, and I found that there was something the matter with the other one; so I stocked the business and unloaded, taking Sir Bors de Ganis into camp financially along with certain of his friends: for the works stopped within a year, and the good saint got him to his rest. But he had earned it. I can say that for him. (pp. 205–6)

There are several things to say before I analyse this passage as a critique of Hank's role as an agent of modernisation. The first is that the hermit is very different from the mass of the population, those 'down-trodden people' (p. 176) whom Hank would free from chains of religious and aristocratic servitude and make independent citizens of a new republic. The hermit's status as a Catholic saint, and the futile nature of his activity (in Hank's mind at least), make him a particularly obvious target for manipulation.[35] None the less, I would argue that the religious animus in the episode disguises the fact that Hank's activity is symptomatic of behaviour and attitudes repeated elsewhere, and in circumstances where such qualifications do not apply. They can thus be taken as paradigmatic. My second comment leads in a similar direction. I would want to recognise that Twain is genuinely funny here, as he opposes the rigidity of the hermit's movements (and consciousness) to Hank's quick and pragmatic wit. Certainly it is easier to laugh at the humour of the scene and to see its dehumanising implications more in terms of Twain being carried away by the comedy of the situation, rather than as a serious critique of Hank's values. In line with my former argument, however, I would see this scene as having exactly that double focus previously described. For the comedy in the passage works to veil the alternative response on which I concentrate.

There is an obvious (though implicit) clash of discourse and conceptualisation here between Hank, the 'impatient modernizer', and the medieval Christian world he is engaging. Werner Sollors, in an intriguing article on 'Ethnicity', discusses the prevalence of 'boundary constructing strategies' in Twain's novel. Hank, a 'solitary bourgeois anachronism'[36] in the Arthurian world, imposes his language and set of values on it. The conditions which form Hank's discourse are those of the capitalist economy which initially locates him. Secular and sacred frames of knowledge clash in the dislocations that fantasy brings: the hermit's assumption of religious devotion and freely chosen action are obliterated – or at least overlaid – by Hank's first-person voice and values.

The entry of the moderniser, Hank, into a different medieval world, becomes a way of opening the rationalisations and efficiencies of late nineteenth-century business practice[37] to comparativist criticism and even ridicule. Frederick Winslow Taylor (the time and motion specialist) had not yet achieved national renown when Twain was writing *A Connecticut Yankee*, but was already 'meticulously pursu[ing] "speed" and "feed" studies at Midvale Steel in the mid-1880s'. The principles which he, and other management experts, were introducing in an attempt to 'determine the "one best way" to increase industrial productivity' and bring 'order, rationality, and efficiency out of the disorder, the irrationality, and the wastefulness of the times' had already been grasped by Hank Morgan, and by his creator. For in this novel, Twain represents and assesses what was in 1889 still no more than a 'shadowy [and] yet unnamed idea' – Taylorisation. Efficiency versus waste is the binary structure which Hank uses to conceptualise the hermit and his actions. If Taylor needed to justify and explain his methods of 'tightly fit[ting] factory workers to their assigned tasks',[38] Hank explains, but feels no need to justify, his use of St Stylite to make those ten shirts a day, in Sollors's phrase, 'immigrant, sweat-shop fashion'.[39]

The principles of Taylorisation, the desire for firm management and for business efficiency, that underpin Hank's language and actions are, though, partly modified to his Arthurian circumstances. Martha Banta, from whose *Taylored Lives: Narrative Productions in the Age of Taylor, Veblen, and Ford* (1993) I extract much of my contextual material here, notes the 'elementary ideas' Taylor applied to the management of the workforce. The first two of these were:

> *First*: Holding a plum for them to climb after.
> *Second*: Cracking the whip over them, with an occasional touch of the lash.[40]

Hank's system is even more efficient, since his worker is self-motivated and self-disciplined. The hermit cracks his own whip, with his 'plum' (eternal life) supplied by the framework of his Christian belief. Hank's place in the process is simply to reap the profits, pull his own secular plum from this particular and productive arrangement.

There are other ways too in which Hank acts as a champion of what would later be known as Taylorisation. Hank taylors the hermit's life and actions to the needs both of an efficient production process and of the consumer society whose growth he is stimulating.[41] He brings time, motion and production together and uses the many repetitions his machinery allows to combat what he sees as unacceptable forms of social and industrial waste.

My last sentence suggests, as does much of the quoted passage, how for Hank man and machine are indistinguishable. The incident in Twain's novel here feeds back into, and provides a reflection on, late nineteenth-century social concerns. The 'robotic motions'[42] of the hermit are disassociated, in Hank's mind, from any notion of consciousness or emotion on his part. Hank's monitorings and surveillances of his underlings are a noticeable factor, not just here, but elsewhere in the novel too.[43] His is the hand that governs this business enterprise; his the hand that draws the thread of rational control through the needle of the hermit's religious sensibility.[44] The hermit, the motive power, drives and becomes Hank's well-managed machinery. Hank, to use Seltzer's terms, 'rewrit[es] . . . the [hermit's] natural body in the idiom of machine culture',[45] couples that body with a sewing-machine, and makes capital from the result.

Henry Ford would later convert 'potential waste into gain'[46] by

using workers whom other industrialists discarded, for he cal-
culated that of the 7882 distinct work operations involved in the
production of his Model T, only 12 per cent needed 'strong,
able-bodied, and practically physically perfect men':[47]

> Inspired by the adage 'waste not, want not,' the Ford Motor
> Company employed a legion of disabled workers: in 1914, 680
> legless men, 2,637 one-legged men, two armless men, 715 one-
> armed men, and ten blind men.[48]

So, similarly, Hank uses his hermit. As far as his plans go, the man
might be handless or armless, or even headless for any but the
purposes of basic survival, for it is the legs and trunk doing the work
(the bowing of the body); nothing else matters here. An emptying
out of human agency takes place as the individual subject is
converted into a mechanical object. In Taylorisation, prior notions of
complete manhood are replaced by the worker's function as an
efficient part of a machine. This section of *A Connecticut Yankee* can
be read paradigmatically as a comment on, and critique of, the
workings of the capitalist economy in the late nineteenth century. In
the individual hermit's fate lies the spectre of a mass work force
made to fit, and bound by, a social and industrial system which
reduces its members to mere ciphers. Martha Banta reaches similar
conclusions when she analyses the relation between Hank, Clarence
and the fifty-two cadets who finally carry out his commands, in terms
of the 'transformations over time of relations between the factory
boss and his boys' as represented in Twain's fiction as a whole.[49]

IV

In *A Connecticut Yankee* then, the use of fantasy, with the conflict
between different forms of language and value systems it introduces
as one world intrudes on another, acts to interrogate late nineteenth-
century norms and assumptions. As a businessman, Twain shared
an enthusiasm for the forms of rationalisation and calculability that
marked an emergent modernised culture in America (see the second
prefacing quote to this chapter). His literary works, though, tell
another and more ambivalent story.

Jackson Lears follows Max Weber in stressing the importance of rationalisation in the modernisation process, describing it as:

the systematic organization of economic life for maximum productivity and of individual life for maximum personal achievement; the drive for efficient control of nature under the body of improving human welfare; the reduction of the world to a disenchanted object to be manipulated by rational technique.[50]

Hank Morgan, 'active, restless, and on the make',[51] is directly associated with the idea of disenchantment. His belief in a 'rationally constructed world' (p. 125) runs alongside his pragmatism. For he has the ability to 'invent, contrive, create, reorganise things; set brain and hand to work', once he is stranded, 'just another Robinson Crusoe' (p. 81), in this other society. Hank, who identifies himself with 'the magic of science', takes on Merlin, representative of medieval necromancy and enchantments, of 'the magic of fol-de-rol' (p. 363). An engineer, a technocrat and a scientist, his set of 'superstitions about *unenchanted* and *unmiraculous* locomotives, balloons and telephones' (p. 181, my emphasis) soon transform the world he has entered.

Though the language Hank uses suggests similarity as well as difference between science and magic (I develop this later), his rationalism combats the power of (occult) superstition, and the anti-modern bias it represents. But Hank's rationalism also proves 'disenchanting' in the broader sense, in the loss of charm or delight it implies. For increasing doubts about late nineteenth-century rationalisation, efficiencies and controls can be identified in Twain's novel as it proceeds. Hank organises, as he modernises, the Arthurian world. He develops a 'system and machinery' to ensure the smooth running of the 'civilization' he will put in place. He relies on expertise – newly trained 'experts in every sort of handiwork and scientific calling' (p. 101) – to do his work for him, and to prepare for the flooding of 'the midnight [sixth century] world with light' (p. 103). Anticipating the direct anti-imperialist satires he was to write at the turn of the century,[52] Twain has Hank Morgan bring 'soap and civilization' (p. 146) to a backward country.[53] He also has him introduce advertising, consumerism and modern business methods there. Hank networks the nation with a modern communications system (ground wires carrying telephone and telegraph –

p. 104), and builds up a 'vast system of clandestine factories and workshops', eventually exposed to the view of 'an astonished world' (p. 364). He sits at the centre of a rational and efficient web of control and brings modernisation to a backward world. The more we learn of Hank's methods and systems, though, the less enchanting they seem. His plan for a 'Man Factory' (p. 130), where promising but common human materials, stifled by unfair and restrictive feudal practices, can be turned from 'groping and grubbing automata into *men*' (p. 159), is apparently based on republican and democratic principles. The implications of reification and rationalisation in its name, however, warn that these men may end up like the hermit – who is no 'man' for Hank, but the tool and agent of a reactionary and corrupt religion. The 'human liberty' (p. 102) Hank espouses operates in highly variable ways. The sound of the Colt factory whistle continues symbolically to resonate here.[54]

If men are made into automata by feudal training, Hank does not necessarily improve their mental condition but simply retrains them to fit his own ideological and social agenda. Thus Ulfius the telephone clerk, 'one of [Hank's] young fellows' (p. 217) met by chance in the Valley of Holiness, has become (like the hermit and his sewing machine) a cog in Hank's system rather than the independent and free-thinking individual his words might promise. Ulfius moves by night and avoids speech with others as he helps in the secret process of getting modern civilisation in place. As he does this, he learns 'naught but that we get by the telephone from Camelot' (p. 218). The plural pronoun used here speaks of Ulfius's status as one of an interchangeable many. In defining himself as Hank's agent, he reveals how narrow are the boundaries of the centralised system of knowledge and information in which he plays his part. For he is uncertain even of his exact location, and is alone, apart from the phone 'back in the gloom' of the cavern, where he has set up his 'office'.

If, in Hank's words, 'the home of the bogus miracle [has] become the home of a real one, the den of a medieval hermit [has been] turned into a telephone office' (p. 217), the underlying ironic turn to this is that little has changed (though in terms of political and religious forms much, of course, has – or will). The hermit's conditioning leads him to a role which only makes sense within the framework of particular religious belief, and where individual identity is measured in terms of the ritual penance undergone. This is not that different from Hank's trainee, whose function and identity exist only as part of the network he is servicing, and who is completely in the dark outside its parameters.[55] Similarly, the boy soldiers who are Hank's 'champions of human liberty and equality' (p. 396) at the narrative's end, are in fact the only fragment of the population not conditioned by prior training (by 'the Church, the nobles, and the gentry' – p. 392) but by Hank's. Thus it is easy to read the Battle of the Sand-Belt in terms of one set of automata fighting another, depending on who has been trained by whom, rather than as standing for any real defence and celebration of democratic principle.

Hank's technological efficiency and scientific knowledge can, by the end of the novel, also be seen from a disenchanted perspective. Hank, speaking undoubtedly for Twain, celebrates modern invention and technical expertise when he looks into the future to criticise England's failures to honour 'the creators of this world – after God – Gutenberg, Watt, Arkwright, Whitney, Morse, Stephenson, Bell' (p. 298).[56] The gap in knowledge and invention between Hank's America and Arthur's England is considerable: 'no gas . . . no candles; a bronze dish half full of boarding-house butter with a blazing rag floating in it was the thing that produced what was regarded as light' (p. 81).[57] Hank has the scientific knowledge to produce (god-like) his own light. By the end of the novel, he is using his 'first great electric plant' (p. 386) to set 'fifty electric suns aflame' (p. 404), and thus to illuminate the slaughter then taking place. Twain's notes for the novel show his interest in the relation between natural and scientific power:

Journal The Sunburst
Electri [sic] Light.[58]

But Hank's drive for an efficient control of nature, and the power and authority it gives him, become identified with mass murder. Indeed the word 'massenmenchemoerder' (p. 212) is part of his incantation in the mending of the holy fountain sequence earlier.

The drive to harness nature's powers was to have disturbing implications in terms of Hank's actions, and in terms, too, of the actions of Twain's late nineteenth-century contemporaries. In both cases, these focused round the 'application of electricity to the human body'.[59] The debate surrounding the introduction of legal electrocution in America took place around the time Twain was writing his novel. Dr Alfred Southwick, a Buffalo dentist and later Professor of Operative Technics at the University Dental School, saw a drunk die instantly after touching an electric wire in 1881. This led him to perform a series of 'lethal electrical experiments on animals'. Following their success, Southwick went on to campaign for a more efficient and less painful form of capital punishment, and, on 1 January 1889, the Electrical Execution Law was passed in New York State. Electrocution thereby replaced hanging, the mode which (as the State-Governor put it) 'has come down to us from the dark ages' as the traditional method for executing criminals. The comparative advance in civilisation that death by electrocution was meant to herald was, however, rather undermined by the fact that the first man to die by this system (William Kemmler, on 6 August 1890) apparently revived after his supposedly lethal shock, and had to be swiftly re-electrocuted.

Kemmler's execution took place at seven in the morning, as 'it was feared that the 1200 convicts at Auburn would be unduly disturbed by a sudden shutdown of the electric power while they were at work in the machine shops'.[60] The connection here between manufacturing needs carried out by an imprisoned and well-supervised labour force, working despite their will, and the use of the same force (electricity) which drove their production to execute one of their fellow criminals seems like a condensed and grotesque version of processes illustrated in Twain's novel. Here Hank gradually moves from his use of the hermit unwittingly to drive his business enterprise to his later use of electricity to slaughter those who oppose his system.

Kemmler's execution took place after *A Connecticut Yankee* was completed. Discussion of electrocution as a mode of criminal execution had been taking place, though, throughout the latter half of the 1880s.[61] Moreover, there were frequent newspaper reports about accidents resulting from electricity, 'deaths resulting from what were called "the deadly wires"'.[62] When Hank sends his electricity through the deadly wires he has set up to trap his enemy, the effect is dramatic:

We would now and then see a blue spark when the knight . . . had touched a charged wire with his sword and been electrocuted . . . ; our current was so tremendous that it killed before the victim could cry out. . . . Our camp was enclosed with a sudden wall of the dead. . . . I shot the current through all the fences and struck the whole host dead in their tracks! *There* was a groan you could *hear*! It voiced the death-pang of eleven thousand men.

(pp. 402–4)

By this point in the novel, Hank's modernisations and rationalisations have come to look very sinister indeed. Twain's nineteenth-century light-bringer becomes a mass-electrocutioner. Scientific and technological knowledge bring destruction and defeat for all the parties involved.

Twain's use of fantasy in *A Connecticut Yankee*, then, interrogates the nature of the 'real' in late nineteenth-century America; confronts and questions generally held norms and assumptions. One such assumption was the 'tendency to equate material and moral progress'.[63] Twain cuts the threads of that particular connection in a novel where material progress, technology and science bring, not human betterment, but moral disaster in an 'annihilating' (p. 396) Civil War, and the Battle of the Sand-Belt that follows.[64] Moreover, the idea of a public order dependent on an individual commitment to, and constraint by, 'an internalized ethic of self-control' (an 'unquestioned norm'[65] at the time) is exploded in a fable of what happens when one self-seeking individual has the edge on his competitors, and how the individual moral gyroscope is upset in such a case. The general belief in a gradual evolution from lower to higher social and historical forms and stages[66] is shattered in a novel whose linear and historical movement ends broken and in tatters.

Again, other readings are possible. Twain has to end his novel in this way, to bring it back in line with the course of real history. The signs of narrative dislocation toward the conclusion and the violence of the Battle of the Sand Belt can be read as Twain's attempts to find a way out of the complicated fictional situation he has set up. It is possible, too, to give equal attention to the defeat of nineteenth-century liberalism by entrenched establishment interests as to Hank's own failings. If, according to my reading, the dominant assumptions of Twain's time are challenged in an explosive text, this is not an interpretation that all critics share. Contradictions and ambivalences have their place in this text too.

V

A further conventional assumption which the use of fantasy in *A Connecticut Yankee* helps to undermine is the belief in 'the most cherished of a human unities: the unity of "character"'. As I have previously shown, anxieties about the sense of self consistently pervade Twain's fictional world. Here, it is possible to read Hank as a consistent and autonomous character, wielding power and sure of his own agency. It is also possible, though, to see an alternative: that the fantastic juxtaposition of the Arthurian and late nineteenth-century worlds acts as a device to illuminate the divided nature of Hank's being. For the use of 'the motif of the double' and of 'otherness' in fantastic texts can provide a way, as Rosemary Jackson suggests, of questioning and destabilising any notion of the coherent subject.[67]

A *Connecticut Yankee* depends on the contrast between the modern and the medieval. Hank's 'other' is Merlin, the arch-enemy who represents all that is backward about Arthurdom. But the opposition between the two figures is far from stable. I noted earlier that the language Hank uses about himself overlaps with that which describes Merlin. While Merlin, for example, is associated with 'absurd necromancy', the Yankee is seen to represent 'the more splendid necromancy of the nineteenth century'.[68] The use of the same word to describe their two practices starts to blur the apparently firm boundaries between them, and between the science and magic they represent. Such a blurring would be familiar to Twain's contemporaries who, for instance, nicknamed Thomas Edison the Wizard of Menlo Park.

Hank's description of himself as a type of representative nineteenth-century culture hero, his apparent identification with a single and coherent subject position, is challenged by a text which repeatedly illustrates the collapse of the differences between him and those he labels as cultural antagonists. Werner Sollors is just one critic who shows the 'pervasive similarity' between the Yankee and his Arthurian host.[69] Thus, though Hank uses his scientific knowledge, particularly that of high explosives, to out-do and overpower Merlin, he consistently uses the language and techniques of the occult to carry out his purposes. Hank's incantation and use of visible display in his 'Restoration of the Fountain' (pp. 207–14) suggests how the gap between his and Merlin's magic tends to disappear, and especially in terms of the knowledge and reactions of their joint audience. As Michael Davitt Bell puts it, Hank, 'in his conflict with Merlin keeps turning *into* Merlin'.[70]

This collapse of difference between Hank and all that constitutes his medieval opposite is signalled in other ways too. So, in the novel, Arthurians start talking like Yankees, and Hank ends (in the prefacing 'Word of Explanation') speaking like an Arthurian: 'Wit ye well. . . . Give you good den, fair sir' (pp. 34, 38). Hank, too, is consistently shown 'doing the same thing or using the same dehumanising words he criticizes in others'. Not only does he rely on 'fake miracles' to fight superstition, but he models the spreading of his own enterprise on the way the church, his prime enemy, works. And he fights 'the "petrified" system of feudalism . . . [by] transforming knights into "statues"', fixing them rigid as he electrocutes them. Hank ends up inhabiting Merlin's cave, and married to Sandy ('wedded to Arthurianism'[71]). He is, despite his own claims to the contrary, a sentimentalist, who is left mourning his 'Lost Land',[72] 'an abyss of thirteen centuries yawning', as he puts it, between him and Sandy; between him and 'all that could make life worth the living!' (p. 409). The boundaries Hank constructs dividing himself from the Arthurians – who represent all the parts of his subjectivity that he would deny[73] – are in complete disarray at the novel's end. The fantastic use of the sixth century double collapses the firm sense of self that Hank, as the progressive representative of nineteenth-century modernism, would take absolutely for granted.

VI

Hank is, in *A Connecticut Yankee*, finally caught between two historical periods, fully at home in neither. His love for his 'home and his friends', for Sandy and his child (both of whom he addresses in his final 'delirium'), provides his last 'pleasure' and 'gladness' (p. 409). Max Weber wrote in 1918 that 'our greatest art is intimate . . . and not monumental', speaking here of the loss of value in public life at a time 'characterized by rationalization and intellectualization and, above all, by the "disenchantment of the world"'. Hank, too, retreats to the intimate, to that same realm of

'direct and personal human relations' to which Weber refers,[74] at
the end of *A Connecticut Yankee* as the world of public history that
his rational and 'disenchanted' techniques have brought into being
goes smash.

In his analysis of realism, the Marxist critic Georg Lukacs
describes the genre as one which allows for the possibility of
grasping the 'real causality of events'. He sees the realist writer as
one who can chart the direction of 'historical sequence' and show
how 'significant human beings' actively participate to effect the lives
of their society.[75] Twain never seems to have had quite this kind of
confidence either in the ability of humans to shape history,[76] or in
the power of the artist to represent it in terms of cause and positive
effect. I read *Huckleberry Finn* in terms of the depiction of an
interracial relationship operating on the fringes of the existing social
system, and pointing in the direction of what might, with great
difficulty, become a future public possibility. Such progressive
impulses (however minimal) seem, though, completely obliterated
at the end of *A Connecticut Yankee*. Hank's final stress on the
importance of interpersonal relationships signals a retreat from
the public (the monumental); a tacit admission of the disastrous
nature of his historical interventions. As so often in this chapter, I
have to stop, though, to remind of the alternative reading available.
The ending can be read as a mere product of the narrative situation
Twain adopts, for Hank *cannot* change history if the basic premises
of the novel are to stand. It is as easy, in other words, to read the
ending in terms of artistic necessity as of a particular view, on
Twain's part, of the historical process and man's relation to it.

But it is the latter interpretation on which I focus. Hank's political
values cannot, in terms of the textual development, be separated
from his desire for personal power and profit. The corporate
civilisation he introduces has dehumanising implications. And the
modern financial machinery (the stock-board) he establishes hastens
the Civil War that brings both his authority and the regime he has
developed to an end. Twain's own fears about the meaning of
democracy in America, and about 'social relations in a capitalist
society', can be traced far back in his career, certainly to *The Gilded
Age*. The shuttling between two worlds he fictionalises in *A
Connecticut Yankee*, and the completeness and apocalyptic nature of
the historical break that finally occurs between them, can be read in
terms of an increasing pessimism about the direction of history, the

state of contemporary American culture, and even about basic human nature, on Twain's part. It is perhaps no coincidence that in his later *The Secret History of Eddypus, The World Empire* (1901–2), he would depict history as cyclic, marked by 'a human tendency toward dictatorship on the one hand and subservience and fanaticism on the other'.[77] Twain would not give up on history: his own political involvements and later satiric writing show this. Undoubtedly, though, his attitude toward it became increasingly more pessimistic. The use of fantasy in *A Connecticut Yankee* can be taken as symptomatic of that fact.

Twain's fictional moves between the American past and present, in *Roughing It, Tom Sawyer* and *Huckleberry Finn*, end similarly. The attraction of the past is modified by an understanding of its flaws, while the seeds of the present, too, are shown to be contained in that past. In *A Connecticut Yankee*, the nostalgic impulse operates too, but the simpler and agrarian landscape that is mourned is at the same time clearly unsupportable, given the tyrannies, injustices and attitudes of mind with which it is associated (and which Hank can never quite remove). And although the modern political and secular values that Hank introduces are lauded, other sides of his late nineteenth-century value scheme doom them, in this fictional context, to defeat. Twain's ambivalences are clear here. The gaps opening up in his work are becoming wider and wider; more difficult, in any way, to bridge.

7

Severed Connections: *Puddn'head Wilson* and *Those Extraordinary Twins*

You see we were twins – defunct and I – and we got mixed in the bath-tub when we were only two weeks old, and one of us was drowned. But we didn't know which. . . . But I will tell you a secret now, which I have never revealed to any creature before. One of us had a peculiar mark – a large mole on the back of his left hand; that was me. That child was the one that was drowned!

('An Encounter with an Interviewer')[1]

It is hard to see clear in a world of twins.

(Arnold L. Weinstein, *Nobody's Home*)[2]

I

Mark Twain was caught between different stories and literary modes as he wrote *Puddn'head Wilson* (1894). His artistic difficulties with his material are suggested in the late change of title from *Those Extraordinary Twins*.[3] They are clear in his account of the 'literary Caesarean operation' he performed, when he 'dug out' farcical material about Siamese twins to leave the 'tragic aspect' of his tale of Roxy and the two changelings intact.[4] Twain's story of this severance is in the first American edition of the text, published as

134

The Tragedy of Puddn'head Wilson and the Comedy of Those Extraordinary Twins. It is told, however, to explain the presence of the farce, which is still retained as supplement to the main narrative.[5] A symbiotic bond, in other words, continues to exist between the two parts of the original body of work. The stories may have been pulled apart, but they remain, none the less, connected.

'Violent separation', as Evan Carton points out, both 'provides a model for the organization of Dawson's Landing' and describes what Twain did in 'severing the double story and disposing of one half'.[6] The twinned publication of the stories, the way they formally interact, and their thematic ties, argue against the success of that disposal. Indeed, as Susan Gillman says:

> *these twin novels must . . . be read together,* despite the fact that the farce makes a mockery of the Siamese twins' grotesque attachment, whereas the tragedy, obsessed with genealogy, race, and miscegenation, offers a critique of an American historical actuality.[7]

One of Twain's most interesting works of fiction is, in other words, made up of two stories still 'tangled together' (p. 229) despite their forced separation. Both *Puddn'head Wilson* and *Those Extraordinary Twins* take as their theme different (but related) types of Siamese connections; share the same textual obsession with violated borderlines, racial and physical. Thus Twain's description in *Those Extraordinary Twins* of Luigi and Angelo as a 'monstrous "freak"' (p. 303)[8] meshes symbolically with Tom's representation in *Puddn'head Wilson* as a mulatto. For, according to one (racist) strand of the racial rhetoric of post-Reconstruction America, the mulatto was defined as 'unnatural hybrid' or '"freak" of natural law'.[9] A cultural scandal replaces a natural one here. Nature, though, is still the court of cultural appeal, as the difference between the two terms is disguised to defend an established and segregated social order. As such overlaps as this occur, additional meanings are released between the two (twinned) narratives which affect our readings of both.

My starting point in this chapter is to lay one twin text against the other to suggest that the tensions and divisions in Twain's work can no longer, here, be contained within a single whole. Cindy Weinstein discusses Twain's 'dis-ease about what does and does not belong in . . . narrative'.[10] She is talking about *Life on the Mississippi*, not about this text, but her comment seems entirely appropriate to it. On one side (*Those Extraordinary Twins*) we have farce, on the other (*Puddn'head Wilson*), tragedy, and Twain cannot reconcile the forms. I suggested in my first chapter that one reading of 'The Stolen White Elephant' implies that extravagant humour (with its anarchic qualities) may not be compatible with a repressive social reality. It is not, however, until this later stage in his career that the gap between the two becomes unbridgeable.[11]

Twain's comedy has already become forced by the end of *A Connecticut Yankee*, as doubts both about dominant American values, and the direction of history itself, are revealed. In *Tom Sawyer* and *Huckleberry Finn*, the use of an ante-bellum setting allows for cultural critique and for nostalgia and escape. The playful and/or idyllic aspects of life on the borders of society carry positive connotations in both novels. Idyll, though, is absent from *Puddn'head Wilson* (set in a similar time and place), and the limits of play are greatly reduced. The view of American history, as seen through a racial perspective, is starkly negative. And wider anxieties about the status of the self, and the determining influence of the environment, are clearly evident. The type of fictional balances found in earlier texts are no longer evident here. And if Twain employs a number of fictional tactics, and particularly the use of the detective genre, which counter the pessimistic tenor of his novel, the use of broadscale humour is no longer one of them.

Cindy Weinstein analyses three of Twain's books (*Life on the Mississippi*, *A Connecticut Yankee* and *No. 44, The Mysterious Stranger*) in terms of a tension in Twain's artistic allegiances between the allegorical representation of personhood and a quite different literary method. On the one hand, character is based – in line with nineteenth-century capitalist values – on 'efficiency and discipline'. Fictional characters come to resemble the 'flattened, mechanical persons . . . in a factory or in a market economy': produced by a determining circumstance and empty of subjectivity. But a different type of *literary* economy competes with that of the market. For literary labour has little to do with the machine-like efficiencies of business. Rather, it 'celebrates an ideal of inefficient . . . narrative that is digressive and, more important, humorous'. This counter-impulse leads in the direction of the type of 'directionless circulations', in which *authorial* efficiency and success consisted. So, in *A Connecticut Yankee*, the comic expansiveness that comes about as a result of Hank's early interactions with Sandy, as their two narrative styles and aesthetic perspectives are contrasted,[12] is subdued at the novel's end as Hank is positioned in the company of 'numbers without stories', the characterless boys he has trained to stand beside him in the cave. Twain's only way of dealing with such 'subversive indistinguishability', in *A Connecticut Yankee* at least, is by 'the killing of those allegorical characters [he] finds so threatening to his view of the world in which people are people and machines are machines'.[13] The Battle of the Sand-Belt which effectively ends the narrative can be read, consequently, as a type of fictional necessity.

Weinstein's insights here can be carried over to a discussion of the relationship between *Pudd'nhead Wilson* and *Those Extraordinary Twins*. Both these texts have allegorical qualities, but it is in *Pudd'nhead Wilson* that the stress on flattened character and forming circumstance becomes most bleakly insistent. Indeed, though Twain speaks of the novel in terms of the tragic, it is better described as deterministic. The history of race, though, and not that of labour (Weinstein's focus), imprints the fictional characters here. The text's strongly allegorical impulse comes from the depiction of a society which rigidly categorises and differentiates its members through artificial racial classification; enslaves its members (both 'black' and 'white') within the narrow boundaries of a twinned system built around fixed notions of racial difference. But the term 'slavery' comes to have a wider significance too, for all the characters are enmeshed and constructed, in one way or another, by the social structures which surround them. Any notion of independent agency is strongly qualified, and the nature of identity itself is interrogated.[14]

Those Extraordinary Twins works as allegory too, but not at the expense of humour. The allegorical aspects only start to take their clearest shape at the end of the text, and more particularly, once it is placed alongside *Pudd'nhead Wilson*. In the story about Siamese twins, we find the type of extended burlesque missing from its novelistic partner. Twain takes artistic delight in letting his comic situation develop and his narrative ramble every which way, from one humorous incident to the next. The mechanics of farce outweigh those of allegory as his pleasure in the absurdist potential of the twinship device overwhelms (when the text is taken alone) any strong production of additional meaning. The expansive nature of the comedy present here disappears in *Puddn'head Wilson*, no longer compatible with a deepening serious and pessimistic social analysis.

Puddn'head Wilson, taken by itself, is marked internally (like so many Twain novels) by its 'generic swerves'.[15] But it is the formal swerve between the ironic and sardonic minimalism which is the novel's predominant *overall* characteristic, and the farcical and fanciful play of *Those Extraordinary Twins*, which particularly catches my interest. For a tension that has always been evident within Twain's texts now becomes a tension *between* texts. The quest for meaning in *Puddn'head Wilson and Those Extraordinary Twins* becomes a form of collaborative project, as the reader puts the two together to find one broken whole. Such a rupture is a sign that established generic forms (or 'conventions of representation'[16]) can no longer contain Twain's complex and tangled web of materials, nor satisfy his diverging artistic needs. *Puddn'head Wilson* can be read as a self-sufficient novel (though, as many critics have pointed out, a number of obvious traces of the twins' Siamese connection still remain within it). I am suggesting, though, that if it is left to stand independently, an added dimension of its fictional life disappears. Its supplementary text both shadows it, and allows its fullest meanings to emerge. *Those Extraordinary Twins*, however, with its many references to its linked text, cannot be read by itself. It is oddly fitting that the narrative in which the twins are Siamese is the one that cannot stand alone.

I do a number of things, then, in this chapter. I show how *Puddn'head Wilson and Those Extraordinary Twins* interrelate: how, as farce vies with deterministic 'tragedy', Twain's fullest fictional meanings are revealed. The mechanics of extravagant farce in *Those Extraordinary Twins* are used to allegorical ends. But I argue that the allegorical aspects of the text only start to take on their deepest resonance at its rather abrupt and unexpected conclusion. Until that point, the more disturbing meanings of the text are hidden as, for the most part, the broad comedy of the story covers up anxieties about individual identity and difference; about agency, how it can be determined, and its relation to forms of social authority and control. The restored equilibrium brought with the final act of community violence then acts, in a different way, to swiftly suppress such troubling issues. Again, in this chapter, it is the presence of such processes, and the way in which the text's more uncomfortable effects are counteracted, that interests me.

Those Extraordinary Twins is a story of a scandal in nature –
Siamese twins, two bodies compellingly and inevitably tied together
– and of the legal and social response to it. It describes the battle
for power between the two parts of this one whole, and the
problems faced by others in telling which twin is master and which
slave when they do act. In focusing on these issues, Twain clearly
parallels and supplements the story of race relations he tells in
Puddn'head Wilson. The interrogation of agency and identity in the
latter text, too, is replayed at another level in *Those Extraordinary
Twins*, to hammer down the point that a belief in autonomy,
independence or separate selfhood is nothing more than a bad
joke.[17] As the twinned texts are severed, so this supplementary effect
is (to significant degree) lost. *Puddn'head Wilson*, too, has its own
conflicting elements. The upsetting of the social order that takes
place, and the instabilities in identity and assumed categories this
reveals, are finally (if not fully) disguised. This happens as the
detective genre takes over the novel, and as, consequently, one of
the disruptive 'twins' is removed from the scene. In *The Extraordinary Twins*, it is both twins who are finally disposed of.

In *Puddn'head Wilson and Those Extraordinary Twins*, Twain leaves
his reader with ragged edges. In the move from one text to its
twinned partner, and from one genre to another, he engages two
forms, neither of which completely meets his artistic needs. For the
world is read both in flatly deterministic and dehumanising terms
and as extravagant and comic farce. Shuttled between diverging but
related stories, and formally torn between different literary modes,
the reader is left finally decentred, the full meaning of this/these
twinned text(s) floating somewhere in the gap between them.

II

Siamese twinship, the subject of *Those Extraordinary Twins*, has
obvious comic possibility and inevitable allegorical resonance.[18]
Two sets of twins seem particularly to have stimulated Twain's
literary interest: Chang and Eng (on whom his 1869 sketch 'Personal
Habits of the Siamese Twins' was based), and the Italian Tocchi
brothers, on whom the physical appearance of Luigi and Angelo is

closely modelled.[19] The enforced biological connection of Siamese twins, and the problems of identity and agency, of separateness and togetherness, raised by their status, have a clear carry-over to the story of inescapable racial links in *Puddn'head Wilson*. Further knowledge of Chang and Eng's lives is relevant here. The twins evidently considered themselves a single person, signing their correspondence Chang Eng. The paralysis which came to afflict one side of Chang meant that Eng increasingly bore his weight. Meanwhile, Chang's 'disability turned him into a clinging, surly child'. Eng's death followed inevitably on that of his brother (on 7 January 1874), but apparently Eng awoke on that particular day unaware that Chang had died in the night. All these details have implications for the themes Twain would explore. Most particularly, Chang and Eng, who lived in ante-bellum North Carolina, owned slaves. The allegorical crossover from a permanent bodily connection (with the various types of interdependency involved) to a particular form of social and racial connection, which Twain explores as he moves from text to text, was thus already present in the circumstances of Chang and Eng's lives.[20]

Twain's early description of *Those Extraordinary Twins* as a 'howling farce'[21] suggests the spirit that motivated him as he started writing. Certainly, his subject matter afforded him ready opportunity for extravagant comic effects based on the physical facts of Siamese twinship, their single and joint selfhood, and the problems they posed in terms of the 'familiar boundaries'[22] of small-town American society. Though this material has allegorical implications concerning Twain's view of individual identity and agency, and though the representation of the twins themselves is consequently flat, much of its impact takes the form of what Gillman calls an 'absurd joke'.[23] This, however, is only true *until* we start to relate it to the plots of race and identity in *Puddn'head Wilson*: to tie it down strongly, in other words, *to social and historical circumstance*. For only in the *allegorical correspondence* between Siamese twinship and the depiction both of individual identity and social relationships in the last-named text is further meaning released. Thematically, then, the overt farce of the one text is tightly bound to the savage irony of the other. The severance Twain made between his interconnected stories can be most readily attributed to their lack of *formal* fit.

The jokes in *Those Extraordinary Twins* are often obvious, but they carry the narrative along with an exuberance which always marks Twain's writing when he is at his ease, and when the flow of his comedy follows, apparently effortlessly, from the one basic situational premise. The humorous 'extravaganza' (p. 234) starts with the difficulty of categorisation, as Aunt Patsy conventionally describes each of the two twins as a 'he' or a 'him', but can only respond to the joint and 'uncanny' presence of this 'double-headed human creature' as a monstrous 'it' (pp. 236–9). Problems with the use of singular and plural forms are part of a similar pattern. Thus, for instance, Rowena and her mother discuss 'that young man' with 'both of his faces' (p. 237).

The comedy swiftly develops with the visual play about the twins' four arms, the problem of determining their ownership, and the confused movements and contorted effects displayed. As Aunt Patsy puts it:

> Nobody could tell [which twin had taken off which hat]. There was just a wormy squirming of arms in the air – seemed to be a couple of dozen of them, all writhing at once, and it just made me dizzy to see them go. (p. 238)

The narrator follows this up with an inspired, and thoroughly Twainian, image, when he describes the tired and wet twins undressing, and says how 'the abundance of sleeve made the partnership-coat hard to get off, for it was like skinning a tarantula' (p. 239). This comic but dehumanising rhetorical turn implies that the twins' main interest for the author lies in their humorous potential. They are one-dimensional pegs on which he is hanging what is for the most part an equally one-dimensional joke.

The thematic thrust of *Those Extraordinary Twins* concerns matters of agency and control: who is in command of the shared body and when, and how any external observer can possibly tell. These issues surface in farcical form during the duel between Luigi and Judge Driscoll. Here, Angelo is first told by Luigi to 'stop dodging' since 'officially you are not here; officially you do not exist' (p. 283).[24] But Angelo then regains use of the mutual legs, to go 'soaring' over a fence, and 'off like a deer' (p. 285), to his brother's utter dismay. The courthouse scene shares in the same joke. For Luigi cannot be found guilty for assault on Tom, when he kicks him off the platform during a meeting of the town's pro-rum party (which is described only in *Puddn'head Wilson*), since no one can prove who possessed 'the battery' (p. 273) – the joint legs – at the time.

The jury verdict, that the 'identity [of one accused] is so merged in his brother's that we have not been able to tell which was him' (p. 278), and the judge's warning ('Look to your homes – look to your property – look to your lives . . . ' – p. 279) begins, however, to sound a more serious note. For the twins' lack of accountability suggests the 'monolothic fixity'[25] of the law: that it has no way of dealing with that which disrupts conventional and communal systems of categorisation.[26] It suggests, too, a potential for violent disruption that the rigid civic rules and conventions of Dawson's Landing cannot entirely hold in check.

In fact, Twain's Siamese twins story does end, abruptly, in violence. This comes, however, from an entirely unexpected source, that of the citizenry itself. And it acts, paradoxically (for it is outside the law), to restore social authority and order, the limits of which have been exposed by the twins' transgressive presence. The farce turns unexpectedly sour, with the political system of the town stalemated and 'rack and ruin' (p. 302) threatened. This results from Luigi's election to alderman, and a court decision that the (unelected) Angelo cannot legally be allowed to sit on the board with him. 'The people', in Twain's ironic words, then 'come to their senses', deciding to restore civic order by lynching the problem alderman. The narrative then concludes with a bad pun, a grim joke, and an ending which, in its suddenness, mirrors the twins' extraordinary fate. As the citizens refer back to Wilson's advice to hire Luigi to resign, the text continues:

'but it's too late now; some of us haven't got anything left to hire him with.'

'Yes, we have,' said another citizen, 'we've got this' – and he produced a halter.

Many shouted; 'That's the ticket.' But others said: 'No – Count Angelo is innocent; we mustn't hang him.'

'Who said anything about hanging him? We are only going to hang the other one.'

'Then that is all right – there is no objection to that.'

So they hanged Luigi. And so ends the history of 'Those Extraordinary Twins'. (p. 302)

Though serious issues about personal agency, law, communal order and violence do come, rather oddly, to take over the story here, their effect is muted. For the main emphasis of *Those Extraordinary Twins* is on vivid farce. Once the disruptive effect of the twins on the community comes to pose any real challenge to its smooth running, they are rapidly disposed of, and the narrative abruptly ends. Its ironic and troublesome aspects are thus swiftly cut short, too. It is only when we read the sketch as a supplement to *Puddn'head Wilson* that its allegorical aspects resonate and multiply. Taken alone, it does read as, what Bruce Michelson calls, a 'dadaist conundrum about the western cult of individuality', with its play on identity and difference between the two twins, and the question that raises about what such differences signify.[27] But further *historical* meaning is released in the connection between this twinned pair, and Tom Driscoll and Valet De Chambre. The link between the two sets of Siamese connections is suggested in the significant (and otherwise pointless) fact that one of the Siamese twins is 'dark complected' and the other light (p. 245; and see *Puddn'head Wilson*, p. 89). Angelo's wish to be '*segregated*' from Luigi, so as to 'be separate individuals, like other men' (p. 253, my emphasis), also provides an ironic cross-over to the racial twinnings of *Puddn'head Wilson*.[28]

Twain's one story of 'conglomerate twins' (p. 234), of two fates compellingly and inevitably tied together, speaks, as parable, to the story of race relations he tells in *Puddn'head Wilson*. The difficulty, in *The Extraordinary Twins*, of telling one twin from the other (p. 238), and of finally identifying where agency and responsibility lie, spills over into *Puddn'head Wilson*.[29] So, too, does the struggle for power between the twins, and the upsets in the relationship of mastery and subordination that accompany it. The issue of sameness and difference, crucial in the case of the Siamese Twins, also prefigures the problems of identity traced in the linked text,[30] not just in the case of racial exchange, but in the use of the fingerprinting motif too. For the latter raises questions that reach beyond the limits of race, about where selfhood lies and how it can be measured, confirmed and defined. In all these areas, *The Extraordinary Twins* supplements the subject matter of *Puddn'head Wilson*. What is considered (in terms of American race relations of the time) an upset in culture is mirrored in an upset of nature.

III

The difficulties readers often have with *Puddn'head Wilson* may, at least in part, stem from its own distinct allegorical nature. Until relatively recently, critics commonly chose to focus on the 'almost geometric' quality of the novel, with its 'iron plot' directed by an author who 'visibly rigs every move',[31] as a sign of its artistic failure. Twain's own admission that he considered Puddn'head Wilson himself not 'as a *character*, but only as a piece of machinery – a button or a crank or a lever, but with no dignity above that',[32] has often been used as further evidence of such a weakness. James M. Cox, who judges the novel flawed, is not atypical. For Cox, 'Puddn'head . . . remains . . . little more than a massive plot device. Neither he nor his "twin," the false Tom Driscoll, is ever freed into character.'[33]

To read the novel as one with a strong allegorical component, however, is to identify exactly the element in it which 'prevents the characters and situations from achieving the dimensions that would give them the illusion of life'.[34] John C. Gerber's suggestion that the text should not 'be measured primarily by the standards of realism' is pertinent here.[35] The chief citizens of Dawson's Landing are described as much as types as in terms of their individual characteristics. They are defined commonly as 'F. F. V.' (First Families of Virginia) and given collective attributes accordingly (p. 139). The highly artificial nature of 'causal relations' in the novel, with its 'improbable visitors . . . coincidental meetings . . . unanticipated conflicts', also works to deny the realist illusion of seamless historical sequence, of 'narrative coherence and continuity', which the specific geographic and historical setting would at first suggest.[36] *Puddn'head Wilson*'s concern with 'allegorical personhood' is evident, too, in its focus on the 'accounting of . . . persons'.[37] For both Roxy's and Tom's identity is decided in terms of fractions of whole numbers: what proportion of their persons is judged 'white' and 'black'. Their loss of civil and legal rights is similarly determined by their categorisation according to the small percentage of 'blackness' their 'blood' contains. In the light of this concern, Puddn'head Wilson's profession as both lawyer and *accountant* takes on further resonance. It is he who conducts the final accounting in the narrative. And in so doing, he reduces Tom once more to owned property, to the non-personhood of slavery.[38]

The allegorical quality of the novel is also clear in the reduction of both the townspeople and main protagonists to elements of geometrical equivalence in a particular narrative formula. Thus the 'group of citizens' who hear Wilson's half-a-dog joke remain indistinguishable, described in the dialogue that follows as numbers (no. 1 to 6, pp. 59–60). Similarly, Wilson's evidence in court at the conclusion of the book depends on a scrutiny of the autographs and pantographs of 'A and B' (p. 219). So Tom and Valet become, literally, interchangeable and equivalent algebraic symbols in a plot over which they have no control:

> A was put into B's cradle in the nursery; B was transferred to the kitchen and became a negro and a slave. . . . From seven months onward until now, A has still been a usurper, and in my finger-records he bears B's name. (p. 222)

The Siamese twins plot of *Those Extraordinary Twins*, and Wilson's early half-a-dog quip in *Puddn'head Wilson*, both reinforce the same sense of interconnection: one half of the dog (or twin) inseparable from the other, their stories symbiotically bound. One figure cannot move without affecting his twin, and, as a Siamese pair, both are finally subject to repressive external force quite beyond their own control. Tom metaphorically ends up losing his bite, for his parricidal aggression and transgressive social role are, at the last, effectively and brutally suppressed with his sale down the river; while Valet (the 'real' Tom Driscoll) has long lost his bark: his use of an African-American vernacular and his lack of social skills bar him from any voice in the community where he is eventually – at least in terms of traditional hierarchies – to become chief citizen. When Tweedledum becomes Tweedledee, both are broken in the exchange.

Puddn'head Wilson not only allegorises the interconnected fates and histories of the two races in America, but also the problematics of identity. Neither the real nor the false Tom Driscoll are 'freed into character', for the very notion of character, of autonomous subjectivity, is interrogated here. 'Conditions', to major extent, '*make* character'.[39] Allegory tends to stark black and white contrasts. The mode is, then, entirely appropriate to a novel where it is the racial status of the protagonists that results in the flattening of their fictional character. Cindy Weinstein shows how allegory, as a rhetorical form, is 'mediated, nuanced, and changed' by its specific historical context.[40] American racial politics, both ante- and post-bellum, form the historical ground for Twain's novel where artificial categories of blackness and whiteness are rigidly determining. The challenge to traditional notions of character that results is, however, not confined to racial politics. For Twain (and this is where the supplementary relevance of the Siamese twins again becomes apparent) destabilises the idea of subjectivity on a more general level too. Indeed, his challenge to 'the fundamental ideology of autonomous individualism in American culture'[41] can be read beside a series of other late nineteenth-century texts where contemporary anxieties about the status of the self are revealed.

First, though, to return to the representation of racial status in *Puddn'head Wilson*. The protagonists of the novel become black and white tokens in the plots of race and identity which structure the text. The novel continually circles round on itself, thus intensifying the thematic sense of entrapment and inevitability. Puddn'head Wilson unwittingly suggests the switch of babies to Roxy at the beginning of the novel (p. 65), only himself to reverse her action (if not all of its consequences) at the end. A stress on the repeated nature of Roxy's thoughts and actions acts to confirm the conditioning effects of race. Roxy threatens suicide three times (pp. 70, 183, 191). Such thoughts, the product of internal and psychological stress, are, however, caused by *external* threats to her physical or emotional well-being; a product of the racially divided society in which she lives. On each occasion, these threats are met with countering acts of aggression or social disruption, and the thoughts of suicide they trigger are accordingly transformed. Roxy's switch of the children first replaces suicide as an option, but both her initial impulse, and the response to it, result from her realisation of the vulnerability of the mother–child bond under slavery. Roxy again acts as racial avenger when she knocks out the Yankee overseer on the Arkansas plantation because he beats a 'little sickly nigger wench 'bout ten year ole dat 'uz good to me, en hadn't no mammy' (p. 183). The suicide decision that follows this act is swiftly replaced, though, by one to flee the plantation. Finally, in St Louis, Roxy carries a knife to kill herself if she should be recaptured by her 'master'. But as she plans an escape from her predicament, she turns the knife onto her son (who has sold her down the river in the first place), threatening to 'jam it into' him if further betrayal occurs (p. 191).

Such repetitions place the reader in a textual world of racial violence and counter-violence. Roxy's illegal and punishable acts here are all responses to the entirely legal cruelties of the slave system in which she is caught. In this repeated cycle, relations of cause and effect spin back on each other. So, for instance, Roxy's first act of switching children originates the novel's sequence of events, but her act is in turn an effect of the social system that harms her. Slavery, its patterns and consequences, come to determine all other relationships and actions. Roxy's disruptive actions are survival tactics in a racial world where self-destruction (suicide), or an acceptance of one's status as will-less property, are the only other options available.

The way race determines events in *Puddn'head Wilson* is also symbolised in the textual motif of the murderous knife. Roxy threatens violence against Tom who, in his role as respectable 'white' master, in turn threatens her freedom. But her action is one element in another three-part repetition. For Luigi too owns a 'murderous blade' with which he has killed a 'native servant' in India, defending his and Angelo's life and property. The native rising 'at the bedside . . . a dirk aimed at [Angelo's] throat' (p. 131) is a nightmare image of that return of the socially and racially repressed on which the larger story expands.[42] Roxy's attitude to 'white' authority is, from early in the novel, a violent one. She reacts to the god-like (p. 68) authority of Percy Driscoll over her life by saying 'I hates him, en I could kill him!' (p. 69). She goes on to talk of her change-ling son as the avenger of the 'crimes against her race' (p. 82).

John Carlos Rowe sees Tom as all but 'a machine' with, so it appears, 'all his actions . . . already determined by cultural or revolutionary forces beyond his control or understanding'.[43] Certainly, Tom acts out a role that seems allotted, as he uses the twins' knife, now in his hands, to commit symbolic parricide. He kills the man who, in a sense, fathered him,[44] and who, in his role as promoter of Dawson's Landing (pp. 96–7) and its chief legal authority ('Judge'), represents law, order and community in his

single person. Tom thinks earlier that 'if his father were only alive
and in reach of assassination his mother would soon find that he
had a very clear notion of the size of his indebtedness to that man'
(p. 157). The text makes clear, in all of this, that murderous impulses
are produced in the African-American by slavery and by its social
system; where a slave-owning father can legally and emotionally
disown his slave son to treat him only as a saleable commodity.
When Tom, consequently, 'drove the knife home – and was free'
(p. 195), these impulses come round to return on that institution's
patriarchal representative. The logic of the action and patternings of
the novel is driven by racial and historical determinants beyond the
ability of any single individual to contain and control.

                                    IV

Race strongly determines both plot and character in *Puddn'head
Wilson*. Though Roxy seems to act as free agent in her chaotic
reversal of the social order of Dawson's Landing, in fact her action
is prompted from without (Puddn'head). It is also psychologically
and historically determined, not just by the general injustices of
slavery as an institution, but also by the gap between a strong
sentimental valuation of the family unit (a dominant cultural trait
which she has imbued)[45] and her own position as a slave mother.
Twain does not offer a single determinate explanation of Roxy's
actions. Rather, he leaves his reader uncertainly hanging between
nature – the strength and power of Roxy's individual personality –
and nurture – the environmental and institutional circumstances
that condition how she speaks and what she does. In a repeated
tactic in this novel, any attempt firmly to distinguish nature from
nurture as the direct cause of plot or action quickly founders in a
spiralling uncertainty of origin. While conditions make character,
then, they are not quite *all* that make it.

None the less, the recognition of individual difference takes
second place to the power of cultural determinants in this novel.
And the efficacy of individual action is strongly questioned here.
Thus a certain irony lies in the fact that Roxy's switch of children
confirms (at the same time that it *secretly* collapses) the inequitable
social structure which dehumanises her. For the master–slave

relationship between changeling son and 'black' servant over-
takes and destroys the bond between mother and child which
caused Roxy initially to act. This stress on the power of racial
circumstance is furthered by the overall structure of the novel, for
'from the opening moment when she decides to drown her child,
to the closing one in which he is sold down the river, death [either
literal or social] is the slave mother's predetermined legacy that
Roxana tries to, but finally cannot, abort'.[46] Her final position,
textually silenced, laughter quashed and 'martial bearing
departed' (p. 225) is a measure of her defeat. Roxy now is reduced
to little more than a shadow, the havoc she has loosed once more
(as it seems to have been determined) safely contained.[47] Any
sense of independent agency on her part vanishes from the novel's
range of possibilities.

Roxy's initial switch of the children completely upsets, and
reveals as a lie, the distinction between supposed racial superiority
and inferiority on which the social system of Dawson's Landing
depends. The switch is made possible because Roxy and her son
are, in terms of physical appearance, both white. They are 'negro . . .
by fiction of law and custom' alone (p. 64, my emphasis), since Roxy
is one-sixteenth, and Tom is one-thirty-second, 'black'. Twain here
shows up the entirely illusory base on which American racial
difference was constructed, and enforced. Shelley Fisher Fishkin ties
Puddn'head Wilson to *Huckleberry Finn* in saying that their 'subliminal
subject is American race relations, not in the time in which the books
were set, but during the period in which they were written'. She
continues:

> In the 1890s . . . laws designed to separate white from black . . .
> proliferated. And what could not be done within the law was
> accomplished extralegally by lynch mobs. The price one paid for
> the color of one's skin was higher than ever before. . . . The fiction
> of 'racial purity' – the notion that it was, in fact, possible to divide
> society into 'white' and 'black' – remained the precious tenet
> which underlay the enormously cumbersome workings of the
> segregation laws. While white society tried to secure the dividing
> line between black and white through the courts and the law on
> the one hand, and through mob terror on the other, the
> population of Americans of mixed blood was increasing
> geometrically.

Fishkin points out that racial categorisation according to a rigid rule of descent – the 'one-drop rule' that meant that 'all descendants of mixed unions' were classed 'with their black progenitors' – stayed, for the most part, 'intact throughout the nineteenth and much of the twentieth century' in America.[48] Susan Gillman, in turn, reveals that 'as late as 1970 . . . in Louisiana the legal fraction defining blackness was still one-thirty-second "Negro blood"'.[49]

In *Puddn'head Wilson*, Twain reduces such discriminatory legal and social classifications to absurdity. Again the Tweedledum and Tweedledee analogy comes to mind. Once Roxy has swopped the officially 'black' and 'white' babies, absolutely no one (until Puddn'head Wilson's late intervention) can tell the difference. If 'black' can be 'white', and vice versa, so easily, then any categorisation of difference in terms of race collapses in on itself. Roxy's initial smearing of jam round Tom and Valet's baby mouths (p. 73) is quite unnecessary as even the 'white' child's father is oblivious of the switch.[50]

Twain is doing several things here. He uses the Tom–Valet twinning motif both to illustrate the starkness of the socially constructed contrast between 'black' and 'white', and to reveal its fraudulence. But he also uses that exchange to question the idea of autonomous subjectivity. For as Twain undermines a social system built on racial difference, he shows the extent to which that system structures the subjectivity of its members. It is the respective environments in which Tom and Valet are brought up that, to major degree, explain their individual differences.

Valet can be quickly dealt with. Entirely the product of his circumstances as a slave, he is 'made' as a man accordingly. When he is restored to his rightful position (a right which rests, of course, on a fundamental moral wrong) he is, in consequence, like a fish out of water, unable to adjust to his new environment. Conditioning is all in his case:

> he could neither read nor write, and his speech was the basest dialect of the negro quarter. His gait, his attitudes, his gestures, his bearing, his laugh – all were vulgar and uncouth; his manners were the manners of a slave. Money and fine clothes could not mend these defects or cover them up. . . . The family pew was a misery to [the poor fellow], yet he could nevermore

enter into the solacing refuge of the 'nigger gallery' – that was closed to him for good and all. (p. 225)

Tom, as most critics have recognised, is a more complicated case, for it is difficult to separate out his 'native viciousness' (p. 79) from his nurtured being. The 'evil light in his eye' (p. 190) and his violent actions may reveal a flawed individual nature. They may, though, reveal a hereditary racial characteristic, the 'one part nigger' (p. 157)[51] in him which makes him first a coward, and then a murderer. But there are further possibilities too. For, if Tom is morally depraved, such depravity may be bred by the social environment in which he has been raised *since* Roxy's switch. And his capacity for violence may relate to yet a further source, determined by race, but not through any equation of racial and moral 'blackness'. For it may arise from an unconscious, or part-conscious, historical conditioning that makes the death of the Judge a 'justifiable homicide', as Tom, now in blackface, acts to avenge past crimes against his race.[52]

Tom's viciousness does seem to distinguish him from the other F.F.V.'s of the class into which he has been raised. On the other hand, Twain writes that he 'was a bad baby from the *very beginning of his usurpation*' (p. 75, my emphasis). In both *A Connecticut Yankee* and *The American Claimant*, Twain appears to show the impossibilty of separating out nature from nurture (or first from second nature, as he puts it in the latter text).[53] So here, one can equally argue that Tom is innately evil (which may or may not be related to his 'blackness') or that, in Rowe's words, his 'dissolute habits are less attributable to his black origins than to the historical deterioration of aristocratic authority'.[54] Whatever the case, as we chase round the nature/nurture argument, it would still seem that much of Tom's 'identity' stems from Roxy's first act in putting him in that other set of clothes and cradle. And if it is at least possible to claim that Tom's worst traits are 'a sign . . . of aristocratic degeneration',[55] then what follows is the implication that if Tom had been Valet and Valet, Tom, the story *could* have remained the same. And if this is so, then the notion of autonomous selfhood collapses. This latter possibility haunts Twain's novel and leads it beyond the boundaries of race to a more general exploration of selfhood itself. As this occurs the links between *Puddn'head Wilson* and *Those Extraordinary Twins* once more clearly emerge.

In making Valet into Tom and Tom into Valet, Twain introduces a theme of identity and imitation which dizzyingly spins his reader in circles. It is difficult even to know how to refer to the novel's characters, but I have followed convention in calling the false Tom, Tom (for this is how he is textually known once the switch has occurred) and the real Tom, Valet. Just the matter of names, then, introduces considerable confusion as far as identity goes. When Tom comes home from Yale, dressed in the height of fashion, his 'fancy Eastern graces' are mocked by the imitations of 'the old deformed negro bell-ringer straddling along in his wake tricked out in a flamboyant curtain-calico exaggeration of his finery' (p. 85). An old black man, in other words, imitates a young white man. That young white man is, though, being imitated by a young 'black' man who is in fact not black at all. In turn, the young white man is imitating this 'black' twin. As Arnold Weinstein puts it: 'One has a "wake" in Twain's book, as if we did not stop where we thought our contours ended'.[56]

When Roxy calls Valet 'you mis'able imitation nigger', and he replies 'If I's imitation, what is you? . . . Bofe of us is imitation *white* . . . – en pow'ful good imitation too' (p. 103), similar doublings and redoublings occur. Roxy's imitation of whiteness is based on the fact that she *is* white, even if social classification denies her that label. When, in her rage, she calls Valet, who is white both by social definition and appearance, an imitation 'nigger', she exactly describes what he is, and what she herself has made him – though this has apparently slipped her mind here. In denying her charge he claims, in self-mockery, imitation whiteness; unconscious that the original he claims to copy is in fact his own self.

This concern with imitation and originality does not merely relate to matters of race. Susan Gillman points to the number of gender as well as racial imitations occuring in the text to assert that 'this is a society radically confused about what people are, who is black and who is white, what is imitation and what is real, a society whose laws create and enforce strict boundaries to mask those confusions'.[57] Tom, who is already disguised as a 'white' man, puts on a further series of disguises when he kills the Judge. First, he makes himself up in blackface (p. 194), so becoming an imitation version of the African-American he is already socially categorised as being. He then puts on a 'suit of girl's clothes' (p. 196) on top of his male attire, veiling his face as he escapes the house. Finally, in the haunted house, he burns both these sets of clothes and disguises himself as a tramp. The question of what identity *is*, how it can be propped up (by social circumstance, and by clothes, title and outward appearance), and how a false role can be distinguished from a real one, resonates through the whole novel.

This question takes us back in turn to the Siamese connection of *Those Extraordinary Twins*, and how twin can be told from twin. For, as Puddn'head Wilson says in the final court scene of *Puddn'head Wilson*: 'You have often heard of twins who were so exactly alike their own parents could not tell them apart' (p. 217). Selfhood becomes even more indefinable in the case of Siamese twins, where singularity and plurality overlap in one confused whole. The question of original and copy collapses with their (transgressive) bodily connection. In the case of this 'twin-monster' (p. 303), it is finally impossible to separate self from self. In *Puddn'head Wilson*, Wilson himself finally sorts out the identity confusion in the novel. In doing so, he ironically (for one who is represented as possessing the 'objective detachment [of] the behavioural scientist'[58]) triumphantly re-establishes the stability of a social order which the whole text has proved to be morally corrupt, and which is founded on the absolute lie of racial inferiority and difference. Twain here uses the detective genre as (through Wilson) he 'clears the world of doubles . . . [and] disposes of . . . the spectre of an open-ended world where lines do not hold between the sexes and the races'.[59] If the cover-up that occurs as Wilson puts the community order back to rights is full of holes, it nonetheless acts (partially) to suppress the more disturbing aspects of the text. For Wilson puts a lid on the deep anxieties about the relation between the individual and her or his social circumstance, and about American racial politics, that would otherwise remain openly apparent. This movement, where uncomfortable issues are raised only then to be disguised or overlooked, as we have come to recognise by now, is a standard feature of Twain's art.

V

As Twain's career progressed, so the anxieties and social criticism apparent in his work became more and more difficult to hide.

Accordingly, the gaps and cracks in his fictional constructs show more and more clearly. Thus the jagged forms of the ending of *A Connecticut Yankee*, and its climactic violence, are signals that the criticism of commonly held assumptions about American culture and the pessimistic view of history that are parts of the novel can no longer be reconciled with their thematic opposites. In *Puddn'head Wilson*, too, a whole series of fissures disturb the apparent logic and aptness of the novel's formal resolution.

This partly relates to the view of American racial history the text implies. It is now generally accepted that here (as in *Huckleberry Finn*) Twain's novel is not just about slavery but also about 'the second slavery'[60] of post-Reconstruction racial practice. Puddn'head Wilson's restoration, by means of the law, of rigid segregation, following the crisis over racial and social boundaries which has occurred, can thus be read as a bleak allegory of the events of this later period. The note of community celebration which accompanies the final cover-up of the novel (Wilson's, and Twain's, restoration of the racial status quo) is, though, questioned by the final position of both 'black' and 'white' twins. For Tom 'goes from black to white to murderer to thing that will be sold down the river';[61] while Valet is left dangling on the fringes of the community, the living symbol of the breakdown of its codes, boundaries and beliefs. The damage done to both parties in a system that depends on binary racial distinctions cannot be hidden here. That *Those Extraordinary Twins* ends with a lynching, a different but more immediate and convenient way to solve a complicated social and legal problem, is no coincidence in a period when this means of *racial* punishment and repression was dramatically on the rise.[62] Again, the fluidity of the boundaries between twinned texts becomes apparent. Twain's story points to the problems of the racial present as everything is put back into its apparently comfortable place in the fictional past.

The cover-up and closure that occurs in the last pages of *Puddn'head Wilson* raises, for the alert reader, as many questions as it solves. The novel ends as a detective story, with Wilson as the possessor of knowledge that allows him to solve the crime and Twain to close his book. The scientific techniques associated with Wilson's hobby of finger-printing allow him to unravel the tangle of identity caused by Roxy's initial act, and, at the same time, to discover the perpetrator of the Judge's murder. Twain's use of the detective genre here partly distracts from the force of his historical materials about race and slavery. For Wilson's investigations, in fact, reveal two 'crimes' at once: the *original* act by which Roxy has upset the town's *racial* order, *and* Tom's later act of murdering his 'uncle', the prompt for the immediate criminial proceedings. These two stories cannot be separated out from one another. The novel brings us back to the broad-scale nature of its racial theme even as its grounds are shifted to the punishment of one black individual for the one black crime. As in 'The Stolen White Elephant' an ironic humour operates as the detective ends up being celebrated by a community that fails to see his, or its, blindness. A similar sense of incongruity exists here, as the disruptive presence which cannot be hidden from sight (race) is entirely overlooked in the shift of focus to the puzzling out of clues that solves a particular murder mystery.

If Wilson's activity distracts from, but also (unwitttingly on his part) draws attention to the racial issue, as far as the larger question of character and self-definition goes, all his intervention does – as he sorts out who is who – is to confirm the instability of subjectivity. The *only* way Tom can be told from Valet, and Valet from Tom (and thus, implicitly, one individual from another) is by their fingerprints. In terms of the exchange that has occurred here, there is absolutely no other way of telling the two individuals apart. Identity is reduced to its basic essence, the lines on one's skin. There is no more to it than that. The idea of the self as fixed, centred and stable in an environment which it can effectively control is revealed here as patent nonsense as Twain questions the fundamentals of nineteenth-century value and belief.

I have suggested how *Puddn'head Wilson and Those Extraordinary Twins* are bound in a Siamese connection. Once this is recognised, the allegorical aspects of the text(s) gain additional resonance. Twain's move from one genre to another, from ironic 'tragedy' to farce, can be seen in terms both of an acceptance of the artistic appropriateness of the rigidities of allegory to the material of *Puddn'head Wilson*, and a counter-impulse toward the extravagant burlesque of the Siamese twins story. This is not to deny the allegorical aspects of the latter, nor the humour of *Puddn'head Wilson*, but to identify a significant tension in the writing – a difference in narrative style and attitude which, despite the symbiotic nature of the two texts, could not be bridged. The peculiar quality of the narratives lies in the lack of formal unity, the sense of incompletion and deferral, that results from their twinning. To suggest this is to see Twain on the verge of the type of artistic understanding which would only become commonplace in later, post-structuralist, times: that our representation of reality can only end in deferral and incompletion.[63]

8

The Late Works: Incompletion, Instability, Contradiction

Damnation! I said to myself, are we real creatures in a real world, all of a sudden, and have we been feeding on dreams in an imaginary one since nobody knows when – or how is it? My head was swimming.

(*The Great Dark*)[1]

I

The general critical consensus is that, with the completion of *Puddn'head Wilson and Those Extraordinary Twins*, Twain's best work was done. But that is not to say that the vast amount he wrote after 1894 (and particularly in the next twelve years[2]) is without interest. Indeed, the range and variety of his writing in this period is extraordinary. Twain published a good part of this material in his lifetime. However, much remained unfinished, or self-censored, and unpublished (or published only in bowdlerised or 'laundered' form[3]) until comparatively recently. *Which Was the Dream? and Other Symbolic Writings* and *Mark Twain's Mysterious Stranger Manuscripts* came out in 1967 and 1969 respectively.[4]

This surge of new material has prompted a re-evaluation of the final stages of Twain's career. Earlier commentary tended to concentrate on his 'slide into despair and artistic impotence'.[5] More recently, Bruce Michelson has warned against 'dividing Mark Twain's career into theater acts', and has emphasised a turbulent, resilient and liberating quality to the late texts matching that found in his earlier writing.[6] Other critics, such as Susan Gillman, Maria Ornella Marotti and David Sewell, focus particularly on Twain's unfinished narratives, especially the dream tales and the different versions of *The Mysterious Stranger*. Though taking different critical perspectives, they agree on the importance of this late work.[7] Each variously recognises that the formal incompletion of these narratives, and their strong sense of deferral, arises out of the duplications, contradictions and relativistic uncertainties, which they obsessively represent. The fragmented nature of these texts point, in Marotti's words, toward 'modern fiction, the open form, and the endless chain of signs'.[8]

I argue in my previous chapter that to read *Puddn'head Wilson and Those Extraordinary Twins* as twinned texts is already to identify a sense of deferral and incompletion in Twain's work. However, *Pudd'nhead Wilson* can still stand alone as a single text, and is brought to an end, albeit with that type of uneasy closure that is a repeated feature of Twain's narratives. The late texts I discuss in this chapter are all unfinished. Formal completion, and the masking of thematic and generic tensions this involved, just could no longer be managed by Twain. Fixed endings could not serve to seal down either the instabilities of the world he was to represent or his conflicting responses to it.

Michelson suggests that earlier critical responses to Twain's late texts were predicated on the basis that he was struggling to create 'shapely, polished' stories. His counter-reading rests instead on their creative instability, which he directly relates to the intellectual and cultural climate of a period when 'structural and thematic unities were . . . coming under unprecedented challenge as aesthetic virtues'. Marotti pursues a similar argument but goes a step further. For while Michelson sets this late work in a modernist context, she stresses, too, its links with postmodernist art. Marotti points to the 'probing of form' which intensifies in the Mark Twain Papers, the generic heterogeneity of these texts, and their thematic content, to conclude that Twain here 'anticipates both our contemporary awareness of the fragmentation of experience and some modern and postmodern literary procedures'.[9]

In my last chapter, I show how the fragmentary and open-ended forms of such narratives as *The Great Dark* (1898), *Three Thousand Years Among the Microbes* (1905) and *No. 44, The Mysterious Stranger* (1902–8), inevitably result from their thematic contradictions, generic instabilities and epistemological uncertainties. While agreeing that Twain anticipates postmodernism here, I would resist identifying him closely with that later movement. For I would argue that, though the fragmentary, repetitious and unfinished nature of these stories reflects Twain's understanding of the relation between text and world, it remains, too, a sign – and here I depart both from Michelson and Marotti – of his artistic frustrations.[10] Twain *could* not finish these texts. That is a very different matter than mounting a fully realised challenge to accepted artistic convention; and from the *deliberate* incompletions and formal ruptures of postmodernism.

II

Twain published a considerable number of finished texts after *Puddn'head Wilson and Those Extraordinary Twins*. My approach in this chapter is once more, and necessarily, highly selective. After brief comment on Twain's last travel book, *Following the Equator* (1897), I focus on two of the dream tales and just one of the *Mysterious Stranger Manuscripts*. I see here a culmination to the thematic and formal anxieties I have traced throughout Twain's career, and which are particularly apparent from *A Connecticut Yankee* onward. The return to fantasy in the late fiction provides, indeed, an important connection with this latter text.

The thematic and generic tensions in Twain's narratives increasingly threatened their artistic shape, so his turn once more to travel narrative can be seen as a temporary reprieve from such concerns. *Following the Equator: A Journey Around the World* (published in England as *More Tramps Abroad*[11]) is the record of Twain's global lecture tour, made to help pay off his debts following the voluntary bankruptcy of 1895. The travel book, as Twain practised it, was a catch-all form. He was never bound by the limits of the conventional non-fiction travelogue, but rather wandered from fact to fiction, from autobiography to history to cultural anthropology, and from burlesque and satire to philosophy and political denunciation, as he wrote. The genre suited Twain's varying artistic needs, perhaps better than any other. He travelled through countries, rather than engaging – in *Following the Equator* at least – in much dialogue with their people. As he went, he commented as he pleased on various individuals, places, aspects of culture and associations,[12] before moving his narrative, at whatever pace suited him, to the next place and topic.

The return to travel writing gave Twain the type of formal looseness that entirely suited him. However, *Following the Equator* lacks the vivacity of his earlier works in the genre. Bruce Michelson notes the fascination with death that pervades the book, and rightly suggests that it is 'not a narrative that waves its hat very much in moments of glee and broad comedy'.[13] The passivity of the narrator, his (often) marginal position in terms of the described environment, histories and events that he recounts, and the noticeable lack of detail concerning his professional activities and personal relationships, are in marked contrast to his construction as an active and fully engaged central persona in *Innocents Abroad* or *Roughing It*.

Susan Gillman links *Following the Equator* to Twain's other late texts in its use of the device of 'occult travel', and in its repeated returns to the matter of race and imperialism. She sharply illustrates how 'the logic of US racial division, based on the "one-drop" rule . . . is exploded within the context of colonial race relations', and looks at examples of Twain's 'close readings of native dress, skin, and bodies' to suggest his 'identification with otherness' here. Tracing such connections, she calls *Following the Equator* the 'companion travel narrative' of the dream tales: where the race problem, she suggests, also strongly figures.[14] I would make a different type of connection. For a sequence of incidents and anecdotes narrated in *Following the Equator*[15] foreshadows other dominating concerns and obsessive repetitions of the late fiction.

In *Following the Equator*, Twain tells a series of (often very short) stories, and uses descriptive terms, which point to his imaginative engagement with a particular set of themes that recur over and over in his writing from this time on. My examples here must necessarily be brief, but are indicative of a more general pattern. Thus Twain's description of a dream he has in Sydney, with the relativistic shifts of scale involved, reads like a close working note for *Three Thousand Years Among the Microbes*:

I dreamed that the visible universe is the physical person of God;

that the vast worlds that we see twinkling millions of miles apart in the fields of space are the blood corpuscles in His veins; and that we and the other creatures are the microbes that charge with multitudinous life the corpuscles. (p. 132)

The possibility of losing one's bearings, a constant threat in the late Twain, connects up with the startling change in perspective described here. The use of charts and maps, and their failure to match known geophysical facts, is a recurrent motif both in *Following the Equator* and the dream tales. When maps, in the former text, are set against direct perception, curious disjunctions occur. So the narrator refers to islands 'so thick on the map that one would hardly expect to find room between them for a canoe: yet we seldom glimpse one' (pp. 80–1). And in this travel book, the type of strange and unsettling events which recur throughout the late fiction take place on Twain's own reported sea journey. As his ship enters the doldrums, so a 'wobbly and drunken motion' overcomes it, and a 'total eclipse of the moon' (p. 65) follows. Exceptional and disturbing changes in the natural environment prefigure the unsettling links between geophysical and psychic disturbance in the dream tales. Descriptions of the 'eternal monotonies' (p. 66) of the voyage at sea, and, later, of a porpoise which takes (as it first appears) the 'corkscrew shape and imposing length of the fabled sea-serpent' (p. 109), are suggestive of the doomed encirclings of *The Enchanted Sea-Wilderness* and the monstrous forms of *The Great Dark* respectively.[16] Such disturbing notes are crucial to Twain's late fiction, and connect with the motif of shipwreck, or disaster at sea which became such a dominant trope there.

If the reuse of the travel genre in *Following the Equator* meant, then, a temporary release from Twain's formal problems as a writer, material in the book anticipates that in the late and unfinished fictional texts. Any attempt to divorce Twain's fictional and non-fictional writing too firmly, or to insist on too rigid a definition of the latter term, cannot be sustained. Biographical detail (Twain's journey round the world in financial disarray; the emotional bombshell of Susy's death from meningitis before his return to America), late nineteenth-century cultural anxieties (about race, technology, knowledge and the status of the self), the travel book he wrote, and the unfinished fictions he would produce, are all bound together in one interrelated whole.

III

In the dream tales and the *Mysterious Stranger Manuscripts*, Twain, as was his normal practice, mixes genres within the same text. Thus *The Great Dark* includes elements of farce, as the invisible Superintendent of Dreams playfully empties and refills the mate's cup of coffee to the latter's consternation: 'I'm dumm'd if *I* recollect drinking that' (p. 115). The story later, however – at least, in the notes Twain made toward a conclusion – turns to tragedy:

> The sea begins to dry up. . . . Capt. & Edwards & others take several days' provisions & walk overland. Arrive too late. All hands dead. They carried the mummied bodies (aged 16 and 25) back to their ship. Too late again. All dead – & he was going to ask forgiveness of her and Jessie. Looks up – is at home – his wife & the children coming to say goodnight. His hair is white.[17]

The narrative shifts between science fiction and fantasy, as Edwards's account of the scientific experiment that reveals a whole ocean in a drop of water is replaced by his shipboard life on that same strange sea.[18] It moves, too, between sentimentalism, with its focus on home and family, and horror story, with the threat of the colossal squid and other 'uncanny brutes' (p. 111). Michelson talks of a 'delight in subverting the ground rules for literary art'[19] running through Twain's whole artistic career, but that does not quite explain what is happening here. The formal choices and instabilities of the late work are inseparable from their *incomplete* status. Twain ends up caught between genres and ideas, unable to finish his texts. His formal frames can no longer accommodate an artistic vision which is marked by a dizzying relativism, and which moves in unreconcilable and contradictory directions. The fragmentation of this work is a measure of Twain's thinking about the nature of identity, the direction of history and the foundations of knowledge. Formal incompletion and thematic instability are the necessary correlatives of his doubts, ambivalences and hesitations on these subjects.

The dream tales and the *Mysterious Stranger Manuscripts* tell, in part, an unfinished story of anxieties about subjectivity and of epistemological uncertainty. Twain's return to fantasy as a genre –

for all the texts I now discuss are fantastic, or contain elements of fantasy[20] – is, accordingly, highly significant. Fantasy's function as a reminder of 'all that has been silenced in the name of establishing a normative bourgeois realism'[21] is particularly relevant. For one of the things Twain does, in these late tales, is to explode with renewed force conventional realist assumptions of the stable, centred and autonomous self.

Rosemary Jackson links the idea of the stable self to the seeing eye. Implicit in the ability to see clearly, and the sense of control that accompanies the eye's dominance over a perceptual field, is that sense of authority and comprehension associated with the sovereign subject. From such a perspective '"I see" [is] synonymous with "I understand". Knowledge, comprehension, reason, are established through the power of the *look*, through the "*eye*" and the "*I*" of the human subject.' Accordingly, so Jackson suggests, the loss of the sense of visual control is a sign of deep uncertainty about identity, the authority of the self, and the relation between self and world. 'Many Victorian fantasies', she writes, 'employ the device of a lens or mirror to introduce an indeterminate area where distortions and deformations of "normal" perception become the norm.'[22]

The use of the microscope in *The Great Dark* has just such a function. Henry Edwards changes from a spectating subject, using the increasingly powerful lenses of his scientific tool to open up the mysteries of nature, to 'observed object'.[23] In the transformation that occurs, he finds himself, and the ship in which he travels, a specimen on the microscope slide. He is still in charge of the narrative he writes but of little else, and, in his change of role and status, he is thrown increasingly off balance. In this other world, 'there ain't any *sun* [and] there *ain't* any . . . moon' (p. 120), and the sky is 'solid black' (p. 119). Vision, beyond the lamps on board ship and the phosphorescence of the sea spray, is 'dimmed to obliteration' (p. 106). The loss of sight is matched by a loss of geographical bearings on the part of the narrating subject and his companions. Compass readings fail completely to match the boat's expected location, thus the mate, for instance, reports that 'the Gulf Stream's gone to the devil!' (p. 118).

The collapse of knowledge and the loss of bearings signify, in line with Jackson's analysis, a slipping sense of authority and identity. Bruce Michelson expresses this very nicely, and suggests the larger implications of the tale, in describing Edwards and his wife as:

middle-class American everybodies and nobodies, distinguished only for their bad luck in losing track of who and where they are. . . . In other words this is a story in which nonpeople from nowhere [typecast fictional characters who come from Springport, a non-existent American town] get lost between realities . . . in an endless nowhere, a nonworld where Pirandello and Stoppard might feel right at home.[24]

Interestingly, though, and in line with other Twain texts at the time, this sense of slipping identity has a double focus to it. For Twain's representations of uncertain subjectivity look in two directions, both outward to the surrounding world, and inward to the psyche. Edwards loses track of things. He finds himself, as middle-class American type, at the absolute mercy of circumstances of which he has no knowledge and which he cannot control. His role, then, is paradigmatic, suggesting Twain's anxieties concerning the status of the subject in a disorienting and unknowable world. But Edwards is also a divided self. In line with his understanding of 'the new psychology of the unconscious', Twain introduces the figure of the Superintendent of Dreams into his story to indicate that the subject is split internally between a dream self and waking self. He then suggests that to insist on the primacy of the waking self is not necessarily an accurate reflection of the way things are.[25] So, according to a holograph note, the Superintendent of Dreams would claim the 'S[uperintendent] of R[ealities]' (p. 131) as his real name, while the life Edwards apparently dreams on shipboard becomes more convincing than his supposedly real prior life (p. 139).

A similar concern with identity loss and self-division also haunts *Three Thousand Years Among the Microbes* and *No. 44, The Mysterious Stranger*. The narrator of the former text, Huck (a diminutive of Huxley[26]), has been transformed by a magician into a cholera germ. He now lives in the bloodstream of Blitzowski, an 'incredibly dirty [and] unspeakably profane' Hungarian-American tramp, whose 'body is a sewer' (p. 436). The value of the individual subject is implicitly mocked in several ways as this (fantastic) change of scale occurs. Blitzowski's name and status contain a veiled reference to contemporary American fears about immigration. A further reminder of this historical context is also present in the description of Huck's own instant naturalisation in his new home: 'I was become intensely, passionately, cholera-germanic; indeed, I outnatived the natives themselves' (p. 435). The allusion to the 'swarming nations of all the different kinds of germ-vermin' (p. 436) that inhabit Blitzowski's body has a double effect. It acts as a reminder that, for many native-born Americans, the new immigrant 'other' (from Eastern Europe) was seen as an alien and proliferating foreign 'germ', lacking any individual identity in its mass infection of the American social body.[27] It also, though, relativises such a perspective in the detached view given of the *universal* body. For, from outside that Blitzowskian cosmos (the narrator's original position), the inhabitants of the host country he will enter lack just as much individualisation as those who would 'invade' them. They are *all*, indeed, 'germ-vermin'.

The destabilising relativism of the narrative, introduced through the use of fantasy, thus provides a way of critiquing both nationalist xenophobia and conventional views of the self as 'unique, distinguishable, irreplaceable'.[28] The microbic world is represented throughout as a microcosmic version of the human one. This opens the way for satire as, for example, the conventional Christian belief that '*all* of God's creatures are included in his Merciful scheme of salvation' (p. 497) is translated to a microbe context. Its effect is both to question the assumed self-importance of the individual human being in the divine scheme of things, and the related sense of the preciousness of distinct identity. Such satiric play continues as Huck claims that American scientists, in their 'torturing' of microbes on microscope slides, commit 'germicide', going on to say that 'there is no moral difference between a germicide and a homicide . . . not even a germ falls to the ground unnoticed' (p. 504).

The interrogation of the idea of stable and autonomous individualism takes a further turn when Huck reveals that, seen from a microbe perspective, all things are alive. Even an atom, he reveals, has 'a certain degree of consciousness [and] a *character*, a character of its own' (p. 448). Death itself does not exist. Rather the molecules which compose living bodies scatter to 'take up new quarters' elsewhere, in 'hundreds of plants and animals'. A complete decentring and radical collapse of the sense of consistent and coherent identity and consciousness occurs here. For as Huck says:

What would become of me if [Blitzowski] should disintegrate? My molecules would scatter all around . . . but where should *I* be?. . . . There would be no more me. . . . I should still be alive, intensely alive, but so scattered that I would not know it. (p. 458)

At this point, Twain's ongoing anxieties about identity reach a climax in the epiphanic vision of subjectivity dissolved into a fluid and boundary-less amorphousness.

No. 44, The Mysterious Stranger, like The Great Dark, throws a double focus on the problem of identity. For August Feldner, the sixteen-year-old apprentice printer and narrator, is divided without and within. The description of his two selves acts to suggest both the subjection of the body to the imprint of historical circumstance (in the allegory of modernisation that is implied), and the split nature of the psyche. For August, and all his fellow printers, have duplicates of themselves brought into being by the young stranger who bears the strange name, No. 44, New Series 864,962.[29] These 'exact reproduction[s]' (p. 305) are a 'flesh and bone' (p. 315) version of 'invisibles'[30] conjured up previously by No. 44 to provide labour when a strike brings the printing works to a standstill. The invisibles then function as more efficient and automatic versions of the original human workforce:

> there before our eyes the press was whirling out printed sheets faster than a person could count them – just *snowing* them onto the pile, as you may say – yet *there wasn't a human creature in sight anywhere!*. . . . When *they* did a thing, they did it right . . . and it hadn't any occasion to be corrected. (pp. 281–2)

This reads like a description of a successful version of the Paige typesetter in which Twain had sunk so much wasted money.

Human forms (the duplicates) of abnormal strength (p. 291), however, replace these invisibles. As this happens, and as the 'original' strikers plan to murder their doubles (p. 387), so an interpretation of such duplication in terms of contemporary anxieties about the status of the subject in a Taylorised work force is prompted. This, in turn, takes us back to Twain's earlier representations of this theme in A Connecticut Yankee and The American Claimant.[31] To read this part of No. 44, The Mysterious Stranger in this way is to see the original workers – with all their inefficiencies, human weaknesses and disruptive economic potential[32] – faced with the threat of conversion into components of a smooth and efficient industrial system, where personal visibility or invisibility is scarcely to the point. But if one can see the duplicates in terms of Twain's concern with the processes of American social and industrial history, there is an alternative and opposite reading contained in the text. For the division in the subject represented here is internal as well as external. August's other duplicate self is, in fact, part of his single first self. When August speaks of the shock he receives 'every time I met myself unexpectedly' (p. 311), that shock comes to signal recognition of internal self-division.[33] For August discovers that his duplicate, Emil Schwartz, is in fact the dream self that has always lived 'Box and Cox lodgers in the one chamber' (p. 343) with his waking self. Only with No. 44's fleshing forth of this duplicate into the waking world has contact between the two selves become any more than hazy.[34] The dream self is, it turns out, far imaginatively superior to the waking self: 'he had all the intensities one suffers or enjoys in a dream!' (p. 344). Twain works his way out of the problems such self-divisions represent for the completion of his narrative by exploding them, together with all that remains of the conventional notion of selfhood, at the end of the manuscript as it stands. Here, No. 44 declares both himself and the universe a dream: a creation of the imagination, of the pure 'thought' of which Feldner is comprised (pp. 404–5). Though the logic of these various interrelationships is problematic, it is clear that Twain's concern with the psychology and composition of the individual subject has taken a sharp turn away here from the social and historical resonance with which the notion of the double is also (previously) invested. The fact that the narrative is unfinished, or part finished, suggests that the different components of the fiction cannot satisfactorily be brought together; that the contradictions in Twain's art can no longer be formally contained.

IV

The fantastic elements of the dream tales and *No. 44, The Mysterious Stranger* disrupt any normative version of centred and coherent subjectivity. They act too, however, to rupture the 'ground rules'[35] by which we conventionally frame and order our world. The displacements and 'disturbing transformation[s]' of Twain's late fantasies undermine what is homely, familiar and 'comfortably "known"', replacing them with a spiralling relativism, where uncertainty and disorder ('areas normally kept out of sight') predominate.[36] The challenge posed to any firm knowledge of 'reality' in these late texts runs hand in hand with a narrative technique which is similarly disconcerting, and to the same ends. A disorienting epistemological uncertainty permeates the late work. This is suggested in the number of times a statement like 'It makes me dizzy; I don't know quite where I am' is echoed by words and phrases connoting acute confusion and estrangement: 'uncanny', 'uncharted', 'dizzy', 'my head was swimming', 'dazed' and 'a good deal jumbled up'.[37] The sense of the ground being removed from under both Twain's characters' and his readers' feet commences in *The Great Dark* with the transformation of the narrator from the scientific controller of a miniature world to a disoriented participant in the uncanny and nightmare sea-scape the lens of his microscope reveals. Then, in the 'Mad Passenger' extract, written as part of the same story, Edwards' children find a microscope in this fellow voyager's shipboard locker. Edwards undergoes a dream-like sense of recall as he watches the Mad Passenger 'put a drop of water on a glass slide', and the children 'exclaiming over the hideous animals they saw darting about and fighting in the bit of moisture'.[38]

A sense of boundless repetition, and an undercutting of any sense of firm narrative and epistemological ground and level occurs here. This latter becomes even more overt in the dialogues concerning the comparative status of shipboard life and the domestic life which (for Edwards, and in the narrative) preceded it. For Edwards starts to loses his hold on which life is dream and which reality. First, the Superintendent of Dreams, on board ship, questions and reverses his assumptions on this matter: 'And this is *real* life. Your other life was the dream!' (p. 124). Then his own wife says that the shared (other) family life they both recall took place in 'dream-homes, not real ones' (p. 130). Finally, Edwards himself starts to recover memories of an earlier shipboard existence. The extreme nature of the uncertainty introduced into this story is evident in the way that the wife's assertion that life on board ship is their joint reality is positioned. For it is given as part of an inner narrative (the sea journey) placed *within* two outer frames. And the first of these two framing statements, which describe and apparently validate –

in their earlier turn – the reality of those events which have occurred in the family *prior* to their fantastic transformation, is also made by her. Edwards' wife, then, validates *both* (unreconcilable) realities.

The text is full too of other destabilising effects. The Superintendent of Dreams has a curious indeterminate status in terms of the two worlds described. The narrator's own acts of writing appear to transgress any clear boundary between the different levels of narrative. And the story itself is incomplete. All these together make Edwards' comment, 'we seldom really know the things we think we know' (p. 125), resonate uncontrollably. The sense of any absolute authority over, or firm knowledge of, experience, and of the ability to represent it in any transparent or straightforward narrative form, disintegrates in the course of the inconclusive and fragmented story.

A similar sense of epistemological uncertainty and narrative incompletion pervades *Three Thousand Years Among the Microbes*. A spiralling sense of cosmic relativism is first prepared for, with the Darwinism of the microbe world – the satire at this point clearly pertains to late nineteenth-century social realities – where the Nobles munch on the SBEs (Soiled-Bread Eaters) and, when the chance is given, the reverse occurs too (p. 512). The chain of eaters and eaten, victimisers and victims, in the natural and social economy that this introduces, is then widened as the narrator, speaking to Franklin, a Yellow Fever germ, undercuts Franklin's providential sense of self-importance with his own knowledge that '[Franklin] and all the swarming billions of his race' were, in complete ignorance, 'gnawing, torturing, defiling, rotting, and murdering a fellow-creature', the tramp, Blitowski. He then continues, to suggest the further implications of this:

> It hints at the possibility that the procession of known and listed devourers and persecutors is not complete. It suggests the possibility, and substantially the certainty, that man is himself a microbe, and his globe a blood-corpuscle drifting with its shining brethren of the Milky Way down a vein of the Master and maker of all things . . . (p. 454)

A mind-stretching relativism develops here, as the initial shift in scale, from human to microbe, prompts the vision of a groundless sequence stretching from the Universal body of God down through layers of infestation to, and implicitly beyond, the 'infinitely microscopic microbes that infest *microbes*' (p. 513).

The loss of centre that such relativism signifies is reinforced by the multi-levelled and inconclusive quality of *Three Thousand Years Among the Microbes*'s narrative form. A kind of double translation appears to take place, as the narrator first writes in 'microbe tongue', then 'laboriously translate[s] it into English' (p. 461). The two framing prefaces further complicate things. For in the first, 'Mark Twain' says that he himself 'translated [the story] from the Original Microbic' (p. 433). In the second, and more consistently,[39] he claims only to have further 'translated the author's style and construction'. He also, however, comments to disorienting effect that the original 'title-page is incorrect' (p. 434). The inside main story is then told from a number of perspectives. So Huck, at one stage, recounts his experience, only to interrupt himself with a later comment on his text. He then interrupts his first interruption to note, from a later perspective still, the inaccuracy of the information he has just added (pp. 439–41). Asterisks, added notes and apparently independent textual fragments ('xxxxx. But really no one was to blame, it was an accident' – p. 43) heighten the sense of dislocation and textual instability. The narrative concludes suddenly with Huck, apparently absorbed in the Blitzowski present, dazzled by the 'incredible wealth' he hopes to mine there (from a gold tooth). The problem of how to reconcile the various levels and voices of the text, and how satisfactorily to end it, is left – one suspects necessarily – unresolved.

The conventional ground rules by which we 'know reality' are also turned topsy-turvy in *No. 44, The Mysterious Stranger*. No. 44 represents the spirit of exuberant play and imagination. He can be seen to stand in self-reflexive relation to Twain himself: a liberating figure who by the means of his artistic imaginings can escape and subvert conventional belief systems and restrictions.[40] If playfulness undermines all normal constraints here, however, it can never be brought into any kind of balanced relationship with the social and historical world it disrupts. To focus just on No. 44's actions, however – for it is these that provide the mainspring of the text – is to see the usual ways of ordering the world completely undermined. Thus No. 44 transcends space and time, for his race is not limited by their rules (p. 331). Accordingly, he brings August canvas-back duck to eat from America, a country not yet discovered

(p. 313), and can transport him, in the instant, to China (p. 399). The human race, to No. 44, is indistinguishable from the 'other bugs' (pp. 319–20), and he reveals to August that the various ways it conducts itself, and socially and morally orders its world, are completely ridiculous.[41]

No. 44 is a boisterous jokester who upsets the frameworks and systems by which those around him pattern their lives, and mocks their rules and customs. He takes human time and history and reverses and rearranges them. He even replays conversations backwards, radically disorienting both August and the reader as he does so (pp. 397–8). August assumes a pious demeanour, in line with his religious beliefs, to pray for the soul of No. 44 when the latter professes his indifference to religion. He is, though, ignored completely, as No. 44 entertains himself, spinning about in the air, making gay and vibrant music with a jew's harp, and whooping with joy as he does so (pp. 298–9).[42] Equally, when Father Adolf invokes divine power against him, No. 44's only response is to indulge in what August calls 'coarse and vulgar horse-play' (pp. 328–9). As Bruce Michelson says, a 'kind of vertigo' affects the reader as the narrative proceeds. For not only does No. 44 playfully upset time, space, history and religion, he undermines confidence in language itself, and its expressive abilities (pp. 318–19); throws the difference between dream and reality, self and world, in doubt. And if everything No. 44 does disorients in one way or another, so does the entire narrative when read as Twain left it. For the story as it stands is marked both by contradiction – between solipsism and historical engagement – and by disjunctive shifts in tone, as satire, deterministic pessimism and (No. 44's) celebratory comic performance each are (separately) introduced. The reader is left 'with every structural and thematic rug pulled out from under'[43] her or his feet. The incomplete quality of the text is a logical result of its internal tensions and vertiginous effects.

V

Fantasy works to produce a form of readerly hesitation as the borders between reality and the unfamiliar or uncanny are blurred. The dislocation that occurs acts to deny the solidity of what is normally taken to be real.[44] But fantasy is not normally associated with textual incompletion and fragmentation. The spiralling relativisms and disturbing vacuums (the self 'alone in shoreless space'[45]) of Twain's late work in this mode problematise any sense of narrative completion. The conventional device of fantasy is to move the central protagonist between two adjacent worlds: as happens, for instance, in *A Connecticut Yankee*. In his late manuscripts, Twain complicates and extends his use of the mode. He denies the centred subjectivity of his characters in exposing the internal divisions that compose the self. Further destabilisation occurs in the final loss of any kind of firm ground. For his protagonists are unmoored, either left with no sense of solid reality at all, or caught between worlds and unable to tell which is real; which has authority over which. All frameworks of knowledge and belief are shown to be arbitrary and untrustworthy. Any sense of narrative resolution or final closure consequently becomes impossible.

This, though, is not quite all. For the sense of internal contradiction and paradox present in all Twain's work to one degree or another becomes, in these late works, overt. Opposed thematic impulses drive these fictions, and no straightforward narrative closure can overcome such inbuilt divisions. So Twain's exploration of individual psychology cuts against his social and historical interests. The focus on the split subject, the dream and waking self, in *The Great Dark* cannot ultimately be thematically reconciled with the allegorical concern with late nineteenth-century science and technology in the same text: the exploration of the 'demonic nature of crossing limits' which the initial use of the microscope introduces.[46] Similarly in *No. 44, The Mysterious Stranger*, the manuscript ends in solipsism; an escape from reality by using the imagination to extinguish it, 'transforming it into a fiction'.[47] But this is desperately at odds with the socio-historical interest in technology and duplication, and the continued anxiety about current events, racial issues and (other) social injustices, that – at times, subliminally, at others, overtly – informs the text.[48] The gap between these two aspects of the narrative is clear as specific references to contemporary occurrence (the Russo-Japanese war, for example, p. 393), and the historical procession described in the penultimate chapter, give way, in a sudden wave of the hand, to the vision of 'an empty and silent world' (p. 403). The structure of dream and the engagement with history are incompatible with one another here, in terms of a coherent narrative.[49]

Thus Twain's continued artistic involvement with, and satiric comment on, late nineteenth-century social and political history stands in contradictory relationship with his impulse to celebrate the creative self-sufficiency of the individual imagination: 'Dream other dreams, and better!' (p. 404). Likewise, the cool detachment and deterministic philosophy that is such a strong element in these late works cannot be reconciled with the 'moral indignation' that continued to motivate their author, and to influence him as he wrote.[50] Something of this contradiction comes across in the moves between satire and comic relativism in *Three Thousand Years Among the Microbes*. In modern forms of black humour, any faith in satire as an instrument of reform is suspended in favour of a comic acceptance of the absurd: that all values are relative, and that humour lies in seeing the joke in the human situation rather than attempting to remedy it.[51] Much of Twain's late work can be placed in this category. The switch in perspective that sees man's 'mission' and 'reason for existing' in providing 'a home and nourishment' for the microbe and bacillus (pp. 447–8) engages just such comic play. The subjective nature of knowledge and belief – 'truth [as] the concoction of the subjective mind'[52] – is also the target of such humour. Thus the narrator's certainties about his previous life and universe are 'dubbed an illusion,' and met with expansive laughter, by the 'able minds' of his microbe friends (p. 492). The conclusion Huck draws from this difference in perception, with each party convinced of its own rationality, is that 'there isn't anybody that isn't right, I don't care what the subject is. It comes of our having reasoning powers' (p. 495). Black humour depends on such relativistic uncertainty as this. It envelops *Three Thousand Years Among the Microbes*, with the relationships and analogies between the worlds of microbes and men on which it plays.

But humour is also used as a satiric weapon in the text. America is satirised in the name given its Blitzowskian equivalent, 'Getrichquick'. Its imperialist policies in the Phillipines are comically savaged in the account given of 'Benevolent Assimilation': the ingenious territorial gain of the 'collection of mud islets inhabited by those harmless bacilli which are the food of the fierce *hispaniola sataniensis*' (pp. 442–3).[53] The textual juxtaposition of remarks about the English monarchy with the account of the long-ruling Pus family of Henryland works to similar satiric effect. Thus Henryland's colonial practices are described, with obvious but none the less apt wit, as the spreading of 'pus and civilisation' (pp. 438–9). Indeed, in *Three Thousand Years Among the Microbes*, Twain aims his comic barbs at a whole range of nineteenth-century practices and institutions. Such satire, based, as it finally is, on the desire for reform, sits uneasily with the comic and cosmic relativism beside it.

Twain, then, was caught between themes and philosophies as he wrote these late texts. Given this, their fragmentary and incomplete nature is no great surprise. In *No. 44, The Mysterious Stranger*, Schwartz, August's dream self, pleads for freedom from 'these bonds of flesh – this decaying vile matter' (p. 369), the human body to which he has become tied. He describes the shape-shiftings and transcendences of 'spirit[s] of air' like him:

> *We* have no morals; the angels have none; morals are for the impure; we have no principles, those chains are for men. . . . We have no character, no *one* character, we have *all* characters. . . . We wear no chains . . . we have no home, no prison, the universe is our province; we do not know time, we do not know space . . . our playgrounds are the constellations and the Milky Way.
>
> (p. 370)

In this dream version of the human self, Twain's imagination works itself free of all the conditioning influences that chain August and his other human protagonists. But the gap between this dream ideal (brought to life in the figure of No. 44) and everyday human realities cannot be closed. In this, it refigures the impossibility of reconciling in one text the 'self-enclosed mental world'[54] of the novel's provisional ending with the external realities of history, time and social being which are there cast aside.

The dream sprite, Schwartz, can scarcely communicate his experiences to August, his 'flesh-brother' and 'Waking-Self'. For to try to do so 'was like "emptying rainbows down a rat-hole"' (p. 378). Twain's late work leaves his reader between incompatible realities, surreally stranded (as the above quote indicates) between transcendent vision and the mundane. To read *No. 44, The Mysterious Stranger* alongside the dream tales is to find Twain still writing extraordinary and interesting narratives, but narratives that cannot be closed or completed. He is artistically trapped here between relativistic black humour and satiric critique; between spinning personal and epistemological disorientation and the desire for community, home and known; between cacophony and incomprehensibility, and a belief in the power of language and communication;[55] between psychology and history; and between a belief in the agency of the subject[56] and a mechanical determinism that undermines the concept of the self as a meaningful category. A separate stress on the divisions within the self also calls coherent subjectivity into question.

There is, of course, much more to the late Twain than the particular works I study here.[57] The divisions, fragments and incompletions of these texts, however, seem an apt conclusion to his writing career. Their inconclusive and anxiously repetitive explorations of individual and social identity, of history and of the status of knowledge, are the end of a long artistic process, with Twain's forms proving increasingly unable to satisfactorily contain his divergent and complex themes. If the fragmentation of these works, moreover, anticipates some aspects of modernist and postmodernist literary practice, it also diverges crucially from them. Twain's formal experiments and incompletions do provide a way artistically to represent his developing understanding of self and world, but he does not produce *finished* texts. Their ragged edges are not formally shaped, there by deliberate choice, but act to signal paradox, contradiction and the artist's *inability* to complete. They are, though, no less valuable for that. To do much more was, one might indeed argue, near to impossible[58] for one writing at the time.

There is a statement attributed to Twain at a school prize-giving, when – so the story goes – he presented a boy with a large Webster's dictionary: 'This is a very interesting and useful book, my son. . . . I have studied it often, but I never could discover the plot.'[59] Whether apocryphal or not, the anecdote provides a suitable note on which to conclude. Twain's study of human behaviour, of philosophy and of socio-historical conditions was finally to leave him, not exactly plotless, but caught between plots; unable formally to contain the spiralling complexities of his vision. The manuscript of *The Great Dark* ends with the ship's captain saying, 'We haven't had an observation for four months, but we are going ahead, and do our best to fetch up somewhere' (p. 150). The words might stand for Twain at his career end, still writing, not quite sure of his direction, left with unfinished manuscripts, but fetching up, despite, as one of the most productive, important and interesting writers of his time.

Notes

Chapter 1 Keeping Both Eyes Open: 'The Stolen White Elephant'

1. Mark Twain, 'The Stolen White Elephant' in *The Stolen White Elephant Etc.* (London: Chatto and Windus, 1897 [1882]) p. 24. Page references to follow quotes hereafter. Twain originally wrote 'The Stolen White Elephant' in November or December 1878, intending it to be part of *A Tramp Abroad*. See James D. Wilson, *A Reader's Guide to the Short Stories of Mark Twain* (Boston, Mass.: G. K. Hall, 1987) p. 247. A version of this, my present, chapter appears in *Studies in American Humor*, new series 3, no. 2 (1995). I am grateful to the American Humor Association for permission to reprint.

2. There is extended critical commentary on Samuel Clemens's use of his pen name, Mark Twain (which he adopted in 1862). For a summary, see R. Kent Rasmussen's *Mark Twain A to Z: The Essential Reference to His Life and Writings* (New York: Facts on File, 1995) pp. 188–9, 303. Recent critics tend to use Twain when speaking of the writer's persona and Clemens as the historical person. For reasons suggested in chapters 2 and 3, I use the former name throughout.

3. Limits of space prevent me analysing this other important story too. But see my 'Caught on the Hop: Interpretive Dislocation in "The Notorious Jumping Frog of Calaveras County"', *Thalia: Studies in Literary Humor*, vol. 15, nos. 1 and 2 (1995) pp. 33–49.

4. The term is borrowed from Gerald Mast's comment on the films of Buster Keaton, and is quoted in Marcel Gutwirth, *Laughing Matter: An Essay on the Comic* (Ithaca, NY: Cornell University Press, 1993) p. 157. I use Gutwirth's book extensively as my theoretical model here, and acknowledge my debt to him.

5. Gutwirth uses this term 'frustrated expectation' in his description of the comic. He links it with another phrase which is particularly provocative once applied to Twain's comic work: a '[rupture] in determinism'. See *Laughing Matter*, pp. 91–3.

6. My move from first-person singular to plural, and the related identification between first- and third-person 'reader', indicates that, in reconstructing the reader's role, I let my own response stand as

representative. For my recognition of the problems involved in such a tactic see the chapter on 'The Dynamics of Reading: *A Lost Lady*' in my *New Readings of the American Novel: Narrative Theory and its Application* (Basingstoke: Macmillan, 1990) pp. 130–61.

7. I reapply the phrase Gutwirth uses to discuss Samuel Beckett's *Waiting for Godot*. See *Laughing Matter*, p. 184. The appropriateness of the implied analogy will emerge later in the chapter.

8. James D. Wilson, *A Reader's Guide to the Short Stories of Mark Twain*, p. 248

9. Twain's own acquaintance with Barnum is noted in Robert Pack Browning, Michael B. Frank and Lin Salamo (eds), *Mark Twain's Notebooks & Journals: Volume III (1883–1891)* (Berkeley: University of California Press, 1979) p. 547. Twain's fictional elephant has, as it happens, the same name as had 'Barnum's celebrated British acquisition, "Jumbo" . . . [which] arrived from London on 9 April 1882'. See Frederick Anderson, Lin Salamo and Bernard L. Stein (eds), *Mark Twain's Notebooks & Journals: Volume II (1877–1883)* (Berkeley: University of California Press, 1975) p. 509. Twain, however, originally wrote his story three and a half years earlier.

10. Susan Gillman, *Dark Twins: Imposture and Identity in Mark Twain's America* (Chicago: University of Chicago Press, 1989) pp. 14–15.

11. Forrest G. Robinson, '"Seeing the Elephant": Some Perspectives on Mark Twain's *Roughing It*', *American Studies*, vol. 21, no. 2 (Fall 1980) pp. 55–6.

12. Marcel Gutwirth, *Laughing Matter*, p. 91.

13. Susan Gillman, *Dark Twins*, p. 22. See too my 'Caught on the Hop'.

14. The fact that the several story frames given are *all* part of the same fictional representation to a degree problematises the making of such distinctions. My repeated use of the words 'seem' and 'appear' suggests, too, the difficulty of any definitive reading of a text which operates as hoax; where the line between deception and the hiding of deception is always marked as problematic. So often in Twain, we cannot be sure who is hoodwinking whom, nor on quite what level we are meant to be reading and responding.

15. Quoted in Marcel Gutwirth, *Laughing Matter*, p. 105.

16. Marcel Gutwirth, *Laughing Matter*, p. 99.

17. Alternatively, or additionally, once we realise that the story does not work satisfactorily as a conventional hoax, we may look for another narrative or allegory which will allow us to make more sense of it. My following sections illustrate what happens when we do this.

18. Marcel Gutwirth, *Laughing Matter*, p. 80.

19. In his valuable study of the sources of Twain's story, 'Of Detectives and Their Derring-Do: The Genesis of Mark Twain's "The Stolen White Elephant"' (*Studies in American Humor*, vol. 2, January 1976, pp. 183–95), Howard G. Baetzhold describes how it had its specific base in the Alexander T. Stewart grave-robbery case of 1878. Twain's contemporary audience would have been aware of the theft of the corpse of the wealthy dry-goods merchant (from St Mark's churchyard

in New York City) on 7 November 1878, and the absurdities of the investigation that followed. Despite reports of a ransom paid and of the recovery of the corpse (in 1880), there still remains some question as to whether the body was in fact ever returned: see Baetzhold, pp. 188–9. Twain's story thus operates first and foremost as burlesque: 'When the detectives were nosing around after Stewart's loud remains, I threw a chapter into [*A Tramp Abroad*] in which I have very extravagantly burlesqued the detective business – if it *is* possible to burlesque that business extravagantly' (*Mark Twain–Howells Letters*, quoted in Baetzhold, p. 184). The 'loudness' of these remains and the 'nosing around' of detectives after a body in a state of two and a half years' decomposition – which rendered it, in the words of the police inspector, Dilks, in charge of the case, 'so offensive that [it] cannot be concealed' (Baetzhold, pp. 186–7) – clearly parallel Twain's depiction of the comic nature of the elephant–detective relationship in his story.

20. Twain's use of foreign names for comic ends indicates his attraction to common forms of ethnocentric humour. See my 'Racial and Colonial Discourse in Mark Twain's *Following the Equator*', in *Essays in Arts and Sciences*, vol. 22 (October 1993) pp. 67–83. The nub of Twain's joke here, however, lies in the reductive move from the formal complexity of the long, ornate and polysyllabic Indian name to the most common and mundane of elephant nicknames. This is a common technique in Twain's comic armoury – that sudden overturning of expectation; the deflationary shift from one level of discourse to another (so-called 'lower' and vernacular) level.

21. Marcel Gutwirth, *Laughing Matter*, p. 85.

22. Marcel Gutwirth, *Laughing Matter*, pp. 97–8.

23. Meanwhile, Blunt may well be playing a double game as he apparently 'cons' the narrator out of $142,000 (the lack of certainty here is a product of Twain's use of the first-person voice).

24. Marcel Gutwirth, *Laughing Matter*, pp. 55, 107.

25. The notion of an allegorical reading of the white elephant tempts further speculation on a possible relationship between this story and Herman Melville's *Moby Dick*. The relation between white whale and white elephant and what each signifies (or *fails* to signify), between the detective (the representative of a secular society, on the trail of the animal for the monetary reward it will bring) and Ahab (whose quest is more of a 'sacred', spiritual and metaphysical, kind), and between the use of tragedy and comedy in the two texts, deserves more extended treatment than I can give it here. The thought of Melville as a literary father figure to this narrative is an intriguing one. The connection with Edgar Allan Poe, and his use of the hidden and the obvious in 'The Purloined Letter', is also worth pursuing.

26. See Marcel Gutwirth, *Laughing Matter*, pp. 50–1, 58, 57.

27. Marcel Gutwirth, *Laughing Matter*, p. 29. This is just one of the series of approaches to the analysis of humour that Gutwirth discusses.

28. Mark Twain, *The Mysterious Stranger*, ed. William M. Gibson (Berkeley: University of California Press, 1969) p. 166.

29. Marcel Gutwirth, *Laughing Matter*, pp. 57, 66
30. See Michael Denning, *Mechanic Accents: Dime Novels and Working-Class Culture in America* (London and New York: Verso, 1987) pp. 118–48. Denning describes both how dime novelists quickly capitalised on the Molly Maguires case and, in relation to this, how the figure of the detective became a common one in American popular fiction of the 1870s and 1880s. There are clear allusions both to the Pinkertons and to detective fiction as a popular genre in Twain's story (and to the two combined, for Allan Pinkerton's fictionalised versions of the cases involving his 'National Detective Agency' were to appear from 1874 onward). The 'wide-staring eye' and the 'WE NEVER SLEEP' legend of the detective badge 'printed in gold on the back of popular novels' ('The Stolen White Elephant' – p. 23) is, as Howard G. Baetzhold points out, that which 'grace[d] the spines – and covers – of Pinkerton's books'. 'What seems to have irked [Twain] most', he continues, 'was the assumption of infallibility implied in the badge and motto, and in Pinkerton's books themselves.' See 'Of Detectives and their Derring-Do', p. 192.
31. See Paul Smith, *A Reader's Guide to the Short Stories of Ernest Hemingway* (Boston, Mass.: G. K. Hall, 1989) p. 208, and Richard Godden, *Fictions of Capital: The American Novel from James to Mailer* (Cambridge: Cambridge University Press, 1990) p. 67. Both refer to Ernest Hemingway's story 'Hills Like White Elephants', a later American narrative which operates round the divergent meanings of the latter term.
32. Though, at the same time, we are aware that part of Twain's joke lies at a simpler level; precisely in the making literal of a figure of speech (something which dreams often do) and the comic move between conceptual boundaries (the real and the surreal) which then follows.
33. Marcel Gutwirth, *Laughing Matter*, pp. 98–9.
34. Marcel Gutwirth, *Laughing Matter*, pp. 108, 99.
35. Marcel Gutwirth, *Laughing Matter*, p. 108 (my emphasis).
36. As my reading of 'Jim Smiley and His Jumping Frog' would confirm (see note 3 above).
37. See Justin Kaplan, *Mr. Clemens and Mark Twain* (Harmondsworth, Middx.: Penguin, 1967 [1966]) pp. 320–3, and Gregg Camfield, *Sentimental Twain: Samuel Clemens in the Maze of Moral Philosophy* (Philadelphia: University of Pennslyvania Press, 1994) pp. 223–4.
38. Though my analytic procedures do not match Mailloux's rigorous interest in 'rhetorical hermeneutics', I am influenced here by his concentration on the way the rhetoric of a text 'participat[es] in the cultural debates of a specific historical period and place', and the way critical analysis then functions to locate 'the intersecting dialogues of the cultural conversation within the social practices, institutional disciplines, and material circumstances that made up American society at the moment the text was produced'. See Steven Mailloux, *Rhetorical Power* (Ithaca, NY: Cornell University Press, 1989) p. 104.
39. See Jane Tompkins, *Sensational Designs: The Cultural Work of American*

Fiction, 1790–1860 (New York: Oxford University Press, 1985) pp. xv–xvii.

Chapter 2 Old World Travel: *The Innocents Abroad*

1. Frederick Anderson, Michael B. Frank and Kenneth M. Sanderson (eds), *Mark Twain's Notebooks & Journals, Volume I (1853–1873)* (Berkeley: University of California Press, 1975) pp. 352, 426, 433.
2. Mark Twain, *The Innocents Abroad or The New Pilgrim's Progress* (1869). I use the version of the text published in *The Innocents Abroad* and *Roughing It* (New York: Library of America, 1984), here p. 17. Page numbers to follow quotes hereafter. Twain also used letters sent to the New York *Tribune* and *Herald* in the writing of his book.
3. The narrator's role in the book varies. At times he apparently speaks for the author; at others, his naive persona is constructed in comic relation to the superior knowledge and sophistication of that author. I use Mark Twain from now on (necessarily uncomfortably) to refer both to author and protagonist.
4. Jeffrey Steinbrink, *Getting to be Mark Twain* (Berkeley: University of California Press, 1991) p. xiii.
5. James Buzard, *The Beaten Track: European Tourism, Literature, and the Ways to Culture, 1800–1918* (Oxford: Clarendon Press, 1993) p. 219. '[S]teamship lines and travel agencies', he continues, 'competed for and stimulated a broadening demand'.
6. See Jeffrey Steinbrink, 'Why the Innocents Went Abroad: Mark Twain and American Tourism in the Late Nineteenth Century', *American Literary Realism*, vol. 16 (1983) p. 279.
7. Michael Kammen also refers to the urge to promote a 'nationally desired note of reconciliation' following the Civil War, which ended just two years before Twain's journey. See *Mystic Chords of Memory: The Transformation of Tradition in American Culture* (New York: Alfred A. Knopf, 1991) p. 103.
8. William W. Stowe, *Going Abroad: European Travel in Nineteenth-Century American Culture* (Princeton University Press, 1994) pp. 36, 17, 34. Stowe provides the best study I have read of *The Innocents Abroad* and the development of American travel writing.
9. I follow Twain in the gender specificity of this phrase. William W. Stowe, in *Going Abroad*, has interesting material on the gendered aspects of *The Innocents Abroad*, and its 'bad-boy bluster', and how they mutually relate to the sense of 'embattled manhood' (p. 128) in the period. J. D. Stahl also discusses the sexual politics of the book in *Mark Twain, Culture and Gender: Envisioning America through Europe* (Athens: University of Georgia Press, 1994).
10. Directly associated by J. D. Stahl with 'the newfound economic and cultural self-confidence of post-Civil War America', in *Mark Twain, Culture and Gender*, p. 31.
11. William W. Stowe, *Going Abroad*, p. 125.

12. Bruce Michelson, 'Mark Twain the Tourist: The Form of *The Innocents Abroad*', *American Literature*, vol. 49 (1977–8) p. 392.
13. In *Going Abroad*, William W. Stowe shows how Twain's tactics and concerns in *The Innocents Abroad* were anticipated by other writers (pp. 129–46). I follow his analysis of what it is that makes Twain's text distinctive (pp. 146–7).
14. Jeffrey Steinbrink describes it as 'the most successful travel book in the country's literary history', with sales of 100,000 within two years of its publication. See *Getting to be Mark Twain*, p. 62, and 'Why the Innocents Went Abroad', p. 278.
15. Alfred Kazin, 'Introduction' to *The Innocents Abroad* (New York: Bantam, 1964) pp. vi, vii.
16. Bruce Michelson's analysis of the text is based on this conflict. See *Mark Twain on the Loose: A Comic Writer and the American Self* (Amherst: University of Massachusetts Press, 1995) pp. 55–63. I acknowledge my critical debt to Michelson, though my commentary runs in different directions.
17. William W. Stowe, *Going Abroad*, p. 126.
18. William W. Stowe, *Going Abroad*, p. 48. Stowe uses the work of Dean MacCannell to suggest the relation between the tourist and the ethnographer here.
19. See Bruce Michelson, *Mark Twain on the Loose*, p. 53.
20. Henry B. Wonham says that as Twain added new episodes to the original travel letters, as he prepared his book for publication, so he prioritised 'dramatization over description'. See *Mark Twain and the Art of the Tall Tale* (New York: Oxford University Press, 1993) p. 81.
21. Richard Bridgman, *Traveling in Mark Twain*, pp. 9, 1. As part of his discussion of the influence of Sentimentalism on Twain, Gregg Camfield discusses the links between Twain's writing and the 'associationist model of human psychology' (p. 45) adopted by some members of the Common Sense school of philosophy. See *Sentimental Twain: Samuel Clemens in the Maze of Moral Philosophy* (Philadelphia: University of Pennsylvania Press, 1994). The importance of this model in terms of Twain's general literary practice cannot be overestimated. See, also, Forrest G. Robinson, 'The Innocent at Large: Mark Twain's Travel Writing', in Robinson (ed.), *The Cambridge Companion to Mark Twain* (Cambridge: Cambridge University Press, 1995) pp. 27–51.
22. Richard Bridgman, *Traveling in Mark Twain*, p. 2.
23. Contemporary reviews were more likely to comment on the distinctive quality of the American brand of humour than anything else, if Frederick Anderson's selection is representative. The review in the *Buffalo Express* spoke of the 'panorama of Europe and the Holy Land as they were seen by one who went abroad with no illusions; who carried about him a shrewd pair of American eyes', but this sounding of a nationalistic note in the context of the Old–New World contrast was the exception, not the rule. British reviewers seem to have been more open to such a reading. See Frederick Anderson (ed.), *Mark Twain:*

The Critical Heritage (London: Routledge & Kegan Paul, 1971) pp. 25–6 and *passim*.

24. William Woodruff, *America's Impact on the World: A Study of the Role of the United States in the World Economy, 1750–1970* (London: Macmillan, 1975) p. 64. William W. Stowe says, of American travel abroad in the period, that 'the tide of the early nineteenth century became a torrent, and the American tourist in Europe became a commonplace'. See *Going Abroad*, p. 8.

25. This episode, where the representative American democrat becomes 'bloated aristocrat' already points to that destabilising of expected polarities which occurs throughout the text. It also raises the question of the nature and consistency of the ironic gap between the author and his narrator. Steinbrink comments on the costs of foreign travel, noting that 'some [Americans] were actually able to economize by going abroad', in 'Why the Innocents Went Abroad', p. 280. See, too, *The Innocents Abroad*, p. 65.

26. J. D. Stahl's analyses the doctor's buying of a kiss from the attractive girl who acts as guide at the Palazzo Simonetti (see *The Innocents Abroad*, p. 156) to show how a relationship based on the 'cash nexus' of tourism is complicated by the sexual politics involved. See *Mark Twain, Culture and Gender*, pp. 41–2. Stahl, William W. Stowe in *Going Abroad*, and Robert Regan, in 'In the Wake of the *Quaker City*', in Robert Sattelmeyer and J. Donald Crowley (eds), *One Hundred Years of Huckleberry Finn: the Boy, His Book, and American Culture* (Columbia: University of Missouri Press, 1985) pp. 231–41, all discuss the gender politics of the text.

27. See 'Why the Innocents Went Abroad', p. 283, for Jeffrey Steinbrink's comments on the 'materialist mindset' of the tourists, and also their buying into both European art and European aristocracies. William W. Stowe's discussion of the guidebook is also relevant here: 'one of [its] most important functions was to endow the traveler with all the freedom and power of the bourgeois consumer by serving as a catalog of tempting products among which he or she was free to choose'. See *Going Abroad*, p. 45.

28. Robert Regan, 'Huck Finn in the Wake of the Quaker City', pp. 233, 234, 236. Regan also suggests that *The Innocents Abroad* invokes a posterior discourse (his term, p. 240); establishes a context for the books he would later write. So, for example, the reference to the monk in the Capuchin Convent in Rome some day being 'taken apart like an engine or a clock' (p. 238) anticipates Twain's later interest in the links between the human body, the machine and the question of identity. Similarly, the puzzle of the veins of oyster shells in the hill of the citadel in Smyrna (pp. 328–9) points forward to the uneasy parody of evolutionary discourse, and a similar lack of firm historical knowledge or ground, in 'Was the World Made for Man?', in Bernard DeVoto (ed.), *Mark Twain: Letters from the Earth* (New York: Harper & Row, 1962) pp. 211–6.

29. Alfred Kazin, 'Introduction' to *The Innocents Abroad*, p. ix.

30. Edward Said, *Culture and Imperialism* (London: Vintage, 1994 [1993]) p. 42.

31. Twain gives an example of this ruinous English in his notebook: 'Muleteers sang "We hang Jaf Deevez on sowly abbla tree/Glory halleluiah – and his soul go"'. In the *Alta* letters, Twain changed this to: 'We 'ang Jeffah Davis on sowlah applah tree,/So we go *molloching* on!' See Frederick Anderson, Michael B. Frank and Kenneth M. Sanderson (eds), *Mark Twain's Notebooks & Journals, Volume I (1853– 1873)*, p. 346. My emphasis anticipates the argument in the final section of this chapter

32. A late comment, where Twain refers to foreign attitudes to America, both obliquely acknowledges, and diverts from, the war: 'When we found that a good many foreigners . . . knew [America] only as a barbarous province away off somewhere, that had lately been at war with somebody, we pitied [their] ignorance' (pp. 515–16).

33. This sense remains intact despite the sailors' burlesque of the passengers, their false humility, and the formal circumlocutions of their rhetoric in the presence of royalty, that follows (pp. 320–2).

34. David E. E. Sloane, 'Toward the Novel', in Sloane (ed.) *Mark Twain's Humor: Critical Essays* (New York: Garland, 1993) pp. 125–6. The essay is reprinted from *Mark Twain as a Literary Comedian* (Baton Rouge: Louisiana State University Press, 1979).

35. Mark Twain, *The Adventures of Huckleberry Finn* (Harmondsworth, Middx.: Penguin, 1987 [1885]) p. 50.

36. See Bruce Michelson on the larger resonances of the 'Is he dead?' gag, *Mark Twain on the Loose*, pp. 49–50, 52–4. The impossibility of such a permanent erasure counterbalances such an episode.

37. So Christopher Mulvey describes transatlantic tourism in the nineteenth century in *Anglo-American Landscapes: A Study of Nineteenth-Century Anglo-American Travel Literature* (Cambridge: Cambridge University Press, 1983), where he speaks of the reduction of 'everything to the condition of things "which tourists travel to see"'. His comment that the word *did* 'was eventually to become the verb to describe the typical activity of the tourist' (all quotes, p. 249) recalls Twain describing his and his fellow tourists' activity as 'we galloped through the Louvre, the Pitti, the Ufizzi, the Vatican – all the galleries' (p. 517), and his first explorings of Marseilles when 'we only wanted to glance and go – to move, keep moving!' (p. 78). James Buzard bases *The Beaten Track* on the 'binary opposition' between travel and tourism that he sees as 'fundamental to and characteristic of modern culture', p. 18.

38. William W. Stowe notes that European art is associated with a repugnant social system. He shows how Twain's 'common-sense solution to the problem of art appreciation' (to look at the painting 'with unprejudiced American eyes and trust one's "natural" judgement') is to deny both that 'beauty is . . . a cultural product' and that the supposedly 'natural eye has already received . . . [an] education' in how to judge it. See *Going Abroad*, pp. 157–9. An implicit

contradiction exists here with comments on art elsewhere in Twain's book.

39. As so often in the book, Twain's position lacks consistency. On other occasions Twain is genuinely moved and impressed by European culture and the aura that surrounds its originals, though such enthusiasm generally refer to places rather than paintings. Even in the case of paintings and sculpture, Twain counter-balances the dismissive quality of his comments by admitting that 'one has no opportunity in America to acquire a critical judgement in art' (p. 187). To read the original/copy relationship in terms of international cultural difference is to problematise any American claim to originality. Such a problematisation is well recognised in any discussion of American cultural identity.

40. The French and the English are represented more positively than other nationalities. That 'otherness' becomes more noticeable in the Holy Land and Africa is unsurprising, for the civilisation/savagery binary had prior existence along European/non-European lines. The Holy Land is also, as I show, associated with the sacred, so representations of the area are not for Twain (or for prior European writers) homogeneous.

41. William W. Stowe uses this term in *Going Abroad*. He usefully describes the complexities and contradictions of the variety of identities Twain assumes in terms of 'a rhetoric of noncommittal enthusiasm' – 'playing every role with brief, sincere commitment and then undercutting the commitment, the sincerity, and the role itself' (p. 156). Bruce Michelson similarly speaks of the quality of 'perilous renewal' in Twain's persona, the trying on of 'new masks, new mentalities, costumes, ways of being', *Mark Twain on the Loose*, p. 44. I would argue (as Michelson also suggests) that the moves between such identities are not always so easily put on and off as Stowe suggests; that the adopting of incompatible roles leads to a sense of some anxiety and dis-ease.

42. Another strain running through the book is its one-dimensional representation of women. Women are consistently described in terms of physical attractiveness alone, or more often the lack of it. An overt misogynistic note appears in the *Alta* letters where the description of the 'atrocious ugliness' of the Moorish women of Tangier that appears in *The Innocents Abroad* (p. 69) is followed by the statement that 'If I had a wife as ugly as some of those I have seen, I would go over her face with a nail-grab and see if I couldn't improve it' (see *Mark Twain's Notebooks & Journals: Volume 1*, p. 365).

43. In the late work, *Three Thousand Years Among the Microbes* (1905), turn-of-the-century colonial practice is satirised as the spreading of 'pus and civilization'. See Chapter 9.

44. David R. Sewell, *Mark Twain's Languages: Discourse, Dialogue and Linguistic Variety* (Berkeley: University of California Press, 1987) p. 60. Sewell has interesting material on Twain's illusion 'that he can pass as a cosmopolitan polyglot', relating it to Emerson's romantic conception of language(s), pp. 64–5.

45. David Sewell refers to the way that 'American gold pieces spea[k] the universal language of economic power' in a prior episode (pp. 42–3) in *Mark Twain's Languages*, p. 61. So, too, the American dollar becomes *like* gold, a *lingua franca*.

46. See David Sewell's astute analysis of the fact that often, in *The Innocents Abroad*, '*less* language equals more power', *Mark Twain's Languages*, pp. 58–9.

47. Forrest G. Robinson, 'The Innocent at Large', p. 31.

48. Alfred Kazin, 'Introduction' to *The Innocents Abroad*, p. x.

49. In both these cases, there are also negative aspects to Twain's descriptions. In the latter, one can also see that 'recoil from the consciousness of the present, proximate, familiar and human' which Forrest G. Robinson identifies as a repeated pattern in the book. See 'Patterns of Consciousness in *The Innocents Abroad*', *American Literature*, vol. 58 (1986) pp. 58, 62.

50. Neither, despite what Robert Regan says in ' Huck Finn in the Wake of the *Quaker City*', can Huck.

51. James Buzard, *The Beaten Track*, p. 158. Buzard has detailed discussion on the problems of asserting 'originality in spite of . . . belatedness'. He describes how: 'nineteenth century visitors to the Continent had to reconcile the essentially repetitive nature of *acculturating* tours – to places known and valued in one's own culture – with that countervailing 'adversary' pressure to demonstrate some measure of originality and independence. . . . Writers . . . saw themselves moving through a domain of texts, seeking the complex satisfaction of participating in a process of cultural accreditation while also standing aloof from such participation as a form of imitation' (p. 161). Though Buzard is speaking of English travellers at this point, his words can be directly applied to Twain's case.

52. I am adapting what Edward Said says here about the 'huge library of *Africanism*', *Culture and Imperialism*, p. 79. Said's comment on the same page that 'there is no such thing as a *direct* experience, or reflection, of the world in the language of a text' is immediately relevant here.

53. Shades of difference between reverence and a deadpan comic version of it, and the exact nature of the tone being used, are not always easy to distinguish in the text. So, for an alternative interpretation, see J. D. Stahl, *Mark Twain, Culture and Gender*, p. 29.

54. Edward W. Said, *Orientalism* (London: Routledge & Kegan Paul, 1980 [1978]) p. 42. See Said's general argument, and especially pp. 65, 71–3, 102.

55. The phrase is Mary Louise Pratt's, though in a different context, in *Imperial Eyes: Travel Writing and Transculturation* (London: Routledge, 1992) p. 125.

56. See William W. Stowe, *Going Abroad*, p. 148.

57. See Bruce Michelson for a penetrating reading of this opposition, in *Mark Twain on the Loose*, pp. 55–63. I follow Michelson's lead here in linking the Holy Sepulchre and Adam's tomb sequences.

58. Dennis Welland, *The Life and Times of Mark Twain* (London: Studio Editions, 1991) p. 42.
59. Twain's worsening relationship with the *Quaker City* party and their complaints about him (and the other 'fast young men') can be traced in Harriet Elinor Smith and Richard Bucci (eds), *Mark Twain's Letters, Volume 2, 1867–1868* (Berkeley: University of California Press, 1990) pp. 102–3, 106, 108, 400–406.
60. See Robert Regan, 'The Reprobate Elect in *The Innocents Abroad*', *American Literature*, vol. 54, no. 2 (May 1982) pp. 240–57.
61. Tony Tanner, 'Writers of the Bible of America', *Times Higher Educational Supplement*, 22 November 1985, p. 17.
62. See Frederick Anderson, Michael B. Frank and Kenneth M. Sanderson (eds), *Mark Twain's Notebooks & Journals, Volume 1*, p. 390.

Chapter 3 *Roughing It* and the American West

1. Edgar Marquess Branch, Michael B. Frank and Kenneth M. Sanderson (eds), *Mark Twain's Letters, Volume 1: 1853–1866* (Berkeley: University of California Press, 1988) p. 150. A close version of this present chapter is scheduled to appear in the *Canadian Review of American Studies*, vol. 26, no. 1 (Winter 1996). My thanks to the journal editors for permission to reprint.
2. From Frederick Jackson Turner, 'The Significance of the Frontier in American History' (1893). See George Rogers Tyler (ed.), *The Turner Thesis Concerning the Role of the Frontier in American History* (Lexington, Mass.: D. C. Heath, 1956) p. 2. Hereafter, 'The Significance of the Frontier'.
3. *Mark Twain's Letters, Volume 1*, p. 132.
4. Stephen Fender, '"The Prodigal in a Far Country Chawing of Husks": Mark Twain's Search for a Style in the West', *Modern Language Review*, vol. 71, no. 4 (October 1976) pp. 740–1. Fender's comments on the rhetorical shaping of the letter for possible publication (p. 741) is confirmed in *Mark Twain's Letters, Volume 1*, p. 139. Twain wrote two versions of this piece, one of which was published in the Keokuk *Gate City*, 20 November 1861.
5. Turner, 'The Significance of the Frontier', pp. 18, 2, 3. Turner first delivered his frontier thesis to the American Historical Association in Chicago. In it, he does distinguish between different types of frontier (farmer's and miner's, for example) and their different rates of development, and allows, too, for geographical discontinuities (the irregularities of such western movement).
6. One that Twain himself would consistently employ (and, as protagonist of *Roughing It*, be the victim of). Stephen Fender discusses the western newspaper hoax, and Twain's breaking of its conventions in his 'A Bloody Massacre' (1863), in '"The Prodigal in a Far Country Chawing of Husks"', pp. 748–50.
7. Turner, 'The Significance of the Frontier', pp. 4–5. Both Lee Clark

Mitchell and Bruce Michelson interpret the Buncombe incident in related ways. Mitchell sees it in terms of the unpredictability of the West, compared to the 'fully predictable' East, in 'Verbally *Roughing It*: The West of Words', *Nineteenth Century Literature*, vol. 44 (1989–90) p. 71. Michelson places Buncombe's 'overthrow' in the context of a West which 'flourishes upon [the] . . . absence' of 'rules, precedents, . . . cultural institutions and common sense . . . '. He sees the 'resistance to "serious" interpretation' here in terms of Twain's general narrative tactics in the book. See *Mark Twain on the Loose: A Comic Writer and the American Self* (Amherst: University of Massachusetts Press, 1995) p. 70.

8. See Bruce Michelson, *Mark Twain on the Loose*, pp. 63–4, 74.

9. Martha Banta, 'The Boys and the Bosses: Twain's Double Take on Work, Play, and the Democratic Ideal', *American Literary History*, vol. 3, no. 3 (Fall 1991) p. 489.

10. Turner, 'The Significance of the Frontier', p. 4.

11. Similar to his method on stage. Within two pages of the start of the transcribed version of the 'Sandwich Islands Lecture' (given by Twain on his return to San Francisco) he says: 'But I am losing time; what I have been saying don't bear strictly on the Sandwich Islands, but one reminiscence leads to another, and I am obliged to bring myself down in this way. . . . It is not safe to come to any important matter in an entirely direct way.' See Paul Fatout (ed.), *Mark Twain Speaking* (Iowa: University of Iowa Press, 1976) p. 5. At this very early stage of his career, Twain is already describing some of the vital techniques of his lecturing (and literary) art.

12. Mark Twain, *Roughing It* (Harmondsworth, Middx.: Penguin, 1985 [1872]), p. 54. Page references to follow quotations henceforth.

13. Turner, 'The Significance of the Frontier', p. 17.

14. Jeffrey Steinbrink, *Getting to be Mark Twain* (Berkeley: University of California Press, 1991) p. 139.

15. Turner, 'The Significance of the Frontier', p. 2. But, pointedly, social pressures too have a major part to play in the clothes and habits the narrator adopts.

16. The book is based on Twain's experiences in the West from the summer of 1861 to December, 1866. The difference between the naive narrator depicted at the start of *Roughing It* and the experienced twenty-five year old who actually made the journey is the subject of extended critical comment. See, for instance, Jeffrey Steinbrink, *Getting to be Mark Twain*, p. 138. Hamlin Hill refers to Twain's 'enormous violation of the facts of his biography' in the construction of his narrative persona in his 'Introduction' to *Roughing It*, p. 16.

17. Henry Nash Smith identified a structural move from innocence to experience in the contrast between these two narrative positions. See 'Mark Twain as an Interpreter of the Far West: The Structure of *Roughing It*', in Walker D. Wyman and Clifton B. Kroeber (eds), *The Frontier in Perspective* (Madison: University of Wisconsin Press, 1957) p. 212. Though, undoubtedly, one of the ways the book works is as a Bildungsroman, the extent and type of maturation associated with the

narrator, and the way it relates to a gradual closing of the gap between the two textual voices, is considerably more problematic than Smith (and the critics who follow his lead) suggests. For the move from tenderfoot to old-timer he describes can, alternatively, be viewed as yet another of the book's 'blind leads'. If the recollecting voice is positioned further back (i.e. identified with the Mark Twain writing in Buffalo and Elmira in 1870–1) some of these problems disappear, though a new one is raised as the tension between naivety and experience has to be reformulated. As in *The Innocents Abroad*, consistent distinction between author and protagonist is problematic. Despite the retrospective gap, at times (and especially when in serious descriptive mode) the narrator's voice becomes one with the author's. 'Mark Twain' accordingly signifies variously.

18. See Turner, 'The Significance of the Frontier', pp. 5, 8. Turner identifies East and West with different orders of the 'civilised'. See note 20 below.

19. Helen L. Harris argues that Twain is 'unfailingly hostile' to American Indians: 'Mark Twain's Response to the Native Americans', *American Literature* vol. 46 (1975) p. 495. Walter Benn Michaels, though, in the context of *A Connecticut Yankee*, sees the Indian as a positive figure of individual resistance to social pressures: 'An American Tragedy, or the Promise of American Life', *Representations* vol. 25 (Winter 1989) pp. 71–98. In my 'Racial and Colonial Discourse in Mark Twain's *Following the Equator*', *Essays in Arts and Sciences*, vol. 22 (October 1993), I argue that there is a sub-text in Twain's late travel book which criticises the dispossessions and depredations to which American Indians were historically subject (see pp. 70–1).

20. As Twain unexpectedly switches his verbal attack to the Baltimore and Washington Railroad Company and its employees (in their resemblance to the Gosiutes), Twain introduces a note of relativistic uncertainty which unsettles his savage–civilised binary. Twain operates here from a similar position that Turner will later adopt, in establishing a three-way set of oppositions between 'savage', frontier and eastern. The advance of capitalism and incorporation associated by Twain with the East, and the corruption that goes with it, are contrasted accordingly with western individualism. I suggest the problematic nature of this contrast later. Any straightforward notion of historical evolution and racial difference is, though, disrupted in the new hierarchy established here. See John E. Bassett, '*Roughing It*: Authority through Comic Performance', *Nineteenth Century Literature*, vol. 43 (1988–9) pp. 227–8.

21. Henry Nash Smith, 'Mark Twain as an Interpreter of the Far West', pp. 214, 212. Forrest G. Robinson argues for a much bleaker reading of the incident and the text, seeing the dog as 'not educated or initiated' by the coyote, but 'utterly crushed', in line with the general movement of a book which recurrently speaks of 'gross self-deception and inevitable failure': '"Seeing the Elephant": Some Perspectives on Mark Twain's *Roughing It*', *American Studies*, vol. 21, no. 2 (Fall 1980) pp. 50, 55.

22. William Bright, quoted in Arnold E. Davidson, *Coyote Country: Fictions of the Canadian West* (Durham, NC: Duke University Press, 1994) p. 2. Warwick Wadlington makes the same connection, writing that 'the coyote is a pivotal metaphor that allows Twain to . . . both . . . establis[h] a pyramid [of superiority] and then pivo[t] it onto its head, giving priority to neither pyramid nor inversion'. See *The Confidence Game in American Literature* (Princeton, NJ: Princeton University Press, 1975) p. 216.
23. Turner, 'The Significance of the Frontier', p. 5.
24. Drewey Wayne Gunn attributes positive value to the dictionary. He says that Twain's 'triump[h] in American letters was in his realization that he must graft the natural speech of the West . . . onto the literary diction of the Eastern establishment': 'The Monomythic Structure of *Roughing It*', *American Literature*, vol. 61 (1989) p. 570. I would resist the assumptions of organic growth and unity behind Gunn's metaphor. The notion of a single pure American form of language (a linguistic gold or silver standard) which could contain the nation's disparate ways of speaking and thinking is shown by Twain also to be illusory. Bruce Michelson suggests a different reading of the sequence, when he discusses 'Life After the Unabridged Dictionary' in terms of a *tension* between constrictive and inherited 'rules of discourse' and a 'tormenting [linguistic] anarchy, a pestilential, "decomposed" composition [the Sphynx]'. See *Mark Twain on the Loose*, pp. 46–7. See also Lee Clark Mitchell, 'Verbally *Roughing It*: The West of Words', p. 82.
25. Kenneth Lynn, *Mark Twain and Southwestern Humor*, quoted in David Sewell, *Mark Twain's Languages: Discourse, Dialogue and Linguistic Variety* (Berkeley: University of California Press, 1987) p. 132.
26. David Sewell, *Mark Twain's Languages*, p. 132.
27. Philip D. Beidler, 'Realistic Style and the Problem of Context in *The Innocents Abroad* and *Roughing It*', *American Literature*, vol. 52 (1980–1) p. 46. These ways of knowing the world are not *quite* separate, thus Briggs leads in with a phrase 'doxology works' which makes use of specialised and sophisticated religious terminology but converts it to his own stylistic needs; reduces its cultivated effect, by combining it with his use of the (formally) inappropriate and (linguistically) casual and imprecise 'works'.
28. M. M. Bakhtin, *The Dialogic Imagination: Four Essays*, trans. Caryl Emerson and Michael Holquist (Austin: University of Texas Press, 1981) p. 297.
29. Philip D. Beidler, 'Realistic Style and the Problem of Context in *The Innocents Abroad* and *Roughing It*', p. 47. Twain's own narrative incorporation of such conflict and difference suggests an understanding of his role as an artist in a heterogeneous society, and a commitment to linguistic (and social) variety. However, such a commitment has its limits, and to speak of the narrator's 'neutrality' is problematic, given the omnipresence of ideological interestedness. The representation of race is ambiguous in *Roughing It*. If, here, Twain interrogates the racist assumptions of Briggs, elsewhere he privileges

the dominant racial and ethnic groups; as when, for instance, he contrasts 'native American' (white) men with Mexican 'Greasers' (p. 435).

30. See Stephen Fender for discussion of the problems involved in Twain's attempt to find a literary style to register a western community which was in itself socially complex (but also deracinated): '"The Prodigal in a Far Country"', pp. 746, 748, 753–5 and *passim*.

31. Lee Clark Mitchell, 'Verbally *Roughing It*: The West of Words', pp. 71–2.

32. John E. Bassett, '*Roughing It*: Authority through Comic Performance', p. 225. Bruce Michelson focuses on the 'refusal of rules, reason, stabilized identities, and recognition of things as they are' the 'blind lead' episode suggests. He associates it with other 'leads' followed and lost, as the narrator attempts to 'inven[t] or discove[r] an identity', and as the narrative itself 'flips and spins' in one direction then another. See *Mark Twain on the Loose*, p. 68. His discussion of unstable identity here usefully connects with my comments on *The Innocents Abroad*. I focus here on other, but related, issues.

33. See Henry Nash Smith (ed.), *Mark Twain of the Enterprise* (Berkeley: University of California Press, 1957) pp. 25–9, for information on the Sanitary Fund controversy, explaining reasons for the move to San Francisco.

34. See Neil Schmitz's stimulating reading of this episode in terms of Twain's use of 'Jacksonian dreaming' as a subject: 'Mark Twain, Henry James, and Jacksonian Dreaming', *Criticism*, vol. 27 (Spring 1985) p. 168.

35. Richard Bridgman, *Traveling in Mark Twain*, p. 56. Twain's attitude in the first Appendix is, I would suggest, itself more ambiguous than Bridgman suggests. His reading of Twain's puzzling third Appendix is, though, illuminating. The analysis Bridgman gives (pp. 39–48) of the Horace Greeley letter about turnips (in the Hawaiian section of *Roughing It*, pp. 501–9) as an embodiment of 'precisely the enigma that Twain himself had to deal with: a scrawled world that yielded a variety of uncertain and by and large unwelcome interpretations' (p. 41) is brilliant (though I disagree with the pessimistic thrust of his general conclusions). In this incident, though the correct version of the letter is finally known, such knowledge comes too late to save the sanity of the preacher.

36. Though I agree with Forrest G. Robinson that any quest for 'knowledge and wisdom' in *Roughing It* is frustrated, I would resist the single stress on self-contempt and cynicism which he reads not only in Twain's own letters from the West but also in his book about it. See his '"Seeing the Elephant"', pp. 44, 53. Twain does, however (as Robinson also notes), seem to have had thoughts of suicide sometime in the last months of 1865 or the very early period of 1866 when he was 'in trouble, & in debt . . . utterly miserable' in San Franciso. See Edgar Marquess Branch, Michael B. Frank and Kenneth M. Sanderson (eds), *Mark Twain's Letters, Volume 1*, pp. 320, 324 (the source of my quote) and 325.

37. Warwick Wadlington, *The Confidence Game in American Literature*, p. 203.

38. As Twain visits the Sandwich Islands, so his narrative continues to bristle with contradictions. Hawaii is both a place of commercial opportunity, and the 'sunniest, balmiest, dreamiest haven of refuge for a worn and weary spirit the surface of the earth can offer'. The latter quote comes from the manuscript fragments of Twain's novel set in Hawaii: see Stephen H. Sumida, 'Reevaluating Mark Twain's Novel of Hawaii', *American Literature*, vol. 61 (1989) p. 593. The attraction of the 'primitive' is obvious in much he says about the country. The missionaries are correspondingly ironically pilloried for the 'improvements' they have brought to these 'simple children of the sun' (p. 481, and see p. 461). But the missionaries are also praised for their improvements, as the idea of savagery as noble is ruthlessly demolished in a description of the violence and 'brutal and unbridled licentiousness' (p. 494) of earlier times.
39. California is described as 'the Garden of Eden reproduced' in one of Twain's 1862 letters from Carson City. See *Mark Twain's Letters, Volume 1*, p. 155.
40. Jeffrey Steinbrink, *Getting to be Mark Twain*, p. 139.
41. Alan Trachtenberg, *The Incorporation of America: Culture and Society in the Gilded Age* (New York: Hill and Wang, 1982) pp. 23, 20.
42. See, too, the reference to the ignorance, of all the Virginia City population but its telegraph operator, of the Civil War victory by Union troops at Gettysburg. This resulted from the 'journalistic monopoly that forbade the slightest revealment of eastern news till a day after its publication in the California papers' (p. 406).
43. See Martha Banta, 'The Boys and the Bosses', pp. 493–4.
44. Howard Horwitz, *By the Law of Nature: Form and Value in Nineteenth-Century America* (New York: Oxford University Press, 1991) p. 112.
45. Edgar Marquess Branch, Michael B. Frank and Kenneth M. Sanderson (eds), *Mark Twain's Letters, Volume 1*, p. 245; and 'Bigler vs. Tahoe', in Edgar Marquess Branch and Robert H. Hirst (eds), *The Works of Mark Twain: Early Tales and Sketches, Volume 1: 1851–1864* (Berkeley: University of California Press, 1979) p. 290.
46. See Leo Marx on Twain's problems of describing nature in any but formulaic and received terms: *The Machine in the Garden: Technology and the Pastoral Ideal in America* (New York: Oxford University Press, 1967 [1964]) pp. 319–25.
47. Peter Stoneley examines this incident in terms of the homoerotic impulse in western literature and life. For him, 'idealized moments of same-sex relationship in *Roughing It* are always curtailed by a retributive violence'. See 'Rewriting the Gold Rush: Twain, Harte and Homosociality', *Journal of American Studies*, forthcoming. Twain implicitly asserts his own manliness (in contrast to a scorned effeminacy) where, for example, he contrasts western horsemanship to 'the silly Miss Nancy fashion of the riding-schools' (p. 197): better to be bucked and jolted by a Genuine Mexican Plug than ride in such a manner.

48. The major thrust of the book, whether through silver mining, speculating, lecturing etc. This episode recalls Locke, for whom 'property results from "workmanship" that "puts[s] the difference of value on everything," which untreated has none'. The West promises such value with only token amounts of work. See Howard Horwitz, *By the Law of Nature*, p. 90.
49. Dan De Quille (William Wright), *The Big Bonanza: An Authentic Account of the Discovery, History, and Working of the World-Renowned Comstock Load of Nevada* (London: Eyre & Spottiswoode, 1969 [1876]) pp. 174–7. See Oscar Lewis's introduction to this edition for an account of Twain's active involvement in, and encouragement of, De Quille's project.
50. See Martha Banta on *Roughing It*'s opposition between playful 'boys' and efficient 'bosses', and the way this affects the book's structure, 'The Boys and the Bosses', pp. 493–7.
51. Martha Banta, 'The Boys and the Bosses', p. 495.
52. See Martha Banta, 'The Boys and the Bosses', p. 496.
53. Walter Benn Michaels, *The Gold Standard and the Logic of Naturalism: American Literature at the Turn of the Century* (Berkeley: University of California Press, 1987) pp. 65–6. He takes the phrase 'fictitious dealings' from a 1921 House Committee enquiry on *Future Trading*.
54. Elisha P. Douglass, *The Coming of Age of American Business: Three Centuries of Enterprise, 1600–1900* (Chapel Hill: University of North Carolina Press, 1971) p. 389. In *The Confidence Game in American Literature*, Warwick Wadlington agrees that 'the importance of financial enterprise in the official national culture finds a dramatic parallel in the flush times of silver and gold mining' but claims that 'the arbitrary luck that usually separates great wealth from hopeful scrounging, as well as the Western habit of spending sprees, completely flaunts the official morality of acquisition through orderly stages of work and capitalization through sober saving' (pp. 203–4). As my argument suggests, I would focus on the similarities of the workings of the capitalist system in the East and the West rather than on their differences, and would ask just how far the type of 'official morality' to which Wadlington refers operated even in the East in Gilded Age America.
55. Earl Pomeroy, *The Pacific Slope: A History of California, Oregon, Washington, Idaho, Utah, and Nevada* (Lincoln: University of Nebraska Press, 1991 [1965]) p. 51.
56. Earl Pomeroy, *The Pacific Slope*, p. 53.
57. See Edgar M. Branch, 'Fact and Fiction in the Blind Lead Episode of *Roughing It*', *Nevada Historical Society Quarterly* 28 (Winter 1985) pp. 234–47. What is suggested in the factual base of this incident is, however, that Twain's ambiguities about individual agency and the market economy may be, in part, a reflection of the rapidity of the changes in American social and economic life. The general relation between fact and fiction in Twain's text is more complicated that Branch's title would imply.
58. Elisha P. Douglass, *The Coming of Age of American Business*, pp. 390–1.

Douglass also gives figures concerning the number and profitability of the Nevada mines: 'Perhaps as many as 5000 claims were located and traded within thirty miles of Virginia City. Only 300 were ever opened, only 20 became mines, and of these only 8 or 9 paid dividends.' Looking at the slim chances of profit from western mining, he comments that 'it is hard to explain the tremendous investment on purely economic grounds' (p. 392).

59. I am extracting here from Walter Benn Michaels's account of late nineteenth-century disputes over the value of money in *The Gold Standard*, pp. 144–9. The quotations given are generally taken from the theorists of the time.

60. Bruce Michelson, accordingly, takes the comic performance which is Jim Blaine's story about his grandfather's old ram as paradigmatic of the conversion to artistic ends of the lack of 'linearity, form, or common sense . . . in the insane world of the American West', *Mark Twain on the Loose*, p. 63.

61. Twain's awareness of such an audience can be implied from the repeated use he makes of the tall tale to reveal its function as a distinctive western type of humour, but also to show its limitations. For the tall tale fails to provide any firm base from which to construct an authoritative version of reality. Instead, deflation (the exaggerations of the tall tale are fabulations, and rest on no solid basis) follows deflation (of the greenhorn victim's naive expectations) in what Neil Schmitz suggests is a kind of 'nihilist joke'. See 'Mark Twain, Henry James, and Jacksonian Dreaming', p. 169. Twain's achievement here is to take that particular western form and represent it as part of a larger literary whole for a *national* audience; allowing that audience both to see the joke, how that joke works and at whose expense, and its final insufficiencies as an alternative and hyperbolic way of representing reality. As a form of humour it does not, like Twain's westward journey itself, finally lead anywhere in terms of constructing a satisfactory stance from which to interpret experience. For an alternative view of Twain's use of this form in *Roughing It*, see Henry B. Wonham, *Mark Twain and the Art of the Tall Tale* (New York: Oxford University Press, 1993) pp. 89–111.

62. See Bruce Michelson, *Mark Twain on the Loose*, pp. 72–4.

63. Lee Clark Mitchell, 'Verbally *Roughing It*', p. 74.

Chapter 4 *Tom Sawyer* and American Cultural Life: Anxieties and Accommodations

1. From *Time* magazine's review of Melvin and Mario Van Peebles's film on the Black Panthers, *Panther*. Quoted in David Gritten, 'The Panthers: Heroes or Villains?', *Independent on Sunday*, 4 June 1995, p. 27.

2. Lee Clark Mitchell, 'Introduction' to *The Adventures of Tom Sawyer* (Oxford: Oxford University Press, World's Classics, 1993) p. x. This is one of the best recent essays on the novel.

3. Described by Gregg Camfield as 'Like the entire park, . . . [offering] a self-contained haven of adventure, where fantasies of piracy and treasure hunting, of endless summertime and endless youth, are colored with enough that is frightful to make them interesting, but are perfectly safe, endlessly repeatable, always charming, and quite saccharine.' See *Sentimental Twain: Samuel Clemens in the Maze of Moral Philosophy* (Philadelphia: University of Pennsylvania Press, 1994) p. 1.

4. Fred G. See, 'Tom Sawyer and Children's Literature', in Gary Scharnhorst (ed.), *Critical Essays on The Adventures of Tom Sawyer* (New York: G. K. Hall, 1993) p. 179.

5. Lee Clark Mitchell, 'Introduction' to *The Adventures of Tom Sawyer*, p. x.

6. Louis J. Budd, 'Mark Twain as an American Icon', in Forrest G. Robinson (ed.), *The Cambridge Companion to Mark Twain* (Cambridge: Cambridge University Press, 1995) p. 6.

7. Cynthia Griffin Wolff, 'The Adventures of Tom Sawyer: A Nightmare Vision of American Boyhood', *Massachusetts Review*, vol. 21, no. 4 (Winter 1980) pp. 99, 94.

8. 'Preface', *The Adventures of Tom Sawyer* (London: Penguin, 1986 [1876]). Page numbers follow quotes from henceforth.

9. Marcia Jacobson, *Being a Boy Again: Autobiography and the American Boy Book* (Tuscaloosa: University of Alabama Press, 1994) pp. 4, 7, 13.

10. Thus Marcia Jacobson's central argument is that the boy book 'could simultaneously be accepted as offering a vicarious escape from and implicit critique of the culture that produced it and as an instrument for furthering the ends of that culture' (*Being a Boy Again*, p. 13). This leads in fruitful directions, as far as *Tom Sawyer* goes, but does not for me quite explain all the complex effects of the book.

11. Lee Clark Mitchell, indeed, discusses the 'mix of contrasts' in *Tom Sawyer* as matching 'the contradictions many have felt about coming of age in American culture', 'Introduction' to *The Adventures of Tom Sawyer*, p. xv.

12. Hannibal was incorporated in 1845. Its citizens (and particularly Twain's father) shared in 'the speculative ferment . . . sparked by the promise of the vast frontier' in the 1830s. The Panic of 1837 and the decade long depression that followed were the most likely cause of Judge Clemens' financial ruin. See John Carlos Rowe, 'Fatal Speculations: Murder, Money, and Manners in *Puddn'head Wilson*', in Susan Gillman and Forrest G. Robinson (eds), *Mark Twain's Puddn'head Wilson: Race, Conflict, and Culture* (Durham, NC: Duke University Press, 1990) pp. 141, 144–5.

13. For a biographical explanation which connects Twain's writing of the book to his marriage to Livy, see, for instance, Charles A. Norton, *Writing Tom Sawyer: The Adventures of a Classic* (Jefferson, NC: McFarland, 1983) pp. 48–51. Although *The Gilded Age* (1873), the novel Twain wrote with his Hartford neighbour, Charles Dudley Warner, was published three years earlier than *Tom Sawyer*, it is generally agreed that Twain had in fact started working on the latter text first. It may be that his work with Warner gave him the confidence for the clear

move away from the autobiographical which takes place as *Tom Sawyer* proceeds.

14. See Alan Gribben, '"I Did Wish Tom Sawyer Was There": Boy-Book Elements in *Tom Sawyer* and *Huckleberry Finn*', in Robert Sattelmeyer and J. Donald Crowley (eds), *One Hundred Years of Huckleberry Finn: The Boy, His Book, and American Culture* (Columbia: University of Missouri Press, 1985) pp. 154, 156.

15. Bruce Michelson argues that Tom's 'psychological immunity, or perhaps superficiality' is seen as he goes from 'mood to mood, sentiment to sentiment, in a flash'. Tom's ability to forget the graveyard murder and the trial for long textual periods has its formal match in the ability of Twain's omniscient narrator to 'contentedly . . . forge[t] with him', *Mark Twain on the Loose: A Comic Writer and the American Self* (Amherst: University of Massachusetts Press, 1995) p. 105.

16. Marcia Jacobson suggests that some of these disjunctions may be explained by the 'constant shifting of attitudes' between 'the narrator and his younger self' that characterises the boy book: 'as the narrator relives his past in recalling it, and brings his present condition to bear on it in interpreting it'. Thus, for example, in *Tom Sawyer*, the narrator takes a clearly ironic position as he mocks, and then literally dashes (possibly cold and certainly dirty) water on, Tom's sentimental maunderings as he lies under what he thinks is Becky Thatcher's window (pp. 25–6). This, however, later gives way to an apparently straightforward romantic perspective in the description of Tom's waking to the new day on Jackson's Island, and in the use of conventional sentimental discourse ('not a sound obtruded upon great Nature's meditation', p. 96) that accompanies it. This latter is 'Childhood . . . seen from the remembered perspective of youth [and] . . . consequently presented in a lyrical or elegiac mode'. See *Being a Boy Again*, pp. 20–3. We are still left here with the rather unexpected fact that Twain uses that type of 'naively romantic perspective' which in his earlier humorous works was generally subject to 'corrective explosion'. See Henry B. Wonham, *Mark Twain and the Art of the Tall Tale* (New York: Oxford University Press, 1993) p. 128. See Wonham, too, for an alternative explanation of such effects as a sign of Twain's 'increasing dexterity as a writer' (pp. 132, 139).

17. Wayne Fields, 'When the Fences are Down: Language and Order in *The Adventures of Tom Sawyer* and *Huckleberry Finn*', *Journal of American Studies*, vol. 24, no. 3 (December 1990) p. 370. Jerry Griswold compares British and American children's books of the period to argue that whereas 'British books . . . move outward to create imaginary paradises', American ones are concerned with 'an internal world we might call the Theater of Feelings'. Though Griswold's description of Tom and his attempts 'to re-create the Protestant Pieta' (as Twain burlesques 'the figure of the literary child as pallid sufferer') is accurate, his attempt to impose outer/inner binaries on the book is (as my use of the fence metaphor suggests) faulty: *Audacious Kids: Coming of Age*

in America's Classic Children's Books (New York: Oxford University Press, 1992) pp. 143, 144, 150, 151.

18. Neil Schmitz, *Of Huck and Alice; Humorous Writing in American Literature* (Minneapolis: University of Minnesota Press, 1983) p. 66.

19. Neil Schmitz, *Of Huck and Alice*, p. 66.

20. Sanford Pinsker writes that 'Tom's . . . abiding sense of play, transmogrifies a dull St Petersburg into a world more attractive'. See *'The Adventures of Tom Sawyer*, Play Theory, and the Critic's Job of Work', *Midwest Quarterly*, vol. 29 (Spring, 1988) p. 360.

21. The Penguin text ('having a holiday') is inaccurate here. I amend accordingly.

22. For *Tom Sawyer* is much concerned with disciplinary practice and its resistance. The world of power that the book sketches (with its judges, teachers, guardians) may be that of the small town rather than of the industrial workplace, but the concern with the socialisation of identity *prefigures* later forms of childhood discipline, by which boys would be trained into efficient workers for an industrial 'economy that has no time for kidding around'. See Martha Banta, 'The Boys and the Bosses: Twain's Double Take on Work, Play, and the Democratic Ideal', *American Literary History*, vol. 3, no. 3 (Fall 1991) p. 511 (see, too, pp. 507–11).

    In 'Sparing the Rod: Discipline and Fiction in America in Antebellum America', Richard H. Brodhead traces the move from corporal correction to a new form of domestic discipline ('correction-by-interiority') in 1830s and 1840s America. The relation between Tom and Aunt Polly might be re-examined in the light of Brodhead's arguments to suggest (though evidence for this is incomplete) that it is through the influence of 'inward colonization, not outward coercion' that Tom's acceptance of the dominant social norms is guaranteed. See *Representations*, no. 21 (Winter 1988) pp. 67–96. I quote from pp. 78, 73.

23. Michael Oriard, *Sporting with the Gods: The Rhetoric of Play and Game in American Culture* (Cambridge: Cambridge University Press, 1991) pp. xi, 11, 369, 394. *Tom Sawyer* is a book written about a boy and one primarily directed toward male readers (see for instance the remark on whistling, p. 11). Oriard is particularly interesting on the difference between boy and girl books at this time, and makes the revealing comment that, if play can be linked to such a 'countercultural desire for work-oriented men', then 'work embodied the reformist desire of play-burdened women' (p. 394; and see pp. 394–9). See also Steven Mailloux's valuable essay, 'The Rhetorical Use and Abuse of Fiction: Eating Books in Late Nineteenth-Century America', in Donald E. Pease, *Revisionary Interventions in the American Canon* (Durham, NC: Duke University Press, 1994) especially pp. 140–50.

24. *Sporting with the Gods* pp. 399, 398.

25. John Seelye, 'Introduction' to *The Adventures of Tom Sawyer* (Penguin) p. xi.

26. My approach, and the terms I use here, are influenced by Scott Michaelsen's unpublished article, 'Tom Sawyer's Capitalisms and the

Destructuring of Huck Finn'. My thanks to him for allowing me to make use of it. Other critics, too, refer to this aspect of the novel. See, for example, Lee Clark Mitchell, who says that Tom anticipates many techniques 'we accept today as commonplace business ploys', 'Introduction' to *The Adventures of Tom Sawyer* (World's Classics) p. xiv.

27. Though Oriard's analysis of the novel and especially his insistence on the 'safe' quality of Tom's play is still to the point: *Sporting with the Gods*, p. 401.

28. Quoted in Alan Gribben, '"I Did Wish Tom Sawyer Was There"', p. 149. Forrest Robinson refers to Tom's 'consummate mastery of face' and calls him 'the leading gamesman in St Petersburg'. He also says that 'in winning his way to the top, Tom outwits and exploits every age group and class in the community', *In Bad Faith*, pp. 31, 28–9, 25.

29. See Karen Halttunen, *Confidence Men and Painted Women: A Study of Middle-class Culture in America, 1830–1870* (New Haven, Conn.: Yale University Press, 1982) pp. 3, 1, 7, 23, 25, 33–4.

30. John Carlos Rowe speaks of the intense economic activity on the ante-bellum southwestern frontier as helping 'Jacksonian America enter the modern industrial age', 'Fatal Speculations', p. 141.

31. See too the links Neil Schmitz makes between Jacksonian values and Twain's representations of the Gilded Age in 'Mark Twain, Henry James, and Jacksonian Dreaming', *Criticism*, vol. 27 (Spring 1985) pp. 155–73.

32. *Confidence Men and Painted Women*, pp. 31, 34, 187, and Michael Oriard, *Sporting with the Gods*, p. 51. Oriard is talking about Southwestern humour here, but his statement bears equal relevance to the city world that Halttunen describes.

33. *Tom Sawyer: A Play*, in Walter Blair (ed.), *Hannibal, Huck & Tom* (Berkeley: University of California Press, 1969) p. 281.

34. Karen Halttunen suggests that by the second half of the nineteenth century, 'aggressiveness, charm, and the arts of the confidence man' had become new components of accepted American success ideology, and were no longer treated with suspicion; rather 'the manipulation of others through artifice was coming to be accepted as a necessary executive skill', *Confidence Men and Painted Women*, pp. 202, 204.

35. See too Cynthia Griffin Wolff, '*the Adventures of Tom Sawyer*: A Nightmare Vision of American Boyhood', pp. 93–105. The fact that both the town doctor and Joe are involved in the grave-robbing also suggests that the relation between community and its 'other' is not as clear cut as one might first imagine.

36. See Scott Michaelsen, 'Tom Sawyer's Capitalisms', unpublished ms, note 26. See, too, Paul Taylor, '*Huckleberry Finn*: The Education of a Young Capitalist', in Robert Sattelmeyer and J. Donald Crowley (eds), *One Hundred Years of Huckleberry Finn*, p. 343. Tom is both like and unlike Joe here. If Tom's intent is robbery, while Joe is innocent of this, Joe's antisocial criminality and displacement of Tom in the cave suggests their likeness.

37. Enterprise and theft continue to stand for one another here. An

alternative interpretation would focus on the *difference* between Tom's earlier exploits and the 'finding of gold in the ground' motif. There are parallels here with *Roughing It*: nostalgia for an imaginary time when individual luck, pluck and financial success went hand in hand, prior to the coming of systematised forms of corporate activity and the creation of a wage-earning middle class. The possibility of such variants suggests the ambiguities of the novel.

38. See Marcia Jacobson, *Being a Boy Again*, p. 16.
39. *Saturday Review*, 8 July 1876. Reprinted in Gary Scharnhorst (ed.), *Critical Essays on the Adventures of Tom Sawyer*, p. 36.
40. T. J. Jackson Lears, *No Place of Grace: Antimodernism and the Transformation of American Culture, 1880–1920* (New York: Pantheon, 1981) p. 146.
41. Eric Sundquist, 'Introduction: The Country of the Blue', in Sundquist (ed.), *American Realism: New Essays* (Baltimore, Md.: The Johns Hopkins University Press, 1982) p. 8.
42. Fred G. See, 'Tom Sawyer and Children's Literature', p. 180.
43. An ironic name, in the light of Twain's own later book, *Following the Equator*; the record of the world lecture tour determined by financial necessity.
44. Cynthia Griffin Wolff, 'The Adventures of Tom Sawyer: A Nightmare Vision of American Boyhood', p. 99. See, too, my earlier note 23 on disciplinary practice.
45. Fred G. See, ' Tom Sawyer and Children's Literature', p. 180.
46. Elizabeth G. Peck, 'Tom Sawyer: Character in Search of an Audience', *American Transcendental Quarterly*, vol. 2 (September 1988) p. 224.
47. See Judith Fetterley, 'The Sanctioned Rebel', *Studies in the Novel*, vol. 3 (Fall 1971) pp. 293–304.
48. My interpretation of *Tom Sawyer* differs considerably from that of Bruce Michelson, who argues that 'the main thematic taproots of *Huckleberry Finn*' are in this earlier novel, present in Tom's 'quest for . . . uncompromised freedom' and his lack of a 'stable self'. See *Mark Twain on the Loose*, p. 102, and, more generally, pp. 101–8.
49. It is a critical commonplace that a central reason for *Huckleberry Finn*'s importance is due to its adoption of the vernacular narrative voice. More acknowledgement, though, should be given to the extent to which *Tom Sawyer* foreshadows this literary revolution. It is noticeable that contemporary English reviews focused repeatedly on the book's distinctive use of language. Thus one reviewer (the London *Standard*) says that 'the language is certainly extraordinary. It is that strange tongue which has grown up on the other side of the Atlantic which, although founded upon English, is yet not English, whose grammar, whose idioms, and whose slang differ wholly from our own'. See Gary Scharnhorst (ed.), *Critical Essays on The Adventures of Tom Sawyer*, p. 35. See too pp. 41, 43. Significantly, the last voice in the main body of the text (to which the distanced narrator then adds his formal closure) is not that of Tom but of Huck. His vigorous vernacular ends with an expression of loyalty to the Widow, suckered into it by Tom's threat

that 'we can't let you into the gang if you ain't respectable' (p. 219): 'I'll stick to the widder till I rot, Tom; and if I git to be a reg'lar ripper of a robber, and everybody talking 'bout it, I reckon she'll be proud she snaked me in out of the wet' (p. 221). The voice that sounds here, and the values that it would speak, cannot, though, be satisfactorily contained either within a conventional narrative frame or by the respectabilities of the small-town world. In *Huckleberry Finn*, Twain would give this voice its fuller freedom.

50. My prior argument about the free expression of self starts here to take on more sinister connotations. Freedom from social convention, being outlaw, has both positive and negative implications in Twain. See, for instance, the difference between Huck and Pap Finn.

51. Cynthia Griffin Wolff, 'The Adventures of Tom Sawyer: A Nightmare Vision of American Boyhood', pp. 102, 100, 99–100, 101, 104. See too Tom H. Towers, '"I Never Thought We Might Want to Come Back": Strategies of Transcendence in *Tom Sawyer*', *Modern Fiction Studies*, vol. 21 (1975–6) pp. 513–14.

52. 'Introduction' to *The Adventures of Tom Sawyer* (Penguin) pp. xix–xx.

53. Tom H. Towers, '"I Never Thought We Might Want to Come Back"', p. 518.

54. *The Adventures of Tom Sawyer* (London: Chatto & Windus, 1885 edition) p. 182. The words 'stark naked' are edited out of the Penguin text!

55. *In Bad Faith*, pp. 97-8.

56. A self-justifying mythologising and mystification of master–slave relations. The master, the head of the plantation 'family', saw himself in the role of fatherly authority and carer to his 'children', the (supposedly) child-like slaves.

57. Robert Tracy, 'Myth and Reality in *The Adventures of Tom Sawyer*', in Gary Scharnhorst (ed.), *Critical Essays on The Adventures of Tom Sawyer*, p. 110.

58. See the London *Times*, 28 August 1876, and also Moncure Conway's two reviews of the book, reprinted in *Critical Essays on The Adventures of Tom Sawyer*, pp. 40, 24, 27.

59. Ronald T. Takaki, *Iron Cages: Race and Culture in Nineteenth-Century America* (London: Athlone Press, 1980 [1979]) p. 84.

60. Dee Brown, *Bury My Heart at Wounded Knee* (London: Pan, 1974 [1970]) p. 11.

61. Robert Tracy, 'Myth and Reality in *The Adventures of Tom Sawyer*', p. 110.

62. Forrest Robinson, *In Bad Faith*, p. 52. See too Robert Tracy, 'Myth and Reality in *The Adventures of Tom Sawyer*', pp. 110–11.

63. Where, none the less, the signs of industry are present in the 'boiler iron' which sheathes the (triple-locked) big doors to McDougal's cave (p. 202) and behind which Indian Joe dies. This is not a pre-industrial society. The actions of the small boy in the school Examination Day ritual who accompanies his recitation 'with the painfully exact and spasmodic gestures which a machine might have used – supposing the machine to be a trifle out of order' and who makes his 'manufactured bow' as he finishes (p. 137) is symptomatic though, I would suggest,

of a post-bellum concern (about man–machine coordinates) that would gradually cause much more anxiety on Twain's part as the century progressed. The description seems irrelevant, though, to the St Petersburg of the 1830s–1840s represented in the text.

64. Only in the superstitions which are so much a part of the imaginative life of both children, and adults, in the village (see pp. 77, 121) do we see signs of interculturalism, of the African-American influence on the dominant culture.

65. Wayne Fields, 'When the Fences are Down', p. 372.

66. Steven Mailloux connects this with the 'more tolerant attitude toward temporary youthful deviance' (p. 147) in the period. He distinguishes strongly, though, between the disciplinary use of juvenile fictions for boys and for girls. See 'The Rhetorical Use and Abuse of Fiction', pp. 140–50. My earlier use of Brodhead suggests a possible bridging of this divide.

Chapter 5 Racial Politics in *Huckleberry Finn*

1. Mark Twain, *The Adventures of Huckleberry Finn* (Harmondsworth, Middx.: Penguin, 1987) p. 348. Page numbers to follow quotes from henceforth. The correct, original title of the novel is *Adventures of Huckleberry Finn*. It was published in the United States in 1885, after prior publication in England and Canada in 1884.

2. John C. Gerber, 'Introduction: The Continuing Adventures of *Huckleberry Finn*', in Robert Sattelmeyer and J. Donald Crowley (eds), *One Hundred Years of Huckleberry Finn: The Boy, His Book, and American Culture* (Columbia: University of Missouri Press, 1985) p. 3.

3. See Laurie Champion (ed.), *The Critical Response to Mark Twain's Huckleberry Finn* (Westport, Conn.: Greenwood Press, 1991) pp. 3, 44.

4. *The New Yorker*, 26 June–3 July 1995, pp. 128–33 (Styron's quote is on this last page). The brief extract, where Jim is ordered, by the medical student who is his master, to warm up the body of a dead man to render him pliable for dissection, rehearses – in comic/grotesque manner – the themes of resurrection (and false resurrection) and of symbolic exchange that run through the whole novel. The sexual undercurrents of the episode readily explain its eventual omission from the novel.

5. Eric Solomon, 'My *Huckleberry Finn*: Thirty Years in the Classroom with Huck and Jim', in Robert Sattelmeyer and J. Donald Crowley (eds), *One Hundred Years of Huckleberry Finn*, p. 246. Solomon's essay provides a good critical account as to why the novel has this canonic status, though he underemphasises the reception of the text in its developing historical context; the way in which each generation of critics has been able (to date) to renegotiate the multiple meanings available in the novel to fit its own academic, cultural and ideological needs.

6. David R. Sewell, *Mark Twain's Languages: Discourse, Dialogue and Linguistic Variety* (Berkeley: University of California Press, 1987) p. 86.

7. See Lee Clark Mitchell, '"Nobody but Our Gang warn't Around": The Authority of Language in *Huckleberry Finn'*, in Louis J. Budd (ed.), *New Essays on Huckleberry Finn* (Cambridge: Cambridge University Press, 1985) especially pp. 88, 102, 104. See too Gregg Camfield, *Sentimental Twain: Samuel Clemens in the Maze of Moral Philosophy* (Philadelphia: University of Pennsylvania Press, 1994) especially pp. 6–13.

8. For a good selection of the more recent critical work on the novel, I would recommend Louis J. Budd (ed.), *New Essays on Huckleberry Finn*; Robert Sattelmeyer and J. Donald Crowley (eds), *One Hundred Years of Huckleberry Finn*; Laurie Champion (ed.), *The Critical Response to Mark Twain's Huckleberry Finn*; and the relevant essays in Forrest G. Robinson (ed.), *The Cambridge Companion to Mark Twain*.

9. See Marcia Jacobson on the use of the narrating adult and of autobiographical and fictional materials in the boy book: *Being a Boy Again: Autobiography and the American Boy Book* (Tuscaloosa: University of Alabama Press, 1994) pp. 20–3. *Huckleberry Finn* is not, according to this definition, in the genre.

10. Steven Mailloux, *Rhetorical Power* (Ithaca, NY: Cornell University Press, 1989) pp. 102, 117. Mailloux sites the book's reception in terms of the 'cultural debates and social practices concerned with juvenile delinquency'.

11. See Laurie Champion (ed.), *The Critical Response to Mark Twain's Huckleberry Finn*, p. 46

12. Jonathan Arac sees such readings as a type of self-reflexive critical activity on the part of a scholarly community, which thus takes its own 'countercultural' stance against 'actually existing America'. See 'Nationalism, Hypercanonization, and *Huckleberry Finn'*, *boundary 2*, vol. 19, no. 1 (1992) pp. 20–4. Arac starts with Henry Nash Smith (1962) and moves forward from there. I would tend rather to contextualise such activity in terms of New Criticism and its legacy, and the focus on myth and symbol it fostered, and would see its influence on criticism post 1970 (though any choice of date will be somewhat arbitrary) as much more limited than Arac suggests.

13. Laurence B. Holland suggests the unstable nature of the difference between liberation and enslavement throughout much of the novel in 'A "Raft of Trouble": Word and Deed in *Huckleberry Finn'*, in Eric Sundquist (ed.), *American Realism: New Essays* (Baltimore, Md.: Johns Hopkins University Press, 1982), p. 71.

14. Shelley Fisher Fishkin, *Was Huck Black? Mark Twain and African-American Voices* (New York: Oxford University Press, 1993) pp. 70–1.

15. R. J. Ellis, '"I Knowed He Was White Inside": Huck Finn's Dangerous Language', *Overhere: Reviews in American Studies*, vol. 14, no. 2 (Winter 1994) p. 10.

16. Jonathan Arac, 'Nationalism, Hypercanonization, and *Huckleberry Finn'*, p. 26. Christine MacLeod argues for exactly such a sense in 'Telling the Truth in a Tight Place: *Huckleberry Finn* and the Reconstruction Era', *The Southern Quarterly*, vol. 34, no. 1 (Fall 1995) pp. 5–15. She contends that the 'social and political implications' of the

novel's subtext are for the reader to reinstate; that 'Twain in *Huckleberry Finn* offered a cogent critique of America's failure to live out the true meaning of the emancipation it had proclaimed. . . . But . . . [Twain] knew that in a society still wedded to the doctrines and practices of white supremacy, direct truth-telling was a high risk strategy. Hence the masks, the narrative displacements, and the signifying silences' (p. 14). The problem of audience response in Twain's own time must remain unresolved. Mailloux's argument in *Rhetorical Power* does not fully explain why a concern with the question of juvenile delinquency should necessarily have meant a complete denial of the race issue. The questions which still need addressing may, as MacLeod starts to suggest, have to do with the relation between humour and hegemonic codes; between realist techniques and countervailing (allegorical) strategies of indirection.

17. Steven Mailloux, *Rhetorical Power*, pp. 103, 64–5, 69.
18. Toni Morrison, *Playing in the Dark: Whiteness and the Literary Imagination* (Cambridge, Mass.: Harvard University Press, 1992) pp. 5, 33.
19. *Was Huck Black?*, pp. 140, 14, 15.
20. Quoting Werner Sollors and Charles Johnson respectively. See *Was Huck Black?*, p. 141.
21. I take my terms from J. L. Dillard, *Black English: Its History and Usage in the United States* (New York: Random House, 1972).
22. For a critical challenge to Fishkin's thesis, see Myra Jehlen, 'Banned in Concord: *Adventures of Huckleberry Finn* and Classic American Literature', in Forrest Robinson (ed.), *The Cambridge Companion to Mark Twain*, p. 113. Jehlen's description of Jimmy's voice as 'impersonated' by Huck does not, though, do entire justice to Fishkin's argument, and her assertions about 'Huck's cultural power' need some modification, at least.
23. *Was Huck Black?*, p. 107.
24. Michael Holquist, 'Introduction' to M. M. Bakhtin, *The Dialogic Imagination: Four Essays*, trans. Caryl Emerson and Michael Holquist (Austin: University of Texas Press, 1981) p. xviii.
25. In *Civil Rights and the Idea of Freedom* (New York: Oxford University Press, 1992), Richard King defines the different meanings of the concept 'freedom' as it has been used in the American (and Western) political context.
26. Neil Schmitz, *Of Huck and Alice: Humorous Writing in American Literature* (Minneapolis: University of Minnesota Press, 1983) p. 103.
27. Both Huck and Jim experience institutional oppression. It is, however, in Huck's case, the internal and psychological results of such oppression that have the most effect. Though Huck's legal status is at issue (as far as his father's rights over his money is concerned), it is not the dominant and determining factor it is for Jim.
28. The terms I use here are all taken from Harriet Jacobs, *Incidents in the Life of a Slave Girl*, in Henry Louis Gates (ed.), *The Classic Slave Narratives* (New York: Mentor, 1987 [1861]) pp. 408, 380, 342. The relation between

Twain's novel and the (ante-bellum) slave narrative becomes more obvious as I proceed.

29. As Howard Horwitz points out there is a Lockean self-legislative charge to this. Our first property is precisely ourselves. See *By the Law of Nature: Form and Value in Nineteenth- Century America* (New York: Oxford University Press, 1991) p. 102.

30. The Exodus motif is a repeated one in the novel. Richard King notes that its particular definition of 'freedom as collective deliverance is ambiguous as to whether it is a story of being freed or of self-liberation, of chosenness or self-initiated rebellion'. Such an ambiguity is relevant to the way Twain's narrative works. See *Civil Rights and the Idea of Freedom*, p. 28.

31. After the threat to Jim posed by the two men in the skiff, he immediately starts to use the first-person plural again (p. 150). The generally fluid nature of pronouns in the text repeatedly raises questions of identity and interest.

32. My use of this term is drawn from Richard King, *Civil Rights and the Idea of Freedom*, p. 13.

33. Laurence B. Holland, '"A Raft of Trouble"', p. 70.

34. Frederick Douglass, *Narrative of the Life of Frederick Douglass, An American Slave* (Harmondsworth, Middx.: Penguin, 1982 [1845]) p. 138.

35. My analysis overlaps and runs parallel to that of Neil Schmitz, in *Of Huck and Alice*, here. I acknowledge my critical debt to this landmark study in my own tracing of Huck and Jim's diverging stories.

36. Huck's double-voicedness, and the way this relates to his sense of self, explains his failure to proceed, to actually betray Jim here. A second discourse has already developed in the context not of the surrounding world, but of the community of two on the river; one which arises out of the shared aspects of their narratives to this point. Huck wavers between these forms of discourse throughout. See my *New Readings of the American Novel* (Basingstoke: Macmillan, 1990) for fuller development of this argument.

37. Neil Schmitz, *Of Huck and Alice*, p. 103.

38. As many critics have pointed out, the more attractive aspects of Tom's character are marginalised in this novel.

39. See Eric Lott, who sees Jim's appearance here as 'recall[ing] the art of blackface at the same time that it explodes the very idea of racial performance'. 'Mr, Clemens and Jim Crow: Twain, Race, and Blackface', in Forrest Robinson, *The Cambridge Companion to Mark Twain*, p. 140. In his fascinating essay, Lott argues that 'blackface minstrelsy underwrote one of the nineteenth century's most powerful antiracist novels – a tribute to the political fractures of minstrelsy and *Huckleberry Finn* both', p. 133.

40. See Myra Jehlen, 'Banned in Concord', p. 100.

41. David L. Smith, 'Huck, Jim, and American Racial Discourse', in James S. Leonard, Thomas A. Tenney, Thadious M. Davis (eds), *Satire or Evasion? Black Perspectives on Huckleberry Finn* (Durham, NC: Duke University Press, 1992) p. 104.

42. I am using terms taken from Eric Lott, 'Love and Theft: The Racial Unconscious of Blackface Minstrelsy', *Representations*, vol. 39 (1992) p. 28.
43. For part of the novel's achievement is in the tension it creates between the *social* powerlessness of Huck's voice and his *narrative* control over the more authoritative social voices represented through it (Jim, with his low social status, is the exception to this rule). Huck is consistently seen in passive relationship to the larger riverbank society, finally bound by its words and value schemes. As narrator, however, he lays out the different voices of southwestern culture for us to hear (in their power, their typicality and their interweavings) and, through that very narrative authority, unwittingly but effectively critiques them. Huck's voice, then, challenges and tears the mask from these languages, even while it cannot escape their influence.
44. Thomas R. R. Cobb, a major legal scholar in the ante-bellum South, wrote that: 'Of the three great absolute rights guaranteed to every citizen by the common law [personal security, personal liberty and private property], the slave, in a state of pure or absolute slavery, is totally deprived.' See James Oakes, *Slavery and Freedom: An Interpretation of the Old South* (New York: Alfred A. Knopf, 1990) pp. 69–70.
45. Huck's voice is not a unified one, and the degree to which Jim's story is, and remains, separate from and subordinate to his, varies. One can argue that Huck's intention to free Jim, articulated in Chapter 31 of the book, remains constant, even when he (disturbingly) acts as Tom's double in the evasion sequence.
46. John H. Wallace, 'The Case Against *Huck Finn*', and David L. Smith, 'Huck, Jim, and American Racial Discourse', both in James S. Leonard, Thomas A. Tenney and Thadious M. Davis (eds), *Satire or Evasion?*, pp. 16, 107. In 'Black Critics and Mark Twain', in Forrest Robinson (ed.), *The Cambridge Companion to Mark Twain*, pp. 116–28, Smith argues that the fact that critics (both black and white) interpret the racial implications of the text so differently is not a sign of 'authorial failings' (p. 122). Rather it indicates their different political position on the question of race. For discussion of the critical debate concerning Jim's role, see too Shelley Fisher Fishkin, *Was Huck Black?*, pp. 79–92. The use of the word 'nigger' does mean that, whatever one thinks of the representation of Jim, and regarding the level of irony in the book, a problem remains in the teaching of it to an American (and British) audience where racism remains a part of everyday life. For one positive response to this, see Jocelyn Chadwick-Jones, 'Mark Twain and the Fires of Controversy: Teaching Racially-Sensitive Literature: Or, "Say That 'N' Word and Out You Go!"', in Laurie Champion (ed.), *The Critical Response to Mark Twain's Huckleberry Finn*, pp. 228–37.
47. Fredrick Woodard and Donnarae MacCann, 'Minstrel Shackles and Nineteenth-Century "Liberality"'; David L. Smith, 'Huck, Jim, and American Racial Discourse'. Both in *Satire or Evasion?*, pp. 142, 112.

48. W. E. Du Bois, *Souls of Black Folk* (Chicago, Ill.: A. C. McClurg, 1903) pp. 2–3.
49. Forrest G. Robinson, 'The Characterization of Jim in *Huckleberry Finn*', in Laurie Champion (ed.), *The Critical Response to Mark Twain's Huckleberry Finn*, p. 220.
50. This is not at all to argue against Jim's intelligence. It is though to posit an unbridgeable gap between what he says and does, and how they can be interpreted.
51. Bruce Michelson examines the whole cycle of texts about Tom and Huck to warn against necessarily seeing them as dissimilar figures. See *Mark Twain on the Loose: A Comic Writer and the American Self* (Amherst: University of Massachusetts Press, 1995) pp. 95–141.
52. From an unpublished paper by William L. Andrews, '*Huckleberry Finn* and the Slave Narrative Tradition', pp. 18–19. My thanks to the author for his permission to quote. I would be more tentative than Andrews in making the connection between Jim's loss of agency and of manhood, again in line with the fact that we are given Jim from the outside only.
53. Robert William Fogel, *Without Consent or Contract: The Rise and Fall of American Slavery* (New York: W. W. Norton, 1989) p. 191. Fogel estimates this at six thousand dollars at 1989 rates.
54. Laurence B. Holland, '"A Raft of Trouble"', p. 71.
55. Victor A. Doyno, *Writing Huck Finn: Mark Twain's Creative Process* (Pennsylvania: University of Philadelphia Press, 1991) p. 230.
56. Ira Berlin, *Slaves Without Masters: The Free Negro in the Antebellum South* (New York: Pantheon, 1974) p. xiv.
57. Quoted in Eric Foner, *Reconstruction: America's Unfinished Revolution, 1863–1877* (New York: Harper and Row, 1989 [1988]) p. 602.
58. Eric Foner, *Reconstruction*, p. 598.
59. Shelley Fisher Fishkin, *Was Huck Black?*, p. 75. Fishkin gives further bibliographical detail.
60. See Christine MacLeod, 'Telling the Truth in a Tight Place', for a full and strong refutation, based on a post-bellum historical contextualisation, of charges that the evasion sequence is artistically inept.
61. Shelley Fisher Fishkin, *Was Huck Black?*, p. 74.
62. Joyce Rowe, *Equivocal Endings in Classic American Novels* (Cambridge: Cambridge University Press, 1988) p. 48.
63. Jonathan Arac, 'Nationalism, Hypercanonization, and *Huckleberry Finn*', pp. 26, 33. I take strong issue here with Arac and his argument that Twain's novel is 'antihistorical' (p. 26). For to use indirect or allegorical methods is not, as he suggests, to '[cut] off the address to . . . acknowledged national concerns' (p. 18). Arac's argument starts by using a four-part scheme (national, local, personal and literary). As it proceeds, though, it comes to turn on the literary/national binary; one which, like all other binaries, is suspect. This may be a useful ploy for suggesting a variable relationship, even an increasing gap, between literary culture and national history as the nineteenth century progressed, but to conclude that Twain's novel rejects the possibility of

public debate – operates in some way outside the province of history – seems to me a bizarre interpretive move. Arac's article is reprinted in Donald E. Pease (ed.), *National Identities and Post-Americanist Narratives* (Durham, NC: Duke University Press, 1994) pp. 14–33.

64. Richard C. Moreland, '"He Wants to Put His Story Next to Hers": Putting Twain's Story Next to Hers in Morrison's *Beloved*', *Modern Fiction Studies*, vol. 39, nos. 3 and 4 (Fall/Winter 1993) p. 505. See Arac, 'Nationalism, Hypercanonization, and *Huckleberry Finn*', pp. 18, 30, 31, for similar arguments.

65. Moreland uses this term just before the above quotation, '"He wants to Put His Story Next to Hers"', p. 505.

66. Other endings have been suggested. For example, John Seelye, in his *The True Adventures of Huckleberry Finn* (New York: Simon and Schuster, 1970) has Jim, weighed down by his chains, drowning in the Mississippi as he attempts escape from the Phelps' and before Huck can get to help him. Though this foregrounds the pessimistic implications kept below the surface in Twain's narrative, I am not sure it engages 'the contingencies of history' any more effectively.

67. See 'Nationalism, Hypercanonization, and *Huckleberry Finn*', pp. 18, 33.

68. I borrow the words used by Richard King in his analysis of Faulkner's *Go Down, Moses* here, and in the passages that directly follow. See *The Southern Renaissance: The Cultural Awakening of the American South, 1930–1955* (New York: Oxford University Press, 1980) p. 138.

69. Richard C. Moreland, '"He Wants to Put His Story Next to Hers"', p. 506. I take the idea of stories being put together from Moreland too as he (mainly) focuses on Paul D. and Sethe in *Beloved*. To stress, this is not to deny the important differences in Huck and Jim's narratives but to argue for sameness too: on the raft, if provisionally, they share at times both interests and story. Sameness and difference are not incompatible, as any theory of multiculturalism would recognise.

70. Roderick Waterman, *Reclaiming the Perverse: Some Readings of Sherwood Anderson and Carson McCullers* (unpublished MA dissertation, University of Nottingham, 1992) p. 24. Waterman uses Bakhtin to argue for a new reading of the grotesque. I redirect here some of his argument to my different context, and thank him for his permission to do so.

71. Leslie A. Fiedler, *Love and Death in the American Novel* (New York: Stein and Day, 1966 [1960]) pp. 352, 355.

72. Mikhail Bakhtin, *The Dialogic Imagination: Four Essays*, trans. Caryl Emerson and Michael Holquist (Austin: University of Texas Press, 1981) p. 229. In writing this, Bakhtin might have been using *Huckleberry Finn* as his model. For more detail on way the rhythms of nature and of human life interrelate in the idyll and in Twain's novel, see my *New Readings of the American Novel*, p. 227.

73. *The Dialogic Imagination*, p. 224, and Katerina Clark and Michael Holquist, *Mikhail Bakhtin* (Cambridge, Mass.: Harvard University Press, 1984) pp. 310–11.

74. See Steven Mailloux, *Rhetorical Power*, pp. 72–6, 83–6.

75. Christine MacLeod, 'Telling the Truth in a Tight Place', p. 7.

76. Harriet Jacobs, *Incidents in the Life of a Slave Girl*, p. 378.
77. For more detail and further analysis, see Steven Mailloux, 'Reading *Huckleberry Finn*: The Rhetoric of Performed Ideology', in Louis J. Budd (ed.), *New Essays On Huckleberry Finn*, pp. 107–33.
78. Christine MacLeod, 'Telling the Truth in a Tight Place', p. 8.

Chapter 6   Fantasy and *A Connecticut Yankee in King Arthur's Court*

1. Lady Emmeline Stuart Wortley, a British traveller in America in the 1840s, quoted by Karen Halttunen in *Confidence Men and Painted Women: A Study of Middle-class Culture in America, 1830–1870* (New Haven, Conn.: Yale University Press, 1982) p. 31.
2. Robert Pack Browning, Michael B. Frank and Lin Salamo (eds), *Mark Twain's Notebooks & Journals, Volume 3 (1883–1891)*, p. 311.
3. Quoted in Arnold Beichman, 'The First Electrocution', *Commentary*, vol. 35 (1963) p. 417.
4. William J. Collins, 'Hank Morgan in the Garden of Forking Paths: *A Connecticut Yankee in King Arthur's Court* as Alternative History', *Modern Fiction Studies*, vol. 32 (1986) p. 111.
5. Shelley Fisher Fishkin says his writings on race are 'complex and ambiguous', *Was Huck Black? Mark Twain and African American Voices* (New York: Oxford University Press, 1993) p. 125.
6. Harold Beaver, *Huckleberry Finn* (London: Allen and Unwin, 1987) pp. 48–9. See my *New Readings of the American Novel* (Basingstoke: Macmillan, 1990) p. 239, for further discussion of the polygeneric aspects of the book.
7. Roger George calls Twain 'one of the pioneers of nineteenth-century realism', in '"The Road Lieth Not Straight": Maps and Mental Models in *A Connecticut Yankee in King Arthur's Court*', *American Transcendental Quarterly*, vol. 5 n.s. (March, 1991) p. 64. See too, with specific reference to *Huckleberry Finn*, Alan Trachtenberg, *The Incorporation of America: Culture and Society in the Gilded Age* (New York: Hill and Wang, 1982) p. 190. Bruce Michelson points to the problems in categorising Twain as a realist, describing 'things as they are', when he writes: 'But what if [the] "real world" . . . is seen to be saturated with delusion, pretence, fantasy? The task of the realist in such straits may call not for box-cameras, but rather for dynamite: disorienting and even violent breakthroughs into the concealed truth about human experience. And if such breakthroughs require strange pyrotechnics – dream-selves, fantasies of time-travel, or 'whoppers' embedded in supposedly factual travel narratives and personal histories – so be it.' See *Twain on the Loose: A Comic Writer and the American Self* (Amherst: University of Massachusetts Press, 1995) pp. 6–7. While I agree with the general thematic lines of Michelsen's analysis, his framing of it in the context of a discussion of realism seems to me to stretch generic boundaries to definitional breaking point. Realism becomes the *same* as fantasy or tall tale here. Michael Davitt Bell, in *The Problem of American Realism: Studies*

in the Cultural History of a Literary Idea (Chicago: University of Chicago Press, 1993), argues that 'the case for connecting *Huckleberry Finn* to the supposed tradition of American realism seems, at every point, an exceptionally weak one' (p. 57). Somewhat unexpectedly, as far as accepted critical opinion goes, he then discusses *A Connecticut Yankee* in terms both of Twain's 'conversion to realist values' (p. 69), and dramatisation of the instability of those values. I would resist the narrow limits of Bell's definitions and conclusions, and would continue to argue for the usefulness and relevance of 'realism' as a discrete generic term despite the problems that surround it. One of the best introductions to the techniques and concept of realism in the context of late nineteenth-century American literature is in June Howard's opening chapter to *Form and History in American Literary Naturalism* (Chapel Hill: University of North Carolina Press, 1985) pp. 3–35.

8. June Howard, *Form and History in American Literary Naturalism*, pp. 11–12.

9. Terry Eagleton, *Literary Theory: An Introduction* (Oxford: Basil Blackwell, 1983) p. 136. The claim that reality can be straightforwardly represented is, as any theory of realism now recognises, naive. As E. H. Gombrich, in *Art and Illusion*, writes, 'All thinking is sorting, classifying' (quoted in June Howard, *Form and History in American Literary Naturalism*, p. 15), and accordingly any representation of reality depends on, and is skewed in one way or another by, the angle of perception and the ideological and historical positioning of the subject involved.

10. 'The Country of the Blue', the introduction to Eric Sundquist (ed.), *American Realism: New Essays* (Baltimore, Md.: Johns Hopkins University Press, 1982) p. 8. This is a good general essay on realism in America as a response to 'the social and psychological effects of industrial capitalism' (p. 6).

11. Rosemary Jackson, *Fantasy: The Literature of Subversion* (London: Methuen, 1981) pp. 82–3. Or as Catherine Belsey puts it, 'Classic realism presents individuals whose traits of character, understood as essential and predominantly given, constrain the choices they make, and whose potential for development depends on what is given. . . . "The mind of man" . . . is shown in classic realism to be the source of understanding, of action and of history', *Critical Practice* (London: Methuen, 1980) pp. 74–5.

12. Lee Clark Mitchell, *Determined Fictions: American Literary Naturalism* (New York: Columbia University Press, 1989) p. xii.

13. *The Adventures of Huckleberry Finn* (Harmondsworth, Middx.: Penguin, 1987) p. 283.

14. The term is Lee Clark Mitchell's. See *Determined Fictions*, p. xii.

15. Rosemary Jackson, *Fantasy*, p. 35.

16. *The Adventures of Huckleberry Finn*, p. 141.

17. M. M. Bakhtin, *The Dialogic Imagination: Four Essays*, trans. Caryl Emerson and Michael Holquist (Austin: University of Texas Press, 1981) p. 404.

18. Tony Bennett, *Formalism and Marxism* (London: Methuen, 1979) p. 21.
19. John Carlos Rowe calls the novel a 'historical romance' in 'How the Boss Played the Game: Twain's Critique of Imperialism in *A Connecticut Yankee in King Arthur's Court*', in Forrest G. Robinson (ed.), *The Cambridge Companion to Mark Twain* (Cambridge: Cambridge University Press, 1995) p. 176. Richard Pressman discusses the relation between sentimentalism and realism in the novel in 'A Connecticut Yankee in Merlin's Cave: The Role of Contradiction in Mark Twain's Novel', *American Literary Realism 1870–1910*, vol. 16 (1983) pp. 58–72. Bruce Michelson discusses the book in terms of the 'battle lines on literary modes' (p. 156) – romance and realism – drawn in it, in *Mark Twain on the Loose*, pp. 150–1. Gregory M. Pfitzer treats it as displaced western in '"Iron Dudes and White Savages in Camelot": The Influence of Dime-Novel Sensationalism on Twain's *A Connecticut Yankee in King Arthur's Court*', *American Literary Realism*, vol. 27, no. 1 (Fall 1994) pp. 42–58. For readings of the novel as science fiction, see, for instance, John Clute, 'Time Travel Past', in Samuel L. Macey (ed.), *Encyclopedia of Time* (New York: Garland, 1994) pp. 646–7. Here Clute equates some forms of science fiction with fantasy. This suggests that the categorisations I mention are by no means exclusive. My thanks to Nick Mount for bringing Clute's entry to my attention. William J. Collins, too, discusses Twain's role as 'innovator of science fiction themes' (p. 111) in 'Hank Morgan in the Garden of Forking Paths: *A Connecticut Yankee in King Arthur's Court* as Alternative History'. His discussion of our readerly hesitation concerning the status of Hank's evidence for his journey through time also leads straight back to definitions of the fantastic.
20. See James M. Cox, who calls the novel 'inverted Utopian fantasy' in *Mark Twain: The Fate of Humor* (Princeton, NJ: Princeton University Press, 1966) p. 203. Winfried Fluck echoes him in saying that 'the novel which can be considered as an inverse utopian novel is clearly a fantasy', 'The Restructuring of History and the Intrusion of Fantasy in Mark Twain's "A Connecticut Yankee in King Arthur's Court"', in Winfried Fluck, Jurgen Peper and Willi Paul Adams (eds), *Forms and Functions of History in American Literature* (Berlin: Erich Schmidt Verlag, 1981) p. 136.
21. Rosemary Jackson, *Fantasy*, p. 34. See my 'Towards the Absurd: Mark Twain's *A Connecticut Yankee*, *Puddn'head Wilson* and *The Great Dark*' in Robert Giddings (ed.), *Mark Twain: A Sumptuous Variety* (London and Totowa, NJ: Vision and Barnes & Noble, 1985) pp. 176–98, for further analysis of the relationship between realism and fantasy, magic and science.
22. See Rosemary Jackson, *Fantasy*, pp. 25–6, 22, 23. She is drawing on the work of other critics (Tzvetan Todorov, Joanna Russ and Irene Bessiere).
23. Mark Twain, *A Connecticut Yankee in King Arthur's Court* (London: Penguin, 1986 [1889]) p. 36. Page references to follow quotes henceforth.

24. See, for instance, William J. Collins, 'Hank Morgan in the Garden of Forking Paths', pp. 112–14.

25. T. J. Jackson Lears's analysis of the 'antimodern impulse' rising out of the dissatisfaction with modern culture in late nineteenth-century America (and Europe), and the terms he uses, provide a particularly useful context for discussion of Twain's novel. See *No Place of Grace; Antimodernism and the Transformation of American Culture, 1880–1920* (New York: Pantheon, 1981).

26. Everett Carter, 'The Meaning of *A Connecticut Yankee*', *American Literature*, vol. 50 (1978–9) pp. 418–40.

27. Louis J. Budd, 'A (Better-Humored) Re-trial for Hank Morgan: Convicted Mass Murderer', *Over Here: Reviews in American Studies*, vol. 15, nos. 1 and 2, (Summer and Winter 1995) p. 6. Budd argues that 'our dismissive hindsight has distorted the interpretations of *A Connecticut Yankee*' (p. 9). I would defend my reading of the novel, while recognising the validity of alternative responses to it.

28. Everett Carter, 'The Meaning of *A Connecticut Yankee*', p. 440.

29. See Mark Seltzer, *Bodies and Machines* (New York: Routledge, 1992) pp. 6–9, 11, 94–5, 153; Martha Banta, 'The Boys and the Bosses: Twain's Double Take on Work, Play, and the Democratic Ideal', *American Literary History*, vol. 3, no. 3 (Fall 1991) pp. 487–520; Ronald T. Takaki, *Iron Cages: Race and Culture in Nineteenth-Century America* (London: Athlone Press, 1979), pp. 147–70; Cindy Weinstein, *The Literature of Labor and the Labors of Literature: Allegory in Nineteenth-Century American Fiction* (Cambridge: Cambridge University Press, 1995) pp. 129–72.

30. Ronald T. Takaki, *Iron Cages*, pp. 166, 169–70.

31. Walter Benn Michaels, *The Gold Standard and the Logic of Naturalism: American Literature at the Turn of the Century* (Berkeley: University of California Press, 1987).

32. Martha Banta, 'The Boys and the Bosses', p. 489.

33. Cindy Weinstein, *The Literature of Labor and the Labors of Literature*, p. 10. The first quote is taken directly from Michel Foucault. In *Bodies and Machines*, Mark Seltzer, too, uses a Foucaultian base to examine tensions concerning body/machine boundaries in 'turn-of-the-century American culture and beyond' (p. 3). As Weinstein indicates, and as any study of twentieth-century modernist literature would confirm, anxieties about agency and technology cannot in fact be confined to a specific 'critical cultural moment' but are generally evident from mid-nineteenth century onward. It can be argued, roughly following Seltzer, that it is toward the end of the century, in a period of considerable social turmoil, that such anxieties reach a climax.

34. Mark Seltzer, *Bodies and Machines*, p. 19.

35. For Twain criticises the hermit and his value system just as much as he does Hank, following his source in this: W. H. Lecky's *History of European Morals* (1872). Lecky focuses especially on the masochistic self-abuse, all performed in the name of self-discipline and God's greater glory, of such hermits. He gives further information on St Stylites and his actions: 'For a whole year, we are told, St Simeon stood

upon one leg, the other being covered with hideous ulcers, while his biographer was commissioned to stand by his side, to pick up the worms that fell from his body, and to replace them in the sores, the saint saying to the worm, "Eat what God has given you".' If Simeon Stylites was a Christian saint to his contemporaries, with biographer at hand to close the gap between the wounding of the self and the writing of the saintliness it signified, to Lecky writing in 1872, to Twain (his Victorian contemporary) and to Hank, such 'hideous maceration of the body', far from being 'the highest proof of excellence' was quite without point or value. The relevant passages from Lecky are quoted in the Norton Critical edition of *A Connecticut Yankee* (New York: W. W. Norton, 1982). Here, see pp. 266, 264.

36. Werner Sollors, 'Ethnicity', in Frank Lentricchia and Thomas McLaughlin (eds), *Critical Terms for Literary Study* (Chicago: University of Chicago Press, 1990) pp. 297, 294, 293.

37. Such methods were taken for granted by those whom T. J. Jackson Lears calls the 'ruling-class custodians of [Victorian] culture'. See *No Place of Grace*, p. 10.

38. Martha Banta, *Taylored Lives: Narrative Productions in the Age of Taylor, Veblen, and Ford* (Chicago: University of Chicago Press, 1993) pp. 43, ix, 235, 3.

39. Werner Sollors, 'Ethnicity', p. 295.

40. Martha Banta, *Taylored Lives*, p. 3.

41. Certainly, at any rate, conspicuous consumption and emulative display, as well as social hierarchy, explain the more decorative versions of the shirt which are produced.

42. See Martha Banta, *Taylored Lives*, p. 9. She is referring to Chaplin's *Modern Times* in her use of the phrase.

43. Again reminding of Foucault, with his emphasis on the forms of regularisation and control, the disciplinary procedures that come together to create 'docile bodies'; reminding too of his analysis of 'panopticism'. See *Discipline and Punish: The Birth of the Prison* (London: Penguin, 1991 [1975]), pp. 135–69 and 195–228.

44. I borrow Banta's terminology here. See *Taylored Lives*, p. 29. I also follow Banta earlier, in my punning on Taylor's name.

45. Mark Seltzer, *Bodies and Machines*, p. 155.

46. Martha Banta, *Taylored Lives*, p. 382.

47. See Mark Seltzer, *Bodies and Machines*, p. 157. Ford's calculations and his concern for exact numbers echo Hank's. See, too, Twain's own obsessive calculations over the Paige typesetter – those given in *Mark Twain's Notebooks & Journals, Volume 3*, p. 585, are typical.

48. Matha Banta, *Taylored Lives*, p. 280.

49. Martha Banta, 'The Boys and the Bosses', p. 487, and see pp. 497–511.

50. T. J. Jackson Lear, *No Place of Grace*, p. 7.

51. Ronald Takaki, *Iron Cages*, p. 167.

52. John Carlos Rowe focuses on this aspect of the novel in 'How the Boss Played the Game'.

53. Soap is undoubtedly (positively) associated with Hank's sanitation

programme. Twain's repeated use in his work of the phrase 'soap and civilization' in an imperialist context carries, though, negative connotations.

54. The following sign was displayed in the Colt Factory Armoury: 'Every man Employed in or about my Armoury Whether by Piecewirk or by Days Wirk is Expected to Wirk Ten Hours During the Running of the Engine [steam power] & No one who Does not Chearfully Concent to Do this need expect to be employed by me. Saml Colt.' See R. C. Wilson, *Colt: An American Legend* (New York: Abbeville, 1985) p. 75.

55. Jennifer L. Rafferty makes similar points in 'Mark Twain, Labor and Technology: *A Connecticut Yankee*, and *No. 44, The Mysterious Stranger*', *Over Here: Reviews in American Studies*, vol. 15, nos. 1 and 2 (Summer and Winter 1995) pp. 24–7.

56. See the notebook entry, written in the period July 1888–May 1889, which echoes this passage: Robert Pack Browning, Michael B. Frank and Lin Salamo (eds), *Mark Twain's Notebooks & Journals: Volume 3*, p. 422.

57. I alter 'a light' as it appears in the Penguin text to 'light' in accord with the authoritative University of California Press edition of the novel.

58. *Mark Twain's Notebooks & Journals, Volume 3*, p. 418.

59. The phrase comes from Tim Armstrong's article, 'The Electrification of the Body at the Turn of the Century', *Textual Practice*, vol. 5, no. 3 (Winter 1991) p. 304.

60. See Arnold Bleichman, 'The First Electrocution', pp. 410, 411, 417, 415.

61. See Arnold Bleichman, 'The First Electrocution', pp. 410–11.

62. See Horst H. Kruse, 'Mark Twain's *A Connecticut Yankee*: Reconsiderations and Revisions', *American Literature*, vol. 62, no. 3 (September 1990) p. 478.

63. T. J. Jackson Lears, *No Place of Grace*, p. 12.

64. As has been often pointed out, Twain alludes in this novel both to the regional differences that were to end in the American Civil War, and to the Indian wars to follow. Thus a common reading of the book is one which sees the conflict between the values of Arthurian England and of Hank in terms of a contrast between a pastoral, feudal and slave-holding ante-bellum South, and a progressive and abolitionist North. Twain's own ambivalent attitude to the South (nostalgia as well as contempt) can then be seen to carry over to his Arthurian materials. Gregory Pfitzer reads the Battle of the Sand-Belt scenes in the different (Indian wars) context; as 'a kind of Custer's Last Stand in which the Indian nation achieves a temporary victory but is ultimately defeated', '"Iron Dudes and White Savages in Camelot"', pp. 48–9.

65. T. J. Jackson Lears, *No Place of Grace*, pp. 12–13. See Lears's remarks concerning the centre of 'nineteenth-century bourgeois morality . . . the autonomous individual, whose only moral master was himself'.

66. See *No Place of Grace*, p. 8.

67. Rosemary Jackson, *Fantasy*, pp. 82, 86.

68. This occurs in a bridging passage Twain wrote for excerpts of the novel

printed in *Century* magazine. See the Norton Critical edition of *A Connecticut Yankee*, note, p. 227.

69. Werner Sollors, 'Ethnicity', p. 302. Sollors uses the instability of the oppositional boundaries constructed in the novel to build a larger argument about the 'invented character' (p. 305) of national and ethnic difference.

70. Michael Davitt Bell, *The Problem of American Realism*, p. 66.

71. Werner Sollors, 'Ethnicity', pp. 303–4, 302.

72. *The Lost Land* was one of Twain's working titles for the novel. See *Mark Twain's Notebooks & Journals, Volume 3*, p. 216.

73. Following Sollors, who writes: ' . . . the Arthurians make themselves felt as mirror images of the Yankee's hidden self: whatever HM denies in himself he may call "Arthurian" – and try to destroy', 'Ethnicity', p. 303.

74. Max Weber, 'Science as a Vocation', quoted in Douglas Tallack, *Twentieth-Century America: The Intellectual and Cultural Context* (London: Longman, 1991) p. 21.

75. Georg Lukacs, 'Narrate or Describe' (1936), in *Writer and Critic and Other Essays*, ed. and trans. Arthur Kahn (London: Merlin, 1978) pp. 133, 125.

76. His *Personal Recollections of Joan of Arc* (1896) might seem to contradict this. Bruce Michelson's comment, though, is relevant here: '*Joan of Arc* turns out to be . . . an escapist work . . . [Joan] lives and dies above the political and moral messes that not only vex everyone else but make them who and what they are', *Mark Twain on the Loose*, p. 206.

77. Maria Ornelli Marotti, *The Duplicating Imagination: Twain and the Twain Papers* (Pennsylvania State University Press, 1990) p. 46.

Chapter 7 Severed Connections: *Puddn'head Wilson* and *Those Extraordinary Twins*

1. Mark Twain, 'An Encounter with an Interviewer,' in *The Stolen White Elephant Etc.* (London: Chatto & Windus, 1897 [1882]) pp. 223–4.

2. Arnold L. Weinstein, *Nobody's Home: Speech, Self, Place in American Fiction from Hawthorne to DeLillo* (New York: Oxford University Press, 1993) p. 67.

3. See Hamlin Hill (ed.), *Mark Twain's Letters to His Publishers: 1867–1894* (Berkeley: University of California Press, 1967) p. 328. Twain later seems to leave the choice of title in his publisher's hands, when he refers to the book as '"Puddn'head Wilson – A Tale." (Or, "Those Extraordinary Twins," if preferable.)', p. 337.

4. Mark Twain, *Puddn'head Wilson and Those Extraordinary Twins* (Harmondsworth, Middx.: Penguin, 1981[1894]) pp. 230, 303. Page references to follow quotes henceforth.

5. A practice which became the rule, rather than the exception, for future editions of the text(s). The first British edition, however, consisted of *Puddn'head Wilson, A Tale* alone.

6. Evan Carter, '*Puddn'head Wilson* and the Fiction of Law and Custom', in Eric J. Sundquist, *American Realism: New Essays* (Baltimore, Md.: The Johns Hopkins University Press, 1982) p. 88.

7. Susan Gillman, *Dark Twins: Imposture and Identity in Mark Twain's America* (Chicago: University of Chicago Press, 1989) p. 55. The emphasis is mine.

8. Twain follows accepted Victorian conventions here. Leslie Fiedler points out that '"monster" is the oldest word in our tongue for human anomolies', in *Freaks: Myths and Images of the Secret Self* (New York: Simon and Schuster, 1978) p. 16. Fiedler's title jars contemporary ears with its binary assumption of normality and complete abnormality. See Susan Gillman for brief comment on late nineteenth-century attitudes to Siamese twins in *Dark Twins*, pp. 55–6.

9. See Eric J. Sundquist, 'Mark Twain and Homer Plessy', in Susan Gillman and Forrest G. Robinson (eds), *Mark Twain's Puddn'head Wilson: Race, Conflict, and Culture* (Durham, NC: Duke University Press, 1990) pp. 66, 64. A revised version of this essay appears in Sundquist's *To Wake the Nations: Race in the Making of American Literature* (Cambridge, Mass.: Belknap Press, 1993) pp. 225–70.

10. Cindy Weinstein, *The Literature of Labor and the Labors of Literature: Allegory in Nineteenth-Century American Fiction* (Cambridge: Cambridge University Press, 1995) p. 139.

11. *Puddn'head Wilson* is still a comic text, but the dominant type of humour is a corrosive irony. I describe a general tendency here. *The American Claimant* (1892) combines farce and social satire, though unsteadily.

12. See Cindy Weinstein, *The Literature of Labor and the Labors of Literature*, pp. 138, 130, 131, 137, 150–2. I condense Weinstein's argument considerably.

13. Cindy Weinstein, *The Literature of Labor and the Labors of Literature*, pp. 159, 130, 160. I would see this process slightly differently. The comedy and expansiveness of the novel comes in Hank's descriptions of, and dialogue with, the medieval world he meets. His narrative accounting of his experience takes the form of an exploration of, and picaresque journey through, an unfamiliar world. As dialogue ends, and as Hank transforms this world into the image of that he already knows, so the comedy and the narrative possibilities close down also. His 'efficient making of persons' (Weinstein, p. 159) to operate as cogs in the system he has created marks the final stage of this process.

14. Arnold Weinstein argues differently. He sees character (and language) as mobile in *Puddn'head Wilson*, engaged in a 'counter-assault' (p. 68) on determinism. Consequently he argues against a one-dimensional 'allegorical' reading (p. 74). Weinstein's argument is strongly made and his account of the figurative play in the text is penetrating. I would, though, challenge his dismissal of the Siamese Twins story. Unlike him, too, I see webs of constraint fixing the terms of Roxy and Tom's actions throughout. Even when they do adopt disguise and shape-shift, it is always within the larger parameters of the racial boundaries which affect their every thought and move. Roxy's subversive act temporarily

upsets the racial order and reveals its arbitrary nature, but does not change its system. I acknowledge, though, the strength of Weinstein's (counter) reading. See *Nobody's Home: Speech, Self, Place in American Fiction from Hawthorne to DeLillo* (New York: Oxford University Press, 1993) pp. 65–88.

15. Eric Lott, 'Mr Clemens and Jim Crow: Twain, Race, and Blackface', in Forrest G. Robinson (ed.), *The Cambridge Companion to Mark Twain* (Cambridge: Cambridge University Press, 1995) p. 144.

16. Bruce Michelson uses this phrase. His description of Twain's subversion of 'basic rules for the framing of narratives' in both *Puddn'head Wilson* and 'The Man who Corrupted Hadleyburg', and his contextual remarks about the wider challenge to 'structural and thematic unities' taking place in 1890s' art, complement my present analysis. See *Mark Twain on the Loose: A Comic Writer and the American Self* (Amherst: University of Massachusetts Press, 1995) pp. 176, 177.

17. As I suggest in my later remarks on Tom and Roxana, Twain's position on the nature–nurture argument is never entirely consistent.

18. As I explore the Siamese twin motif, I recognise my critical debts here to the following: Susan Gillman, *Dark Twins*; Susan K. Gillman and Robert L. Patten, 'Dickens: Doubles:: Twain: Twins', *Nineteenth-Century Fiction*, vol. 39, no. 4 (March 1985) pp. 441–458; and Nancy Fredericks, 'Twain's Indelible Twins', *Nineteenth-Century Literature*, vol. 43, no. 4 (March 1989) pp. 484–99.

19. The Tocchis each had a head and arms but were joined from the sixth rib down. Their main difference from Twain's twins lies in the fact that, due to the different stages of development of their two legs, the Tocchis were unable to walk. See Leslie Fiedler, *Freaks*, p. 211.

20. Leslie Fiedler, *Freaks* pp. 217, 214, 213.

21. Hamlin Hill (ed.), *Mark Twain's Letters to his Publishers*, p. 319

22. Forrest G. Robinson, 'The Sense of Disorder in *Puddn'head Wilson*', in Susan Gillman and Forrest G. Robinson (eds), *Mark Twain's Puddn'head Wilson*, p. 32. The twins' status in terms of legal and political boundaries is particularly important.

23. Susan Gillman, *Dark Twins*, p. 63. She refers here just to the twins' 'problematic leg power'.

24. To cross between the two texts, this comment would have considerable resonance for a pre-Civil War slave, twinned in Siamese connection with a socially powerful master.

25. Arnold Weinstein, *Nobody's Home*, p. 68.

26. Again to cross to *Puddn'head Wilson*, Tom, as mulatto 'freak', can cause such disruption because Southern law and society, both ante- and post-bellum, only categorised racial difference in terms of 'black' and 'white'. The 'black–white binary that defines the US racial system and the master narrative of US race relations' contrasts with more complex systems of racial classification elsewhere. See Susan Gillman, 'Mark Twain's Travels in the Racial Occult', in Forrest G. Robinson (ed.), *The Cambridge Companion to Mark Twain*, pp. 201, 206.

27. Bruce Michelson, *Mark Twain on the Loose*, p. 200. His analysis is sharp

here: 'Joined at the waist . . . the Twins are indistinguishable in ways so gross that distinctions in identity, as this culture belabors them, become ludicrous. Luigi smokes, drinks coffee, reads heresy and votes Democrat, boozes heavily and brawls; Angelo stays a pious peaceful, nonsmoking, teetotalling Whig. Satiric fire rains upon such vices, virtues, and political inclinations, not in themselves but as preposterous indicators and measures of identity, as plausible definitions of human difference. Thus a deep-running theme of this sketch: that every Tweedledum or Tweedledee, with alterations in a few trivial habits, could really be anybody else, and that possibly everybody is fundamentally and inescapably just that: Tweedledum or Tweedledee.' See *Mark Twain on the Loose*, pp. 200–1. I make my own critical use of the Tweedledum/Tweedledee motif.

28. Eric J. Sundquist reads *Puddn'head Wilson* in the context of the *Plessy* v. *Ferguson* case (finally settled in 1896). Homer Plessy challenged the 1890 law establishing segregated railroad accommodation (in theory, but not in fact, 'equal but separate') in Louisiana. See *To Wake the Nations*, especially pp. 233–49.

29. Susan Gillman ponts out that Roxy's exchange is set in motion by her master's actions, thus 'in a peculiar way . . . the master is responsible for enslaving his own son', *Dark Twins*, pp. 63–4.

30. The fact that one twin is 'very masculine', the other 'much less so' (pp. 247–8), may accordingly connect with the crossings of gender boundaries in *Puddn'head Wilson*. Gillman notes that Twain, after this novel, 'explicitly pursue[s]' implications of the race/gender connection introduced here: 'if "male" and "female" are as readily interchanged as "black" and "white," then gender difference may prove to be as culturally constituted, as much "a fiction of law and custom" as racial difference.' *Dark Twins*, p. 79. See elsewhere in Gillman's book for other material on Twain and gender. This subject, increasingly the focus of critical interest, is explored by such scholars as Peter Stoneley in *Mark Twain and the Feminine Aesthetic* (Cambridge: Cambridge University Press, 1992), Laura Skondera-Trombley, *Mark Twain in the Company of Women* (Philadelphia: University of Pennsylvania Press, 1994), and Shelley Fisher Fishkin, 'Mark Twain and Women', in Forrest G. Robinson (ed.), *The Cambridge Companion to Mark Twain*, pp. 52–73. Particularly useful bibliographical information is contained in the footnotes to the latter essay.

31. Richard Chase, *The American Novel and Its Tradition* (1957). See *Critical Essays* in Sidney E. Berger (ed.), *Puddn'head Wilson and Those Extraordinary Twins* (New York: Norton Critical Edition, 1980) p. 247. And James Cox, 'Puddn'head Wilson Revisited', in Susan Gillman and Forrest G. Robinson (eds), *Mark Twain's Puddn'head Wilson*, p. 18. These two collections of essays, taken together, provide a useful indicator of the changing nature of the critical response to Twain's book.

32. Quoted in Frederick Anderson, '[The Writing of *Puddn'head Wilson*]' (1968), reprinted in the Norton Critical Edition of the text, p. 293.

33. From James M. Cox, *Mark Twain: The Fate of Humor* (1966). See the

Norton Critical Edition, p. 267. Cox's argument is that the novel's irony overwhelms the attractive vernacular character of Roxy. His choice to twin Tom with Puddn'head rather than Valet suggests how widely critical readings of the text diverge.

34. John Carlos Rowe, *Through the Custom-House: Nineteenth-Century Fiction and Modern Theory* (Baltimore, Md.: The Johns Hopkins University Press, 1982) p. 167.

35. John C. Gerber, 'Puddn'head Wilson as Fabulation' (1975), reprinted in the Norton Critical Edition, p. 361. Gerber's reference to 'the charm of fabulation' (p. 366) may indicate why I do not think this generic term a useful one to apply to Twain's novel.

36. See John Carlos Rowe, *Through the Custom-House*, p. 148.

37. That is, African-Americans as part-people and pieces of property. Cindy Weinstein uses the quoted terms in *The Literature of Labor and the Labors of Literature*, p. 140, in her discussion of the allegorical aspects of *Life on the Mississippi*. Eric J. Sundquist reminds his reader that 'the Constitution had originally counted the African American slave as three-fifths of a person', *To Save the Nations*, p. 239.

38. Susan Gillman points to 'the anguished tangle of contradictions surrounding the slave system' revealed by the trial and what follows it. As Roxy's son is redefined as property so he becomes, by definition (a 'will-less chattel') incapable of the murder he has committed, and 'not to be held accountable for human antisocial acts'. See *Dark Twins*, p. 92.

39. William Dean Howells, *A Hazard of New Fortunes* (Oxford: Oxford University Press, 1965 [1889]) p. 396. The statement comes from Basil March when he is at his most despairing about American society. It has come, though, to be generally applied to Naturalist writing.

40. Cindy Weinstein, *The Literature of Labor and the Labors of Literature*, p. 52.

41. George E. Marcus, '"What did he reckon would become of the other half if he killed his half?": Doubled, Divided, and Crossed Selves in *Puddn'head Wilson*; or, Mark Twain as Cultural Critic in His Own Times and Ours', in Susan Gillman and Forrest G. Robinson (eds), *Mark Twain's Puddn'head Wilson*, p. 197.

42. Though Arnold Weinstein approaches the novel from a different interpretive position, his reading of the symbolic resonances of the scene is particularly interesting. See *Nobody's Home*, pp. 79–80.

43. John Carlos Rowe, *Through the Custom-House*, p. 163. Rowe exempts 'that one uncanny moment in which he experiences his own divided identity as imitation black/imitation white'. Lee Clark Mitchell, too, follows Rowe in calling 'Tom' a 'deterministic machine'. He sees Roxy, too, as 'similarly a product of cultural forces'. See '"De Nigger in You": Race or Training in *Puddn'head Wilson*', *Nineteenth-Century Literature*, vol. 42, no. 3 (December 1987) pp. 304–5.

44. Susan Gillman points out that, in his working notes, 'Twain made Judge Driscoll himself the father of Tom'. See 'Mark Twain's Travels in the Racial Occult', p. 197. See too Arlin Turner, 'Mark Twain and the South: *Puddn'head Wilson*' (1968), reprinted in the Norton Critical

Edition. Turner quotes from Twain's notes and manuscript scraps to show that Twain planned at one stage to have 'Tom' confront and kill his own father: 'when his father pleads, "spare me! – I am your father!" Tom cries, "Now for *that*, you shall die," and kills him' (p. 276).

45. Though John Carlos Rowe's approach differs from mine, his comments on the 'illusion of . . . family instincts' is relevant here. See *Through the Custom-House*, p. 161.

46. Carolyn Porter, 'Roxana's Plot', in Susan Gillman and Forrest G. Robinson (eds), *Mark Twain's Puddn'head Wilson*, pp. 133, 134.

47. And contained, anyway, in its very secretness. If no one had found out that Tom was 'black', then the social system would have continued unaltered.

48. Shelley Fisher Fishkin, 'Race and Culture at the Century's End: A Social Context for Puddn'head Wilson', *Essays in Arts and Sciences*, vol. 19 (May 1990) pp. 2, 5, 6. Fishkin quotes George M. Frederickson in the definition given of the 'one-drop rule'.

49. Susan Gillman, *Dark Twins*, p. 85.

50. Standing in for his class here, 'too concerned with their speculations to notice any substitutions in the specific bodies that are the vehicles of their capital', Carolyn Porter, 'Roxana's Plot', p. 135. See John Carlos Rowe, 'Fatal Speculations: Murder, Money, and Manners in *Puddn'head Wilson*', in Susan Gillman and Forrest G. Robinson (eds), *Mark Twain's Puddn'head Wilson*, for discussion of the novel as 'a commentary on the shared economics of slavery and the new speculative economy that would carry us through the Civil War into the Gilded Age', p. 141. See too George M. Spangler, '*Puddn'head Wilson*: A Parable of Property' (1970), reprinted in the Norton Critical edition, pp. 295–303.

51. It is Roxy who uses this phrase. It can accordingly be read entirely ironically as part of Roxy's acceptance of hegemonic values.

52. See Eric Lott, 'Mr. Clemens and Jim Crow', pp. 148–9. While I agree with the general lines of Lott's argument, I differ in my conclusions.

53. In *The American Claimant* (New York: Charles L. Webster, 1892) young Lord Berkeley sees the forms and customs of European society as having become 'second nature'. They need casting off in favour of what can thus be called first or original nature – making one's own judgements and reverencing one's own ideals (pp. 99–100). In the incident which shortly follows this, when Berkeley is introduced to Puss, the daughter of the boarding-house keeper, Twain comments that 'his natural, lifelong self' which 'sprang to the front' did not know how to respond to this introduction to a chambermaid, but that his 'other self – the self which recognized the equality of all men – would have managed the thing better, if it hadn't been caught off guard' (pp. 108–9). The distinction between first and second nature, the natural self and that conditioned by environment and training, is here absolutely blurred. Cindy Weinstein similarly analyses Hank's opposition of nature and training ('that one microscopic atom that is truly *me*' versus 'training is everything', *A Connecticut Yankee*, p. 161)

to illustrate its collapse. See *The Literature of Labor and the Labors of Literature*, p. 154.

54. John Carlos Rowe, *Through the Custom-House*, p. 156. See, too, the passage in Twain's working notes for the novel where he writes, in regard to Tom's refusal of the duel, 'what was high came from either blood, & was the monopoly of neither color; but that which was base was the white blood in him debased by the brutalizing effects of a long-drawn heredity of slave-owning . . . '. Quoted in Shelley Fisher Fishkin, 'Race and Culture at the Century's End', p. 16.

55. Eric J. Sundquist, 'Mark Twain and Homer Plessy', in Susan Gillman and Forrest G. Robinson (eds), *Mark Twain's Puddn'head Wilson*, p. 71. The wording here differs from the version of the essay in *To Wake the Nations*, and is contradictory. Sundquist first claims that Tom's criminality may be *either* such aristocratic degeneration or a sign of his 'blackness', but goes on to argue that 'Tom's worst traits, like his "color" . . . can be traced neither to birth nor to training alone, neither to black nor to white'.

56. Arnold Weinstein, *Nobody's Home*, pp. 68–9.

57. Susan Gillman, *Dark Twins*, p. 78.

58. John Carlos Rowe, *Through the Custom-House*, p. 144.

59. Arnold Weinstein, *Nobody's Home*, pp. 86–7.

60. Eric Sundquist, *To Wake the Nations*, p. 228. See Sundquist's book for a reading of *Puddn'head Wilson and Those Extraordinary Twins* as 'an allegory of the 1880s and 1890s' (p. 232).

61. Arnold Weinstein, *Nobody's Home*, p. 87.

62. Sundquist describes how 'lynching in the 1890s was not reserved for African-Americans alone but had spread like an epidemic across . . . racial lines'. Focusing on the lynching of eleven Italians In New Orleans in 1891, he reads the twinned texts in terms of anti-immigrationist as well as anti-racist responses, and in terms of national as well as Southern prejudices. *To Wake the Nations*, pp. 261–3.

63. Twain adds one more element to this sense of necessary incompletion in the thematic development of the provisionality of knowledge itself. This theme appears in both *Those Extraordinary Twins* and *Puddn'head Wilson*. Unfortunately, my imposed textual limits prevent me from dealing fully with this important subject, though it returns as an issue as I discuss Twain's late writings in my final chapter. I merely indicate here, then, the grounds of an argument.

Fingerprinting in *Puddn'head Wilson* is not a neutral science ('pure' knowledge) but an ideological tool, used to confirm the racial prejudices of a particular community. The 'truth' of Tom's final identity as 'nigger' which the fingerprinting reveals, is only a fiction of law, based in turn on a fiction of race classification. 'Scientific' knowledge, in other words, is relative, dependent on the political framework that contains and produces it.

Equally Wilson's position as both a lawyer and a scientist in the trial scene raises theoretical (though only theoretical) questions about how anyone can *know* he tells the truth. In the trial scene, Wilson steps down from one role to give evidence in another. The only person with the 'scientific' knowledge to explain the case is also the one in whose professional interest (as lawyer) it is to win his case as convincingly as possible. It is clear Wilson does not falsify his evidence, but as a legal and scientific expert he does have his audience in the palm of his knowledgeable hand, should he wish to 'swindle' them (the word comes from Luigi's hoax in *Those Extraordinary Twins*, p. 261). At every turn in the text we are confronted with the potential unreliability of knowledge; the reminder that expertise and authority carry no guarantee of disinterested truth.

A final acknowledgement of the former fact lies in the play between fingerprinting and palmistry in *Puddn'head Wilson*. It is only palmistry that is seriously called a 'science' in the novel (p. 126). If we now dismiss palmistry as a science, and if fingerprinting has been validated by long practice, this was not the case as Twain wrote. In the comparative use made of the two 'sciences', the text provides a hint that knowledge is not always stable, and that our definitions of science always have something provisional about them.

For critical texts that address such issues, see especially Susan Gillman, *Dark Twins*; Evan Carter, '*Puddn'head Wilson* and the Fiction of Law and Custom'; John Carlos Rowe, *Through the Custom House*; and Brook Thomas, 'Tragedies of Race, Training, Birth and Communities of Competent Puddn'heads', *American Literary History*, vol. 1, no. 4 (Winter 1989) pp. 754–85.

Chapter 8 The Late Works: Incompletion, Instability, Contradiction

1. Mark Twain, *The Great Dark*, in John S. Tuckey (ed.), *Mark Twain's Which was the Dream? and Other Symbolic Writings of the Later Years* (Berkeley: University of California Press, 1967) p. 130. All page references from this, and *Three Thousand Years Among the Microbes* (also published in this edition), to follow quotes henceforth.

2. William R. Macnaughton, in *Mark Twain's Last Years as a Writer* (Columbia: University of Missouri Press, 1979), suggests that, from the end of 1906 till his death in 1910, 'Mark Twain seldom wrote well or finished what he began . . . ' (p. 241).

3. The best-known editorial manipulation of Twain's later work was the version of *The Mysterious Stranger* (1916) 'laundered and pasted together by Albert Bigelow Paine and Frederick A. Duneka'. See William R. Macnaughton, *Mark Twain's Last Years as a Writer*, p. 2. Maria Ornella Marotti alludes to other 'violation[s]' (p. 8) of Twain's work, discusses his self-censorings (pp. 3–6, 9–10), and gives a history of the publication of the Mark Twain Papers, in her important book, *The Duplicating Imagination: Twain and the Twain Papers* (Pennsylvania State University Press, 1990).

4. William M. Gibson (ed.), *Mark Twain's Mysterious Stranger Manuscripts* (Berkeley; University of California Press, 1969). The edition I use in this

chapter is the paperback version of this: Mark Twain, *The Mysterious Stranger*.

5. So Bruce Michelson categorises this critical tendency in *Mark Twain on the Loose: A Comic Writer and the American Self* (Amherst: University of Massachusetts Press, 1995) p. 175. See, too, his footnote, p. 253.

6. Bruce Michelson, *Mark Twain on the Loose*, pp. 173, 174, 212. Michelson's final chapter, 'The Wilderness of Ideas', discusses Twain's work after 1890. See pp. 173–229.

7. See Susan Gillman, *Dark Twins: Imposture and Identity in Mark Twain's America* (Chicago: University of Chicago Press, 1989) pp. 136–80; Susan Gillman, 'Mark Twain's Travels in the Racial Occult', in Forrest G. Robinson (ed.), *The Cambridge Companion to Mark Twain* (Cambridge: Cambridge University Press, 1995) pp. 193–219; Maria Ornella Marotti, *The Duplicating Imagination*; David R. Sewell, *Mark Twain's Languages: Discourse, Dialogue, and Linguistic Variety* (Berkeley: University of California Press, 1987) pp. 126–54. See, too, Susan K. Harris, *Mark Twain's Escape from Time: A Study of Patterns and Images* (Columbia: University of Missouri Press, 1982); Bruce Michelson, 'Deus Ludens: The Shaping of Mark Twain's Mysterious Stranger', *Novel*, vol. 14, no. 1 (Fall 1980) pp. 44–56; Cindy Weinstein, *The Literature of Labor and the Labors of Literature* (Cambridge: Cambridge University Press, 1995) pp. 160–72. I note here only those critics who have influenced my thinking. An increasing stress on the value of the late work (in all its variety) is now becoming standard.

8. Maria Ornella Marotti, *The Duplicating Imagination*, p. 62.

9. See Bruce Michelsen, *Mark Twain on the Loose*, pp. 223–5, and Maria Ornella Marotti, *The Duplicating Imagination*, pp. 31, 64, 152. Michelson uses Conrad as a 'handsome opposite' to Twain. To do so is also, though, to reveal, in terms of literary context, the nature of the difference between the two writers. If Conrad shows how Marlow's 'self press[es] on in full awareness of its own contingency' and finds a kind of healing and authority over experience in the telling of his well-shaped story (*Mark Twain on the Loose*, pp. 224–5), Twain's narratives cannot be brought to completion, and his fictional characters are often subjects who lack Marlow's self-awareness. Marotti's study focuses on fictions from all the posthumously published Twain Papers. My range is narrower. By the dream tales, I refer primarily to those fictions published in *Mark Twain's Which Was the Dream?* (though I do not discuss all the texts published there). Susan Gillman puts *The Mysterious Stranger Manuscripts* in the same category (see *Dark Twins*, p. 139). I prefer, here, to refer to *No. 44, The Mysterious Stranger* separately.

10. I would query Bruce Michelson's suggestion in *Mark Twain on the Loose* that Twain is consciously rebelling 'against cultural and rationalist expectations governing narrative and the written word' (p. 222). The large number of incomplete, fragmented and (at that time) unpublished texts suggest to me no such deliberate *intent*.

11. Dennis Welland points out that the two versions of the text were far

from identical, but that there is no evidence that Twain was aware of this. See *The Life and Times of Mark Twain* (London: Studio Editions, 1991) pp. 134–6. For fuller discussion of the differences between the two texts, see Welland's 'Mark Twain's Last Travel Book', *Bulletin of the New York Public Library*, vol. 69, no. 1 (January 1965) pp. 31–48.

12. I comment in chapter 2 on the importance of the associationist mode in Twain. The notion of 'occult travel' (p. 204) that Susan Gillman introduces in 'Mark Twain's Travels in the Racial Occult' is a reworking of the same principle, but one that also takes into account Twain's later interest in 'spirit communication and disembodied space-and-time travel, made newly respectable . . . by the investigations of psychical researchers' (p. 194). Gillman's analysis of Twain's writing on race, as, in *Following the Equator*, he mentally shifts from Bombay to his Missouri childhood home, and accordingly discovers a 'more forgiving cultural relativism' (p. 204), is astute.

13. Bruce Michelson, *Mark Twain on the Loose*, p. 77.

14. Susan Gillman, 'Mark Twain's Travels in the Racial Occult', pp. 204, 206, 194; and *Dark Twins*, pp. 99, 100. In my 'Racial and Colonial Discourse in Mark Twain's *Following the Equator*', I place emphasis, rather, on the divided nature of Twain's racial discourse in the text. See *Essays in Arts and Sciences*, vol. 22 (October 1993) pp. 67–83.

15. The repeated nature of these patterns signal, for me, a move from conventional non-fiction reportage to the deliberate patternings, equivalences and symmetries normally associated with the fictional and/or poetic. 'The Enchanted Sea-Wilderness' was, in fact, initially written as a story to be included in *Following the Equator*. See the introduction to John S. Tuckey (ed.), *Mark Twain's Which was the Dream?*, p. 8.

16. Other similar and related motifs appear in *Following the Equator* which relate to the late fictions. (i). Accounts of family disaster, the separation of families, and the loss of home (see pp. 63, 75, 99–100, 110–12, 121: not all these examples necessarily carry the psychologically disturbing or pessimistic implications of the late fiction). (ii) Relativistic uncertainty and the way different sets of coordinates, or frameworks of knowledge, meet to dislocatory effect; the failure of contact and communication (see p. 57, and the examples in my main text). (iii) Sudden reversal of fortune, both upward (pp. 141–50 – the story of Cecil Rhodes as a type of 'mysterious stranger' figure) and downward (p. 179 – I see an analogy between this description of the Adeleide crash and Twain's own financial disaster, especially in its forceful language, and in the metaphor with which he describes the story's final reversal: 'the corpse got up and danced'). On pp. 156–7 Twain alludes to the Tichborne trial: a story of twinned and confused identities, claimants, the conflicting status of dream and reality, and the loss of fortune and status.

17. Quoted in William R. Macnaughton, *Mark Twain's Last Years as a Writer*, p. 99. See too Bernard DeVoto (ed.), *Mark Twain: Letters from the Earth* (Greenwich, Conn.: Fawcett, 1962) pp. 226–7.

18. If fantasy as a genre gains its effects from hesitation concerning the nature of the 'real', an odd effect occurs at the start of *The Great Dark*. For rather than directly moving between one world (Jessie's birthday and the scientific experiment) to another (on shipboard), there is an intervening passage where the narrator talks to the Superintendent of Dreams about his projected voyage. We are left uncertain as to exactly where the rupture with 'reality' occurs; whether the narrator is already dreaming (if this is what happens to him) or not. This contributes to the sense of uncertainty over the status of the real in the text.

19. Bruce Michelson, *Mark Twain on the Loose*, p. 173.

20. Maria Ornella Marotti, in *The Duplicating Imagination*, calls the predominant mode of *The Mysterious Stranger Manuscripts* that of romance, but 'interspersed with fantastic, satirical, and burlesque motifs' (p. 99).

21. Rosemary Jackson, *Fantasy: The Literature of Subversion* (London: Methuen, 1981) p. 124. She discusses the intrusion of the Gothic in Victorian novels here, but it relates equally to the Fantastic.

22. Rosemary Jackson, *Fantasy*, pp. 45, 44.

23. Maria Ornella Marotti, *The Duplicating Imagination*, p. 92.

24. Bruce Michelson, *Mark Twain on the Loose*, p. 218.

25. See Susan Gillman, *Dark Twins*, pp. 149, 159–60. Gillman identifies Twain's representation of the dream and waking self with the theories of the psychic researcher, F. W. H. Myers. Gillman's valuable chapter on 'The Dream Writings' shows them to be 'thoroughly saturated in the context of late-nineteenth-century psychology' (p. 178), and links Twain's interest in this area to his own 'problems of authorial intentionality and control' (p. 138).

26. But, of course, also a duplication of the name of Twain's best known protagonist. In an unpublished article, 'Tom Sawyer's Capitalisms and the Destructuring of Huck Finn', Scott Michaelsen pursues the implications of this. His argument that Huck finally emerges as Tom Sawyer here, and that Huck's 'inability [in his microbic world] to resist capitalist occupation' (p. 33) provides a bleak rethinking of Twain's thirty years of work on aspiring capitalists (p. 22), should stimulate critical reassessment of the story. Michaelsen's description of the narrative's 'radical account of personhood', its portrayal of 'the self as entirely in flux' (p. 31), parallels and complements my own thinking on this subject. His further historicist move, in connecting this notion of the self to the allegorical representation of capitalism, is especially intriguing. My thanks to the author for allowing me to refer to his work.

27. For details of Eastern European immigration, see Roger Daniels, *Coming to America: A History of Immigration and Ethnicity* (New York: Harper Perennial, 1991 [1990]). Daniels writes that 'many Americans at the turn of the century felt that their way of life was threatened by what they called the "immigrant invasion"' (p. 275). Mary Douglas's remark that 'our ideas of dirt . . . express symbolic systems' is also to

the point here. See *Purity and Danger: An Analysis of Concepts of Pollution and Taboo* (London; Routledge & Kegan Paul, 1966) p. 35.

28. Catherine Belsey, *Critical Practice* (London: Methuen, 1980) p. 58.

29. Cindy Weinstein writes that 'His full name . . . registers his birth on the assembly line and his membership in an allegorical population [of workers]', *The Literature of Labor and the Labors of Literature*, p. 163. No. 44's role and identity cannot, however, be so narrowly contained.

30. Mark Twain, *The Mysterious Stranger*, edited by William M. Gibson (Berkeley: University of California Press, 1969) pp. 305, 315, 282. Page references follow quotations henceforth.

31. See my 'Afterword' to *The American Claimant* in the forthcoming edition of *The Oxford Mark Twain*. In my present interpretation of the duplicates, I take my initial cue from Cindy Weinstein in *The Literature of Labor and the Labors of Literature*. Weinstein's analysis takes a different direction, though, as she describes the confusions resulting from the failure to distinguish original from duplicate in terms of the disintegration of 'the efficiency of [Frederick Winslow] Taylor's utopia' (p. 165).

32. Though it must be said that neither these workers, nor their way of asserting their industrial rights, are presented sympathetically here. This serves to remind of Twain's deep ambivalence about labour–capital relationships.

33. The text closely parallels *Puddn'head Wilson and Those Extraordinary Twins* in its play with confused subjectivity. Similarly, it reverts to farce in the stage business about the twin wooing of Marget/Lisbet von Arnim by August and his double (see pp. 342–53).

34. Twain further complicates his narrative by giving August three selves. The Soul is the immortal spirit, capable of great force and passion, existing beyond the 'physical and mortal' properties of the other two selves. See pp. 342–3.

35. Maria Ornella Marotti, *The Duplicating Imagination*, p. 65.

36. Rosemary Jackson, *Fantasy*, p. 65.

37. *No. 44, The Mysterious Stranger*, pp. 318, 311; *The Great Dark*, pp. 104, 122, 130; *Three Thousand Years Among the Microbes*, p. 482.

38. *The Mad Passenger*, Appendix to John S. Tuckey (ed.), *Mark Twain's Which was the Dream?*, p. 567.

39. This bears all the marks of the confusions that inevitably attend the later editing of unfinished manuscripts. There seems every reason for seeing the second 'Preface' as a replacement for the first.

40. See especially Bruce Michelson, '*Deus Ludens*: The Shaping of Mark Twain's *Mysterious Stranger*', pp. 55–6; also, Maria Ornella Marotti, *The Duplicating Imagination*, pp. 126, 128.

41. See Maria Ornella Marotti, *The Duplicating Imagination*, p. 113.

42. I follow Bruce Michelson here. See '*Deus Ludens*: The Shaping of Mark Twain's *Mysterious Stranger*', p. 53. Michelson argues that, in such sequences, 'through play, a vital, enduring hopeful festivity and life have been restored to Mark Twain's fiction' (p. 56).

43. Bruce Michelson, '*Deus Ludens*: The Shaping of Mark Twain's *Mysterious Stranger*', p. 56.

44. I paraphrase Rosemary Jackson, *Fantasy*, p. 22.

45. Mark Twain, *The Mysterious Stranger*, p. 404.

46. See Eric Mottram, 'The Location of Dangerous Shoals: American Fictions on the Science of Power', *Over Here: An American Studies Journal*, vol. 3, no. 2 (Autumn 1983) p. 23. Mottram's brief but provocative reading of the text focuses on Twain's 'sense of catastrophe in the modern age': 'Henry Edwards' despair', he writes, 'increases as exploration of the unknown looks like going on for ever. . . . Adaptation to conditions causes amnesia. . . . [Henry] has become a flying Dutchman of American technological fears, dreaming of family, home, and land'.

47. Susan Gillman, *Dark Twins*, p. 167.

48. Susan Gillman, in 'Mark Twain's Travels in the Racial Occult', focuses on the historical resonances of the various versions of *The Mysterious Stranger*. She concentrates on Twain's representation of race and ethnicity, and shows how 'the black-Jewish parallel' (p. 213) made in the narratives extends into a 'final vision of universal human enslavement, containing and collapsing within it all of the historically specific nationalist, religious, and ethnic persecutions encompassed by *The Mysterious Stranger*, from the medieval witch-hunt, to the French revolution, to European missionary and colonial violence in China and India' (p. 216).

49. See Susan Gillman, *Dark Twins*, pp. 170–1.

50. Forrest G. Robinson, *In Bad Faith: The Dynamics of Deception in Mark Twain's America* (Cambridge, Mass.: Harvard University Press, 1986) p. 222. Robinson discusses the incompatibility of the free choice and determinist poles of Twain's thought, with specific reference to the late works, in the final chapter of his book.

51. Richard Boyd Hauck's discussion of Twain in *A Cheerful Nihilism: Confidence and the 'Absurd' in American Humorous Fiction* (Bloomington: Indiana University Press, 1971), pp. 133–66, is of relevance here, though I do not always agree with his conclusions.

52. Gregg Camfield, *Sentimental Twain: Samuel Clemens in the Maze of Moral Philosophy* (Philadelphia: University of Pennsylvania Press, 1994) p. 215.

53. Twain's concern with this area of American foreign policy can be traced in Jim Zwick (ed.), *Mark Twain's Weapons of Satire: Anti-Imperialist Writings on the Philippine–American War* (New York: Syracuse University Press, 1992).

54. Susan Gillman, *Dark Twins*, p. 170.

55. See David Sewell, *Mark Twain's Languages*, Chapter 7, 'Toward a Chaos of Incomprehensibilities', pp. 126–54.

56. Bruce Michelson refers, for instance, to the breezy resilience of children in Twain's late narratives (*Mark Twain on the Loose*, p. 212).

57. Indeed in his *Autobiography*, Twain did find a method that could, in its meandering variety, its free associations, repetitions and intersections, shape his materials. His formal approach there was based on the principle that 'in following no plan but the plan to follow no plan, he

allowed his memories to speak out in spite of himself' (Camfield, p. 229). The problem, though, is that if this appears to become a paradigmatic postmodernist text (the recounting of a life that formally defies closure; a 'measur[ing]' of the truth by a self who fully acknowledges the variability and inconsistency of his 'tapeline', and builds this changeable subjectivity into his text), its extreme length and necessary formal and thematic indiscipline has made it, to the present, unpublishable in any final version – though the Mark Twain Papers project is evidently preparing 'something approximating a definitive edition': see R. Kent Rasmussen, *Mark Twain A to Z: The Essential Reference to His Life and Writings* (New York: Facts on File, 1995) p. 23. Critical interest in the *Autobiography* is growing, and Gregg Camfield has a particularly interesting section on it in his *Sentimental Twain*, pp. 220–36. The quote I use to describe Twain's method has its source in (one version of) the *Autobiography* itself, where Twain writes of Susy 'measur[ing] her disasters . . . with her own tape-line': see Michael Kiskis (ed.), *Mark Twain's Own Autobiography* (Madison: University of Wisconsin Press, 1990) pp. 29–30. This reminds me, in its application to Twain's own textual methodology, of Henry Adams' historian, seeking 'no absolute truth . . . only a spool on which to wind the thread of history without breaking it', *The Education of Henry Adams* (New York: The Modern Library, 1931[1918]) p. 472.

In *Mark Twain on the Loose*, Bruce Michelson concentrates too on the 'anti-story configurations' (p. 222) of the late texts, and gives a particularly interesting reading of the neglected *Extract from Captain Stormfield's Visit to Heaven* (1909) pp. 219–23.

58. Perhaps Henry Adams, in his *The Education of Henry Adams*, provides a notable exception to this rule.
59. Alex Ayres (ed.), *The Wit and Wisdom of Mark Twain* (Harmondsworth, Middx.: Penguin [Meridian], 1987) p. 58.

Select Bibliography

This bibliography is necessarily highly selective. Twain wrote a vast amount and, since his death, much more of his work has been published, and republished, most especially in the authoritative University of California Press Editions. At least four versions of his *Autobiography* (as this suggests, a highly problematic text) have appeared, as well as various editions of his letters. The fourth volume of *Mark Twain's Letters* (1995), published in chronological sequence by the University of California Press, still only takes Twain's life up to 1871. There are also three volumes of *Mark Twain's Notebooks & Journals* (running to 1891) published by the same press. The amount of critical work, too, that has appeared on Twain is mountainous. I keep to narrow limits here, listing a selection of books that Twain produced during his lifetime, but then naming those texts that have been most useful for my own critical purposes. For a longer, up-to-date, but not overwhelming, bibliography, I would direct my reader to the 'Books by Mark Twain' and 'Suggested Reading' sections of one of the most useful reference works on Twain, R. Kent Rasmussen's *Mark Twain A to Z* (details below). I only refer to full studies of Twain's work. For information on critical articles and chapters in books, see my notes.

In my book, I use the Penguin edition of the text (when there is one) for ease of readerly access.

TWAIN'S MAJOR WORKS

The Celebrated Jumping Frog of Calaveras County and Other Sketches (1867).
The Innocents Abroad, or The New Pilgrim's Progress (1869).
Roughing It (1872).
The Gilded Age (1873).
Sketches New and Old (1875).
The Adventures of Tom Sawyer (1876).
The Prince and the Pauper (1881).
The Stolen White Elephant, Etc. (1882).
Life on the Mississippi (1883).

Adventures of Huckleberry Finn (1885).
A Connecticut Yankee in King Arthur's Court (1889).
The American Claimant (1892).
The £1,000,000 Bank-Note and Other New Stories (1893).
Puddn'head Wilson and Those Extraordinary Twins (1894).
Personal Recollections of Joan of Arc (1896).
Following the Equator (1897).
The Man that Corrupted Hadleyburg and Other Stories and Essays (1900).
Letters from the Earth (1962).
Mark Twain's Which Was the Dream? and Other Symbolic Writings of the Later Years (1967).
Mark Twain's Mysterious Stranger Manuscripts (1969).

Letters, Speeches, Etc.

Mark Twain–Howells Letters: The Correspondence of Samuel L. Clemens and William D. Howells, 1872–1910, ed. Henry Nash Smith and William M. Gibson (Cambridge, Mass.: Harvard University Press, 1960).
Mark Twain's Letters to His Publishers, 1867–1894, ed. Hamlin Hill (Berkeley: University of California Press, 1967).
Mark Twain's Correspondence with Henry Huttleston Rogers, 1893–1909, ed. Lewis Leary (Berkeley: University of California Press, 1969).
Mark Twain Speaking, ed. Paul Fatout (Ames: University of Iowa Press, 1976).

See too the various editions of *Mark Twain's Letters* and *Mark Twain's Notebooks & Journals* published by the University of California Press.

SECONDARY CRITICISM

Biographical Studies

Budd, Louis J., *Our Mark Twain: The Making of His Public Personality* (Philadelphia: University of Pennsylvania Press, 1983).
Emerson, Everett, *The Authentic Mark Twain: A Literary Biography of Samuel L. Clemens* (Philadelphia: University of Pennsylvania Press, 1976).
Hill, Hamlin, *Mark Twain: God's Fool* (New York: Harper & Row, 1973).
Hoffman, Andrew, *Inventing Mark Twain* (William Morrow, forthcoming).
Kaplan, Justin, *Mr Clemens and Mark Twain* (New York: Simon & Schuster, 1966).
Skandera-Trombley, Laura, *Mark Twain in the Company of Women* (Philadelphia: University of Pennsylvania Press, 1994).
Steinbrink, Jeffrey, *Getting to be Mark Twain* (Berkeley: University of California Press, 1991).
Welland, Dennis, *The Life and Times of Mark Twain* (London: Studio Editions, 1991).

Critical Studies

My book is deeply influenced by the generation of scholars who, in the late 1950s and 1960s, did the critical groundwork on which most later responses to Twain depend. Though I have made little direct reference to these texts, they inform much of what I have written. I list a selection of these below, and then leave a space before separately listing the more recent books which I have found most useful.

Blair, Walter, *Mark Twain & Huck Finn* (Berkeley: University of California Press, 1960).

Budd, Louis J., *Mark Twain: Social Philosopher* (Bloomington: Indiana University Press, 1962).

Cox, James M., *Mark Twain: The Fate of Humor* (Princeton, NJ: Princeton University Press, 1966).

Lynn, Kenneth S., *Mark Twain and Southwestern Humor* (Boston, Mass.: Little, Brown, 1959).

Regan, Robert, *Unpromising Heroes: Mark Twain and His Characters* (Berkeley: University of California Press, 1966).

Smith, Henry Nash, *Mark Twain: The Development of a Writer* (Cambridge, Mass.: Harvard University Press, 1962).

Bridgman, Richard, *Traveling in Mark Twain* (Berkeley: University of California Press, 1987).

Louis J. Budd (ed.), *New Essays on Adventures of Huckleberry Finn* (Cambridge: Cambridge University Press, 1985).

Camfield, Gregg, *Sentimental Twain: Samuel Clemens in the Maze of Moral Philosophy* (Philadelphia: University of Pennsylvania Press, 1994).

Champion, Laurie (ed.), *The Critical Response to Mark Twain's Huckleberry Finn* (Westport, Conn.: Greenwood Press, 1991).

Doyno, Victor A., *Writing Huck Finn: Mark Twain's Creative Process* (Philadelphia: University of Pennsylvania Press, 1991).

Fishkin, Shelley Fisher, *Was Huck Black? Mark Twain and African-American Voices* (New York: Oxford University Press, 1993).

Gillman, Susan, *Dark Twins: Imposture and Identity in Mark Twain's America* (Chicago: University of Chicago Press, 1989).

Gillman, Susan and Robinson, Forrest G. (eds), *Mark Twain's Puddn'head Wilson: Race, Conflict, and Culture* (Durham, NC: Duke University Press, 1990).

Gribben, Alan, *Mark Twain's Library: A Reconstruction*, 2 vols. (Boston: G. K. Hall, 1980).

LeMaster J. R. and Wilson, James D. (eds), *The Mark Twain Encyclopedia* (New York: Garland, 1993).

Leonard, James S., Tenney, Thomas A. and Davis, Thadious M. (eds), *Satire or Evasion? Black Perspectives on Huckleberry Finn* (Durham, NC: Duke University Press, 1991).

Marotti, Maria Ornelli, *The Duplicating Imagination: Twain and the Twain Papers* (Pennsylvania State University Press, 1990).
Michelson, Bruce, *Mark Twain on the Loose: A Comic Writer and the American Self* (Amherst: University of Massachusetts Press, 1995).
Rasmussen, R. Kent, *Mark Twain A to Z: The Essential Reference to His Life and Writings* (New York: Facts on File, 1995).
Robinson, Forrest G., *In Bad Faith: The Dynamics of Deception in Mark Twain's America* (Cambridge, Mass.: Harvard University Press, 1986).
Robinson, Forrest G. (ed.), *The Cambridge Companion to Mark Twain* (Cambridge: Cambridge University Press, 1995).
Sattelmeyer, Robert and Crowley, J. Donald (eds), *One Hundred Years of Huckleberry Finn: The Boy, His Book, and American Culture* (Columbia: University of Missouri Press, 1985).
Scharnhorst, Gary (ed.), *Critical Essays on The Adventures of Tom Sawyer* (New York: G. K. Hall, 1993).
Sewell, David R., *Mark Twain's Languages: Discourse, Dialogue, and Linguistic Variety* (Berkeley: University of California Press, 1987).
Sloane, David E. E., *Mark Twain as a Literary Comedian* (Baton Rouge: Louisiana State University Press, 1979).
Stahl, J. D., *Mark Twain, Culture and Gender: Envisioning America Through Europe* (Athens: University of Georgia Press, 1994).
Stoneley, Peter, *Mark Twain and the Feminine Aesthetic* (Cambridge: Cambridge University Press, 1992).
Sundquist, Eric J. (ed.), *Mark Twain: A Collection of Critical Essays* (Englewood Cliffs, NJ: Prentice Hall, 1994).
Tenney, Thomas A., *Mark Twain: A Reference Guide* (Boston, Mass.: G. K. Hall, 1977).
Wilson, James D., *A Reader's Guide to the Short Stories of Mark Twain* (Boston, Mass.: G. K. Hall, 1987).
Wonham, Henry B., *Mark Twain and the Art of the Tall Tale* (New York: Oxford University Press, 1993).

Index

Adventures of Huckleberry Finn 18,
    20, 67, **86–109, 111–15**, 132,
    133, 136, 149
  'evasion' sequence 88, 89–90,
    96, 99, 101, 102, 104, 109
  freedom 92–8, 99, 100, 101, 104,
    105, 108–9
  genre 111–5
  Huck's voice 87, 91–9, 101–2,
    103–8, 112–13, 114–15
  idyll 87–8, 103–8
  Jim, representation of 87, 88,
    90, 91–108
  'Jim and the Dead Man' 86
  narrative incompletion 87–8,
    103–9
  race 86–109, 111–12, 114
    positive depiction 87–8,
      102–9, 132
    post-Reconstruction 88–90,
      99–100, 102, 104, 105, 109,
      111–12, 115
    see too Jim, representation of
  realism 112–15
  status of subject 112–14
Adventures of Tom Sawyer, The 1,
    65–85, 111, 133, 136
  anti-modernism 65–7, 73, 76,
    81, 83, 85
  boy book 66, 67, 71, 76, 81, 111
  Huckleberry Finn 80
  Indian Joe 74, 80–2, 84–5
  Jacksonianism 72–3, 75, 84
  race 81, 82–5

  sexuality 81–2
  status of subject 76–9
  theatricality 76–7
  Tom as proto-capitalist 67,
    70–2, 73–6
  Tom as confidence man 72–4
  whitewashing scene 68–72
  work–play relation 70–2, 75–6
Aldrich, Thomas Bailey 67
American Claimant, The 151, 166
American West
  see Roughing It
Andrews, William L. 99
Arac, Jonathan 104, 105, 107
Authorial intentionality 13, 18–21,
    89, 105, 111, 115–16, 117, 119,
    138, 175–6

Bakhtin, Mikhail 92, 106, 115
Banta, Martha 46, 60, 118, 119, 123
Barnum, P. T. 4
Bell, Michael Davitt 131
Bennett, Tony 115
Big Bonanza, The 60
Bridgman, Richard 26
Budd, Louis J. 65

Cable, George Washington 90
Carter, Everett 117, 118, 119
Carton, Evan 135
Civil War 20, 23, 28–9, 42, 66, 68,
    73, 119
*Confidence Men and Painted
    Women* 72

Connecticut Yankee in King Arthur's Court, A 19, **110–11, 115–33,** 136–7, 151, 154, 166
  Battle of the Sand-Belt 127, 128–9, 137
  body–machine interaction 119–24, 126
  cultural anxieties 117–33, 154
  electrocution 110, 127–9
  fantasy 110–11, 115–33
  history 131–3
  Hank–Merlin relation 125, 130–1
  St Stylite 119–24, 126–7, 128
  status of subject 119–24, 130–1, 136–7
  Taylorisation 122–4

De Quille, Dan 60
Douglass, Frederick 95
Doyno, Victor 100
Dream Tales 157–9, 160, 161, **162–6, 167–70, 171–6**
  see also Enchanted Sea-Wilderness, The; Great Dark, The; Three Thousand Years Among the Microbes
DuBois, W. E. B. 97, 100

Edison, Thomas 130
Eliot, T. S. 86, 89
Ellis, R. J. 90
Enchanted Sea-Wilderness, The 161
'Ethnicity' 122
European–American relations
  see Innocents Abroad

Fender, Stephen 44
Fiedler, Leslie 106
Fishkin, Shelley Fisher 90, 91, 92, 100, 149–50
Following the Equator **159–61**
  race 160
  travel writing 159–60, 161
Foner, Eric 100
Ford, Henry 123
Foucault, Michel 119, 120
'Freedman's Case in Equity, The' 90

Gilded Age, The 35, 132
Gillman, Susan 4, 135, 140, 150, 152, 158, 160
Grandissimes, The 90
Great Dark, The 159, **162–4,** 166, **168–9, 172,** 175
  epistemological uncertainty 162, 163–4, 167–9, 172, 175
  fantasy 162–3, 167–8, 171–2
  farce 162
  narrative problems 158–9, 162, 168, 169, 172, 175
  status of the subject 162–4, 167, 172, 175
Gribben, Alan 67
Gutwirth, Marcel 4, 8, 9, 10, 14, 15, 16

Haltunnen, Karen 72
Holland, Laurence B. 95
Homestead Strike 12
Horwitz, Howard 58
Howard, June 113
Howells, William Dean 113
Humour 1–21 and *passim*
  ambivalence about 9–13

Incidents in the Life of a Slave Girl 108
Innocents Abroad, The **22–43,** 47, 48, 160
  aesthetics 30–1, 36, 37, 38
  Civil War 23, 28–9, 42
  Columbus's discovery 29–30
  economics 22–4, 27–8, 31, 32, 33, 43
  ethnocentrism 28–34, 38
  epistemological uncertainty 25, 35–6
  Milan bath-house 32–4
  Orientalism 38
  'pilgrim'–'sinner' contrast 41–3
  status of subject 24–5, 32, 34, 36
  tourism 22–4, 27, 30–1, 33
  travel writing 22–4, 26, 36–40

Jackson, Rosemary 113, 116–17, 163
Jacobson, Marcia 66, 67
Jacobs, Harriet 93, 108

'Jim Smiley and His Jumping Frog' 2, 5

Kazin, Alfred 28, 35
Kemmler, William 128
King, Martin Luther 109

Lears, T. Jackson 77, 125
Life on the Mississippi 58, 67, 90, 135, 136
Lukacs, Georg 132
Lynn, Kenneth 51

MacLeod, Christine 108
Mailloux, Steven 19, 88, 90
Marotti, Maria Ornella 158
Michaels, Walter Benn 61, 119
Michelson, Bruce 24, 143, 158, 160, 163, 171
Mitchell, Lee Clark 53, 64, 113
Molly Maguires 12
More Tramps Abroad
   see *Following the Equator*
Moreland, Richard C. 104, 105
Morrison, Toni 91
Mysterious Stranger, The,
   manuscripts 11, 157, 158, 159, 162
   see also *No 44, The Mysterious Stranger*

No 44, The Mysterious Stranger 136, 159, 164, **166–7**, **170–1**, **172–3**, **174–5**
   epistemological uncertainty 162, 167–8, 170–1, 175
   fantasy 162–3, 167–8, 172
   narrative problems 158–9, 167, 171, 172–3, 174, 175
   status of the subject 162, 164, 166–7, 172, 174, 175
   Taylorisation 166–7

Oriard, Michael 71

Paige typesetter 166
Pinkerton Detective Agency 12

see also Homestead Strike, Molly Maguires
Puddn'head Wilson and Those Extraordinary Twins 18, 67, 79, 83, **134–56**, 157, 158, 159
   allegory 136, 137, 138, 139, 140, 144–6, 154, 155
   Chang and Eng 139–40
   detective genre 136, 153, 154–5
   farce 134–5, 137, 138, 140–3
   finger-printing 155
   narrative tensions 134, 135–6, 139, 140, 153–4, 155–6
   Puddn'head Wilson 134–9, 140, 142, 143, **144–56**, 158
   Puddn'head Wilson 144, 145, 146, 148, 153, 154–5
   race 135, 137, 140, 143–55
      post-Reconstruction 135, 143–4, 146, 149–50, 154
   Roxy 144–52, 154–5
   Siamese Twins 134, 137, 139–43, 153, 155
   status of subject 136–7, 140, 141–3, 145–6, 148, 150–3, 155
   Those Extraordinary Twins 134–9, **139–44**, 145, 153, 154
   Tocchi brothers 139–40
   Tom Driscoll 134, 144–5, 147–55
   twinnings 134–43 and *passim*
   Valet de Chambre 145, 150–5

Regan, Robert 28
Robinson, Forrest G. 4
Roughing It 26, 34, **44–64**, 66, 111, 133, 160
   Buck Fanshawe's funeral 50–2
   American Indian 49–50
   emergent capitalism 46–7, 57–63
   epistemological uncertainty 46, 53–7
   Great Landslide Case, The 45–6
   Hawaii 56–7
   Lake Tahoe 59–61
   Mining 54, 60–2
   Mountain Meadows Massacre 54–5
   Slade 53

travel narrative 47, 56, 64, 111
see also Turner, Frederick Jackson

Said, Edward 28, 38
San Francisco *Alta* 22
Secret History of Eddypus, The 133
'Seeing the Elephant' 4
Seltzer, Mark 118, 120, 123
Sewell, David 32, 51, 158
Smith, David L. 97
'Sociable Jimmy' 91
Sollors, Werner 122, 130
Southwick, Dr Alfred 110, 128
Steinbrink, Jeffrey 48
'Stolen White Elephant, The'
    1–21, 25, 136, 155
  allegory 10–13, 20
  detective genre 1–2, 4, 5–8, 10,
    12, 17–18
  epistemological uncertainty
    2–3, 14–18
  hoax 4–6, 16, 20
  narrators 3–5, 13
  'seeing the Elephant' 4
Story of a Bad Boy, The 67
Stowe, William W. 23, 25, 43
Sundquist, Eric 77

Takaki, Ronald 118
Taylor, Frederick Winslow
  see Connecticut Yankee, A:
    Taylorisation
Taylored Lives 123
*Three Thousand Years Among the
    Microbes* 159, 160, **164–6,
    169–70, 173–4**

black humour 173, 175
epistemological uncertainty
    162, 165, 167, 169–70, 172,
    173, 175
  fantasy 162–3, 164–5, 167–8,
    171–2
  historical context 164–5, 173–4
  narrative problems 158, 170,
    172, 173–4, 174–5
  status of the subject 162, 164,
    165–6, 167, 172, 173, 175
Todorov 117
Trachtenberg, Alan 57–8
Turner, Frederick Jackson 44, 45,
    46, 47, 48, 49, 50
Twain, Mark
  as fictional persona 22, 32,
    33–4, 36–7, 48–9
  Notebooks 43, 110

Virginia City *Enterprise* 4, 60

Wallace, John H. 97
Was Huck Black? 91
Weber, Max 125, 131–2
Webster & Company 110
Weinstein, Cindy 118, 119, 136–7,
    146
*Which Was the Dream? and Other
    Symbolic Writings* 157
  *see also The Great Dark, Three
    Thousand Years Among the
    Microbes*
Whittier birthday dinner 19
Wolff, Cynthia Griffin 66